READING THE HEBREW BIBLE WITH ANIMAL STUDIES

READING THE HEBREW BIBLE WITH ANIMAL STUDIES

Ken Stone

STANFORD UNIVERSITY PRESS

STANFORD, CALIFORNIA

Stanford University Press
Stanford, California

© 2018 by the Board of Trustees of the Leland Stanford Junior University. All rights reserved.

No part of this book may be reproduced or transmitted in any form or by any means, electronic or mechanical, including photocopying and recording, or in any information storage or retrieval system without the prior written permission of Stanford University Press.

Printed in the United States of America on acid-free, archival-quality paper

Library of Congress Cataloging-in-Publication Data

Names: Stone, Ken (Kenneth A.), 1962– author.
Title: Reading the Hebrew Bible with animal studies / Ken Stone.
Description: Stanford, California : Stanford University Press, 2017. | Includes bibliographical references and index.
Identifiers: LCCN 2017005554 (print) | LCCN 2017012935 (ebook) | ISBN 9781503603769 | ISBN 9780804799751 | ISBN 9780804799751Q (cloth :qalk. paper) | ISBN 9781503603752 (pbk. :alk. paper)
Subjects: LCSH: Animals in the Bible. | Bible. Old Testament—Criticism, interpretation, etc. | Animal welfare—Biblical teaching. | Animals—Religious aspects.
Classification: LCC BS1199.A57 (ebook) | LCC BS1199.A57 S76 2017 (print) | DDC 221.8/59—dc23
LC record available at https://lccn.loc.gov/2017005554

Contents

Acknowledgments		*vii*
	Introduction	1
1	Israel's Companion Species and the Creation of Bibles	21
2	Tracking the Dogs of Exodus	45
3	The Chimera of Biblical Sacrifice	66
4	From Animal Hermeneutics to Animal Ethics	91
5	Israel's Wild Neighbors in the Zoological Gaze	116
6	The Psalmist, the Primatologist, and the Place of Animals in Biblical Religion	140
7	Reading the Hebrew Bible in an Age of Extinction	164
	Notes	*183*
	Index	*217*

Acknowledgments

Donna Haraway, whose influence on my thinking will become clear throughout this book, has reminded us that we all live in, and as, multispecies worlds. None of us exist as independent individuals. So, too, writing and scholarship are collective enterprises in ways that we do not always articulate. Because it is impossible to thank everyone who supported me during the time I worked on this project, I want to acknowledge first the feedback and suggestions I received from many people, too numerous to list, who responded to my ideas in a wide range of contexts, both formal and informal.

Several organizations and program organizers deserve particular appreciation for giving me opportunities to further my thinking and writing about animal studies and biblical interpretation while I was writing this book. These include a Transdisciplinary Theological Colloquium at Drew Theological School in 2011, organized by Stephen D. Moore; the Reading, Theory, and the Bible Section of the Society of Biblical Literature, coordinated by Jennifer Koosed, Robert Seesengood, and Jay Twomey; a panel on "difference" and biblical interpretation, coordinated for the Society of Biblical Literature in 2012 by Erin Runions; the Visiting Scholar Colloquium at Swarthmore and Haverford Colleges in 2013, coordinated by Gwynn Kessler; the Gay Men's Issues Group of the American Academy of Religion, which in 2013 organized a session on sexuality and animality coordinated by Scott Haldeman; a lecture for the Department of Philosophy and Religious Studies at Ball State University, organized by Joseph Marchal in 2015; the Eastern Great Lakes Biblical Society meeting in 2016, organized by Susan Haddox and Jonathan Lawrence; and the Feminist Hermeneutics Section and Ecological Hermeneutics Section of the Society of Biblical Literature.

My colleagues at Chicago Theological Seminary, including its Board of Trustees, President Alice Hunt, faculty, staff, and many students, supported the project through sabbatical leaves, patience with my distraction from other duties, and enthusiastic responses to presentations of my ideas. I am especially grateful to students in my course "Animals, Ecology, and Biblical Interpretation."

A few individuals deserve a special word of appreciation. Tat-siong Benny Liew, Theodore Jennings, and Laurel Schneider prodded me for several years, and in several different ways, to bring animal studies to bear on biblical interpretation. Barbara J. King, an inspiration to all of us who are interested in animals, graciously read two of my chapters and encouraged the project. Jared Beverly read my entire manuscript and assisted me in the final stages of its preparation. Two anonymous readers for Stanford University Press gave me crucial feedback. Emily-Jane Cohen shepherded the project for Stanford University Press in ways that were always helpful.

It has become conventional in projects related to animal studies to acknowledge the support of one's companion animals. During the time that I worked on this book, I benefited deeply from living alongside several of them, including Baldwin, Bayard, Duncan, and especially Mack, who patiently waited for me to get up from my computer and get out in the world.

But most of all I thank Adolfo Santos for his untiring support and encouragement, his companionship on occasions that brought us closer to animals, and our endless conversations about animals and the earth.

READING THE HEBREW BIBLE WITH ANIMAL STUDIES

Introduction

If media provide any indication of our culture's primary concerns, fascination with animals is on the rise. Magazines, newspapers, web sites, and television and radio outlets regularly release stories about new discoveries in animal research or conservation. Nature documentaries generate significant interest. A different genre of media stories features individual animals who have been observed doing something unexpected, even heroic, or just plain cute. Even if one sometimes wonders about the quality of the output, the ongoing production of such stories testifies to a widespread interest in the nonhuman creatures who share the earth with us.

But how new is this fascination with animals? In her book *Being with Animals: Why We Are Obsessed with the Furry, Scaly, Feathered Creatures Who Populate Our World*, the anthropologist Barbara J. King points out that cave paintings of animals, some as old as 30,000 years or more, found at such famous sites as Chauvet and Lascaux (and more recently at newly discovered sites in Sulawesi and elsewhere), provide us with the oldest known surviving symbolic representations created by humans. Strikingly, such paintings seldom represent humans, focusing primarily on other animals. While cautious in her interpretations of the meanings of specific artifacts, King connects these ancient animal paintings to a wide variety of objects and practices that testify to a recurring interest in animals across time and space. This interest is no doubt related in part to the use of animals for food and the fear of potentially dangerous animals with whom humans have long had to contend. King notes, however, that many types of art, myth, and ritual—elements of human culture that we frequently associate with religion—have also involved animals, from ancient dog burials to aboriginal Australian "dreamtime" narratives to blessings of animals in contemporary North American Christian churches. *"Animals mattered always,"* King writes; and they still do.[1]

If King is right to suggest that animals have "mattered always," as I believe she is, one would expect to find an interest in animals in both the writings of the Bible and the interpretations of those who read it. King herself calls attention to "the complex treatment of animals in the Bible" (80), where animals are sometimes held in high regard and at other times subordinated explicitly to humans. As an example of a text in which animals play a prominent role, she points to the story of Daniel and the lions, which she connects to other stories about lions, religious and secular, ancient and modern, that reveal our recurring preoccupation with these great cats. Elsewhere in her reflections on religion, King also reminds her readers of such biblical tales as "Noah's preservation of all animal species with his ark."[2]

Indeed, animals wander in and out of biblical literature from beginning to end. In the opening chapter of Genesis, diverse categories of animals are created across two days, recognized as good by God, blessed, and commanded to reproduce and multiply throughout their habitats. At the other end of the Christian Bible, in the closing chapter of Revelation, a lamb sits on a throne in a city populated by God's servants, while dogs are excluded from the city, together with several species of evildoers. The books between Genesis and Revelation are variously populated with different types of animals, who appear, disappear, and reappear in numerous passages and multiple genres. Few readers of the Bible who are watching for animals will fail to spot them.

Surprisingly, however, the Bible's animals and animal symbolism have, until recently, received only limited attention. For much of the twentieth century, scholarship on the Hebrew Bible assumed a sharp distinction between nature and history, and associated biblical literature more closely with history than with nature.[3] Any significant interest in nature was said to be characteristic of the non-Israelite religions from which, it was claimed, biblical theology should be sharply distinguished. Within this framework, the Bible's animals attracted little attention from biblical scholars. It is striking, in fact, that another anthropologist rather than a biblical scholar wrote what was arguably the most influential discussion of biblical animals published during the twentieth century, the chapter on food laws and unclean animals in Mary Douglas's 1966 landmark study *Purity and Danger*.[4] Biblical scholars themselves, however, acknowledged animals mostly in passing as evidence for the social niche inhabited by certain Israelites (often said to be "pastoralists" or "small cattle farmers"), or as minor props in an epic story focused on humans and God.

More recently, however, the Bible's animals have started to creep back into the literature of biblical studies. This reemergence has taken several forms. Following the path opened by Douglas, some scholars use the distinction between clean and unclean animals to interpret biblical religion.[5] Others, cognizant of new developments in archaeology such as zooarchaeology (or archaeozoology), give animals a more prominent place in reconstructions of the history and material world of ancient Israel and the ancient Near East.[6] An increasing number of studies explore the Bible's use of animal symbols to represent both humans and God, interpreting such symbolism by focusing on either specific species or particular books.[7] And the growing literature on ecological hermeneutics includes animals within its purview, though often in a wider frame.[8]

Alongside these approaches, only a few scholars have called attention to the potential relevance for biblical interpretation of a growing body of interdisciplinary animal studies emerging outside of biblical scholarship.[9] While zoological and ethological fields associated with animal biology, behavior, and cognition continue to expand our knowledge of animals in significant ways, questions about animals are also being raised today in literary and cultural studies, philosophy and philosophical ethics, history, sociology, and anthropology as part of what is sometimes called an "animal turn" in the humanities and social sciences.[10] Indeed, this heterogeneous body of animal writing is already having an impact on the attention given to animals in non-biblical religious studies.[11]

If scholars from multiple disciplines, including religious studies, have made us aware of the importance of what one volume of essays calls "making animal meaning,"[12] then biblical scholars, too, may wish to reconsider the significance of animals and animal symbolism in biblical literature, in the ancient world that bequeathed it to us, and among its diverse readers. One of the primary goals of this book is to suggest that contemporary animal studies can prove useful to readers of the Hebrew Bible who wish to carry out such a task. Thus each of the chapters that follow reexamines some section or sections of biblical literature in dialogue with various resources or questions from contemporary animal studies. Taken together, the chapters argue that the importance of both animals and animal symbols has been significantly underemphasized by biblical scholars and underestimated by other readers of the Hebrew Bible. Indeed, I will go so far as to suggest that, without the presence of the specific animals known to the writers of the Hebrew Bible, neither biblical theologies nor the religions of Judaism and Christianity that make use of the Hebrew Bible would exist in anything like their current forms. The literature and religion of the Hebrew Bible emerge from, and are made possible by, particular multispecies contexts.

But in a world with as many pressing issues as our own, what is the relevance of either animal studies generally or animal studies and the Hebrew Bible in particular? Can we afford to spend our time thinking about animals when so many urgent matters demand attention? The frequency with which questions such as these are asked indicates that, in spite of our fascination with animals, concerns about them are still usually considered secondary to human concerns. Indeed, most humans appear to feel little compunction about using animals in ways that require their deaths (e.g., for food, clothing, or experimentation), or about making life more difficult for them (e.g., by destroying their habitats by harvesting trees, growing crops, or human settlement). If asked to justify such behavior, many people would probably refer to the Hebrew Bible itself. For a long tradition of biblical interpretation appeals to a handful of passages in order to argue that animals are not only ontologically different from humans but also rightly subordinated to us and to our interests and concerns. Those who argue thus emphasize Genesis 1:26–28, in particular, where a contrast appears to be made between humans, who are said to be created "in the image of God," and "the fish of the sea, the birds of the air, and every living creature that moves on the earth," over which humans are said to have "dominion." Lifting this passage from its larger literary context, readers sometimes conclude that we as humans need not worry too much about other living creatures. Although we may wish to treat animals more kindly, many would insist that we should not allow animal issues to distract us from the more important human issues of our time.

I will be returning to some of the biblical passages that are used to draw such sharp, hierarchical distinctions between humans and animals. My goal in doing so will not be to deny the anthropocentric force of Genesis 1:26–28, but rather to re-read it in the context of numerous other passages, from Genesis and elsewhere, that reveal far more complicated, and sometimes contradictory, relationships among humans, other animals, and God. Indeed, Genesis 1 places much more emphasis on the flourishing of animal life than most readers acknowledge. For the moment, however, I will make a few points briefly about the importance of paying greater attention to the Bible's animals, in dialogue with animal studies.

First, as I hope will soon become clear, a reexamination of biblical literature in dialogue with animal studies need not limit one's focus to questions about nonhuman animals. Although the animals referred to in the Hebrew Bible will receive much attention here, those animals are mediated to us through the words of the humans who bequeathed it to us. To be sure, our interpretation of the Bible's animal references can be, and will be here, supplemented by our growing archaeological knowledge of the actual animals who lived in Israel and elsewhere in the ancient world. But the frequent references to animals in the Bible do not only shed light on those animals. The animal world provided the writers of biblical literature with a rich set of symbols that they used to speak about themselves, their human neighbors, the religion they practiced or advocated, and the God or gods they worshipped. Claude Lévi-Strauss famously observed that animals are not only "good to eat" but also "good to think."[13] Biblical literature, like many other human cultural expressions, amply demonstrates that this is true. When the writers of biblical literature "thought" *with* animals, however, they were not only thinking *about* animals. They were, in addition, using their observations about and relations with animals to understand themselves, their relations with one another (including the relations of power and subordination that structured their societies), their relations with other peoples and nations, their relations with God, and the relations they imagined God to have with the larger natural world and the nonhuman creatures who inhabit it. All of these relations will concern us here, as will our own relations to these ancient texts as modern readers.

On the other hand, even if one believes that concerns about animals are rightly subordinated to human concerns, it is important to recognize that we read the Bible today in a context in which ethical questions about our interactions with animals grow ever more pressing.[14] Centuries-old questions about eating animals have been transformed by the rise of so-called factory farms and industrial slaughterhouses, which create intense suffering not only for animals but also for the human workers, mostly nonwhite and from lower socioeconomic classes, who labor in them.[15] A series of developments caused wholly or in part by humans, including habitat loss, deforestation, unsustainable hunting and fishing, overpopulation, and climate change, are leading toward what some scientists call the "sixth great extinction," a catastrophe comparable to other massive extinction events such as the one that famously wiped out the dinosaurs.[16] Ironically, these and other animal crises are intensifying at a time when new advances in animal research are demonstrating cognitive, behavioral, and emotional abilities in animals that previously were believed to exist only in humans.[17] Such research also highlights many remarkable animal traits that are quite different from our own, of course. But we are creating more suffering for more animals, and more threats to the continued existence of more species, even as we learn more every year about the ways in which animal abilities exceed the limited conceptions we have had about them in the past. To be sure, the writers of the Hebrew Bible could not have anticipated the very different world in which we are now reading their texts. But if our interpretations of the Bible are contributing to a disregard for animals that produces suffering on a massive scale, we have to ask whether those interpretations are as persuasive or inevitable as we have been led to believe.

And this leads to another reason for reexamining the Bible in dialogue with animal studies. Such reexamination is valuable in part because it may lead to a better understanding of the Hebrew Bible itself. In making this statement, I do not wish to be understood as relying on outdated assumptions that a single, correct meaning can simply be extracted from biblical texts through the proper application of modern exegetical principles. I have made it clear elsewhere, in the context of queer readings and gender analyses of the Bible, that in my view biblical meanings have as much to do with the questions, assumptions, and rhetorical reading strategies that we bring to biblical texts, and to the contexts in which we interpret those texts, as they do with empirical facts about the texts themselves.[18] As a practical matter, however, we do still rely upon shared conventions of reading (including conventions of translation, contextualization, intertextual reference, and so forth) to produce interpretations that are considered plausible and interesting to others. One of my contentions here is that, even within the framework of shared conventions for biblical interpretation, the significance of animals in the Hebrew Bible has been distorted by our anthropocentric assumptions about biblical literature and the religion it promotes. Thus a reading strategy that intentionally takes an opposite approach, relying in part on insights from animal studies to highlight the Bible's animal references and interpret them in new ways, provides a useful counterbalance in our attempts to understand and engage these ancient texts in our contemporary world.

Each of the chapters that follow, then, explores the possible significance of animals and animal studies for biblical interpretation by starting from specific points of departure in the Hebrew Bible, in contemporary animal studies, and in the literature of biblical interpretation. Because the issues raised from animal studies vary by chapter, in several places I return to biblical texts that have already been discussed earlier in the book to consider how they might be re-read in the context of different interpretive issues and additional biblical texts. From chapter to chapter, however, the biblical references cover different animal species appearing in multiple genres. Taken together, such references underscore the significant numbers of animals and types of animals who actually do roam through the Bible's pages.

The diversity of animals who appear in the Bible coexist, here, with a diversity of questions that one can ask about them. Indeed, the chapters that follow do not rely upon or provide a single "method" of animal studies. New approaches to biblical interpretation are often presented in exactly this fashion, as new methods that can be "applied" to various texts in a series of neat, methodological steps. I am certainly not opposed to making methodological recommendations for biblical interpretation on the basis of new areas of study.[19] But as Stephen Moore and Yvonne Sherwood note, this way of thinking about interdisciplinary biblical interpretation, which they refer to critically as biblical scholarship's "methodolatry and methodone addiction," often stands in some tension with practices of contemporary non-biblical literary criticism.[20] By focusing on interpretive moves that can easily be summarized and replicated as exegetical steps, biblical studies tends to tame or domesticate insights from other fields.

More important for my purposes here, the distillation of a single method from animal studies is made impossible by the heterogeneity of this rapidly growing body of interdisciplinary scholarship. Even the term, "animal studies," which I have been using as if it were unproblematic, exists alongside competing ways of referring to at least portions of the literature in question ("critical animal studies," "animality studies," "human–animal studies," "zooanthropology," and so forth). These terminological differences are not simply interchangeable ways of describing the field. In many cases they represent diverse foci and philosophical or methodological assumptions undergirding different projects in animal studies. Such diversity can make it difficult for the scholar who brings animal studies to bear in a new area, such as biblical studies, even to specify what animal studies *is*.

Some scholars attempt to define animal studies in as inclusive a way as possible, underscoring work being done across many academic disciplines. Margo DeMello, for example, defines animal studies or "human–animal studies" as "an interdisciplinary field that explores the spaces that animals occupy in human social and cultural worlds and the interactions humans have with them." Her expansive overview thus gives attention to such diverse issues as domestication, recreation, food production, pet-keeping, scientific experimentation, art, religion, literature, film, and more. While DeMello distinguishes such studies from "animal behavior disciplines," she also suggests that the latter disciplines are relevant for animal studies since "we can better understand human interactions with" animals when we are informed by new research on "the behavior of animals, animal learning, cognition, communication, emotions, and culture."[21] Paul Waldau suggests, even more ambitiously, that "Animal Studies engages the many ways that human individuals and cultures are now interacting with and exploring other-than-human animals, in the past have engaged the living beings beyond our species, and in the future might develop ways of living in a world shared with other animals."[22] This broad definition allows Waldau to reflect on the study of animals across a wide number of disciplines, including the biological sciences, history, public policy and law, the "creative arts" (including literature), philosophy, religion, anthropology, archaeology, and more. While acknowledging the complexity of "integrating knowledge" across so many disciplines, Waldau imagines a future in which animal studies exists as a kind of multidisciplinary "megafield" (300–301), expanding the university by paying more, and more careful, attention to animals. As DeMello notes, however, animal studies in this expansive sense, precisely because of its wide scope, cannot be defined by a single method. It tends, rather, to be shaped by methodological debates taking place within the various disciplines that contribute to it. This methodological pluralism may raise difficulties for shared knowledge. "How then," DeMello asks, "do we know what we know?"[23]

And the challenges that animals present to our knowledge are not limited to challenges of methodological diversity. Attempts to understand animals quickly run up against obstacles that we at least assume are not as severe when we study other humans. We cannot usually ask an animal questions for clarification, for example. If we are attempting to read texts in which human concerns are privileged over animal concerns, moreover, our conventional ways of handling texts that privilege some concerns over others may not work as well with animals. For example, our recognition that biblical and other ancient texts are largely written by men, and reflect the concerns and perspectives of an elite male class, sometimes lead us to find creative ways to give ancient women a voice.[24] But animals complicate such strategies, since the very assumption that spoken or written language is the best medium for giving back agency clearly privileges human linguistic abilities, and is in that sense anthropocentric. As Kari Weil observes,

> animal studies thus stretches to the limit questions of language, epistemology, and ethics that have been raised in various ways by women's studies and postcolonial studies: how to understand and give voice to others or to experiences that seem impervious to our means of understanding; how to attend to difference without appropriating or distorting it; how to hear and acknowledge what it may not be possible to say.[25]

Species differences may prove to be challenging for many of our critical interpretive habits.

Paradoxically, however, animal studies does not only highlight ways in which animals are different from us. It also undermines long-standing assumptions about the absolute, ontological distinction between humans and animals. Although this distinction and the anthropocentrism that it fuels are, as I have noted already, sometimes grounded in appeals to biblical literature, they also undergird much philosophical and psychological discourse as well as societal and institutional practice. Yet as more characteristics that were assumed in the past to distinguish humans from other animals are found in some form among one or more animal species, the boundary between humans and animals has become increasingly less clear. Even language may not provide as secure a criterion for distinguishing humans from other animals as has long been assumed. After all, some nonhuman animals do learn to communicate with humans in ways that rely, in part, on elements of human language; and it has become increasingly apparent that many animal species have developed their own complex systems of communication.[26] Both human and nonhuman animals rely upon semiotic systems external to ourselves to communicate with one another and to become who we are. Partly for this reason, some scholars argue that animal studies rightly moves us beyond many of the traditional assumptions of humanism into something closer to posthumanism (though the latter topic also touches on matters that have little to do with animals).[27]

Challenges to traditional ways of construing the boundary between humans and animals are themselves diverse, however, and do not always proceed from the same ontological assumptions or carry the same implications for ethics. Matthew Calarco has recently attempted to map animal studies, not by giving it a comprehensive definition, but rather by categorizing a number of critical philosophical works on animals according to three ways of construing this boundary. He refers to these three categories with the terms identity, difference, and indistinction.[28] The identity approach takes its point of departure from Darwin's recognition that humans are also animals, situated on the tree of life alongside other mammals. While our evolution has produced characteristics that distinguish us among animal species, there remains "a deep continuity among human beings and animals with respect to certain ethically salient traits and capacities, such as sentience, cognition, subjectivity, and so on" (13).

Introduction 11

Many animals share *interests* with humans that are ethically relevant, such as the interest of sentient beings in pleasure rather than pain. To refuse to take these interests into account simply because animals do not belong to the human species is an "unjustifiable prejudice . . . a kind of speciesism, or granting unjustified privilege to our own species" (14). Against such prejudice, identity theorists argue that beings with similar interests and capacities deserve similar consideration when ethical decisions are made.

Calarco associates several philosophers with the identity approach, including Peter Singer, who attempts to apply the utilitarian principle of "the greatest good for the greatest number" to all sentient lives, whether human or animal; Tom Regan, who argues for animal rights on the basis that many animals as well as humans are "subjects of a life"; and Paola Cavalieri, who suggests that, since many animals possess the intentional agency protected by human rights, such rights ought to be extended to animals.[29] The ideas put forward by these thinkers have lent credibility to various proposals for both individual change (e.g., the reduction or elimination of meat in our diets at a time when factory farming has increased the suffering of animals we eat) and institutional change (e.g., attempts to extend basic rights to great apes on the basis of their similarities to us).[30] That latter example, however, also indicates one of the weaknesses of this approach. By specifying particular features, shared by humans with some animals, as qualifications for ethical consideration, identity theorists leave out animals who do not display these features to the same degree. Even some humans may fail to qualify for ethical consideration under certain definitions of ethically relevant characteristics.

Calarco thus turns to a second set of approaches to philosophy and ethics that are "based not on similarity, continuity, or identity but instead on an appreciation of the manifold differences that exist between and among human beings and animals."[31] Calarco's primary example here is Jacques Derrida, whose work is discussed further in my first three chapters. Rather than highlighting similarities between humans and other animals as identity theorists do, Derrida emphasizes heterogeneities that cut across both categories. The particularities of human differences (e.g., sexual or racial differences) and the particularities of animal differences (e.g., between species, or those discovered in encounters with individual animals such as Derrida's famous description of being seen naked by his cat)[32] need to be taken into account for an ethical response. As difference theorists, including some feminist thinkers, note, liberalism's focus on rights and rationality runs the risk of reinscribing hierarchies that exclude not only animals but also humans considered less rational than the Western subject of rights.[33]

Although Calarco is clearly sympathetic to the emphasis on difference, he does note weaknesses in its approach to animals. In comparison with identity theorists, thinkers of difference have been relatively restrained in their political recommendations, supporting initiatives on behalf of animals pragmatically but without devoting much attention to matters of policy or activism.[34] In making this assessment, Calarco acknowledges Derrida's "hyperethical . . . desire to change the status quo in view of justice," which Derrida emphasizes over the calculations of interests and rights found in some animal writings. Calarco suggests, however, that the premises of difference theorists should lead to greater "experimentation with the very kinds of alternative practices and modes of thought" for which they call.[35] Moreover, Calarco notes that the desire to avoid homogeneity among humans and animals can lead difference theorists, as it apparently led Derrida, to retain a sense of "radical discontinuity" between humans and animals, which Calarco finds problematic (47). Although Derrida wishes to complicate the boundary between humans and animals rather than maintain its traditional binary form, Calarco's dissatisfaction with this boundary leads him to a third approach.

The thinkers discussed by Calarco under the rubric "indistinction" include such diverse figures as Giorgio Agamben, Donna Haraway, Gilles Deleuze, and the environmental philosopher Val Plumwood. Like writers associated with Calarco's other two approaches, indistinction theorists challenge conventional ways of drawing ontological and ethical lines between humans and animals. Rather than arguing that some animals are like humans, however, indistinction theorists tend to emphasize, from a less anthropocentric direction, that humans are always already animals. Our fundamental animality is obscured by what Agamben calls "anthropogenesis" or the "anthropological machine," whereby Western thought and politics produce human being through a separation from animal life.[36] Calarco observes that "the anthropological machine is what philosophers would call a *performative* apparatus, inasmuch as it enacts and calls into being (which is to say, performs) a certain reality. It is the machine itself that creates, reproduces, and maintains the distinction between human life and animal life."[37] While Agamben underscores the impact of the anthropological machine on humans who come to be associated with animality, his call for moving beyond the anthropological machine also resonates with animal theorists who are concerned about the impact of that machine on nonhuman animal as well as human lives.

In order to think beyond the negative effects of the anthropological machine, Calarco calls attention to several efforts at reconceptualizing relationships among human beings and animals in less anthropocentric ways. These efforts include Plumwood's reflections on her experience of being attacked by a crocodile, which led to "a 'shocking reduction' away from her privileged subject position to a shared zone of coexistence with other edible beings."[38] But Calarco rightly notes that the anthropological machine is more than a set of ideas. It is also "a series of institutions and apparatuses that capture and reproduce but also constrain and kill animal life." Challenging the anthropological machine therefore requires a "pro-animal politics" (64), intersectional alliances between animal activists and other social justice causes, and direct actions taken against capitalist economies that generate suffering, on a massive scale, among both humans and animals.

"Indistinction" remains the least distinct among Calarco's three categories. Yet the heterogeneity of thinkers and issues covered under this framework seems, somehow, appropriate. One of the points made by Calarco and other animal studies thinkers, including Derrida and Agamben, is that the founding distinction between humans and other animals has explicitly or implicitly structured Western thought and practice. Thus, approaches that try to think beyond this constitutive distinction are bound to seem experimental and, like animals them/ourselves, heterogeneous.

Significantly for my purposes here, Calarco's discussion demonstrates the multiplicity of approaches to animal studies as a field. His three categories are simultaneously different from one another and internally diverse. His attention to writers who are not so often associated with animal studies, such as Plumwood, points us toward the benefits of being willing to draw upon other areas of interdisciplinary work that reflect on animals, including environmental or ecological thinking.[39]

Thus, while I will continue to use the phrase "animal studies" for the sake of convenience, it is important to acknowledge that the phrase is used here to refer to diverse styles of reading and analysis rather than a single methodological approach. Although I will attempt to make explicit the methodological and hermeneutical assumptions at work in the chapters that follow, these chapters do not all engage the same interdisciplinary partners or proceed in the same fashion. They might be understood rather as constituting what Mel Y. Chen calls "a multipoint engagement" between biblical literature and animal studies.[40] Or perhaps it would be more appropriate, in light of the attention given here to animals, to borrow Judith Halberstam's observation about queer reading and say that I am adopting "*a scavenger methodology* that uses different methods to collect and produce information on subjects who have been deliberately or accidentally excluded from traditional studies" of biblical literature.[41] But however one puts it, methodological respect for multiplicity and difference is in my view appropriate to the natures of the diverse texts that we refer to collectively as "the Hebrew Bible," the heterogeneous literature appearing in animal studies, and even the variable forms of life that we refer to collectively if simplistically as "animals."

Moreover, a reexamination of biblical literature in dialogue with animal studies does not require one to abandon insights from more traditional biblical studies. To the contrary, biblical scholarship has much to offer the study of animals and animal symbolism. Thus I will draw frequently on numerous types of biblical scholarship in the pages that follow, including both traditional modes of scholarship such as archaeology, historical contextualization, and close literary reading as well as less traditional modes. Some of my chapters will engage contemporary biblical scholarship more heavily than others, but none of them will ignore it.

My first chapter, then, takes its point of departure from what may seem a rather mundane animal fact: the crucial role of goatskins in the historical production of biblical scrolls, and in the biblical story of Jacob and the blessing that secures his place as ancestor of the Israelites. How might we explicate this enabling role of animal bodies in both the material history and the literary content of the Hebrew Bible? I explore this question by introducing three analytical frames from contemporary animal studies: (1) the constitutive importance of "companion species" relationships in specific contexts, emphasized by the feminist biologist and cultural theorist Donna Haraway, and illustrated in particular, in Israel's case, by flocks of goats and sheep; (2) the instability of the human/animal binary opposition, noted by philosophers such as Derrida and Calarco, among others; and (3) ubiquitous associations between species difference and differences among humans, particularly, in the case of biblical literature, gender and ethnic differences. Though all three of these frames are used in chapter 1 to shed light on stories from Genesis, they also recur throughout most of the chapters that follow.

Chapter 2 focuses on a companion species that is likely to be much better known by contemporary readers of the Bible than goats or sheep. Dogs, the earliest domesticated animals, may interact with more humans around the world today than any other species of living mammal. In the Hebrew Bible, however, their roles are not only limited but also usually considered negative. This chapter attempts to stage a more productive relationship to the Bible's dogs by engaging a short essay by Emmanuel Levinas, "The Name of a Dog, or Natural Rights." Although many writers associated with animal studies have discussed "The Name of a Dog," only a few give attention to two references to dogs in Exodus (one found in narrative, and one found in legal literature) that Levinas, following his rabbinic sources, engages. By reading these texts together, as Levinas and his rabbinic sources do, and reading them in relation to other texts from Exodus that stand alongside them, I attempt to highlight some of the complexities involved in the Bible's attitudes to animals. On the one hand, some texts from Exodus point to a positive concern for animal lives and animal welfare, and include the Israelites' animals among the multitude delivered from Egypt. On the other hand, texts from Exodus also prescribe animal sacrifice, raise the possibility of human sacrifice, and include Egyptian animals among the population who are slaughtered in Egypt, including children and slaves. These and other ambiguities in the Bible's treatment of animals parallel complications in attempts to use the Exodus story or other biblical narratives as straightforward resources for human liberation. Nevertheless, such texts do underscore recognition by the Bible's writers that the fates of humans and the fates of animals are inextricably intertwined.

Chapter 3 grapples more directly with the question of sacrifice raised in the previous chapter. Although many biblical texts command or assume the legitimacy of sacrifice, the motivations for and meanings of it remain obscure and at times contradictory. Rather than attempting to resolve all the questions that have traditionally been raised about it, I approach sacrifice from an unconventional direction by first engaging Derrida's brief reflection on the story of Cain and Abel and their respective offerings in *The Animal That Therefore I Am*. That reflection is embedded in a longer section on the Chimera, an ancient mythical beast who combines features from several animal species in a single body. I use Derrida's framing of the biblical story to ask whether "biblical sacrifice"—that is, the collection of biblical and scholarly texts that represent sacrifice—is not itself "chimeric" in nature. Although sacrifice is easily taken as a practice that functions to distinguish humans from animals, biblical sacrifice simultaneously produces divisions among animals (by making some animals available for sacrifice and other animals unavailable), produces divisions among humans (by distinguishing humans who can sacrifice from those who cannot), and blurs lines between humans and other animals (by raising the possibility of child sacrifice and holy war, and identifying certain animals as appropriate substitutes for humans who might otherwise be sacrificed). I also discuss Jonathan Klawans's symbolic theory of Israelite sacrifice as a ritual process that draws analogies between, on the one hand, domesticated animals and Israelites and, on the other hand, Israelites and God. Klawans articulates these analogies with biblical passages such as Psalm 23 that use relations between domesticated animals and humans as metaphors for relations between humans and God. I suggest that his theory also helps us understand ancient child sacrifice as a logical consequence of analogies that structure the biblical sacrifice of animals. Paradoxically, by reading biblical sacrifice in dialogue with the otherwise opposed accounts of Derrida and Klawans, we may find ourselves better able to recognize that, rather than simply reinforcing the boundary between human and animal, biblical sacrifice, like the story of the Chimera, simultaneously assumes, undermines, and redraws lines among humans, animals, and the divine.

In chapter 4, my biblical focus shifts to the story of Balaam's ass and to attempts by scholars to read her story alongside those of other animals in the Hebrew Bible and beyond. While I attempt elsewhere to read the story of Balaam's ass as a reflection on difficulties we face whenever we try to understand human, animal, and divine others,[42] here I shift my interpretive questions to animal ethics and "animal hermeneutics."[43] Matters of animal ethics may seem rather distant from this donkey's story, but Jewish tradition sometimes appeals to her story in order to encourage kindness to animals. Indeed, the story explicitly calls attention to Balaam's mistreatment of the donkey and his prior relationship to her; and, unusually, it supplies her with agency and perspective. With only rare exceptions, biblical scholarship seldom raises questions about the treatment of animals in connection with Balaam's donkey. Since biblical scholars themselves do not agree on how, best, to read her story, however, or where to place her among the Bible's other animals, I consider the ways in which multiple approaches to the text allow us to see the story and the donkeys who inspire it in a new light. By allowing for diversity and difference in our interpretations of the Bible's animals, as among animal species, and by paying more attention to the words of the donkey herself as well as the messenger of God, I suggest that we may find opportunities to move from animal hermeneutics to animal ethics. The particular form of animal ethics stimulated by the story, however, is less about abstract principles and more about the empathy and affect that some animal studies scholars emphasize.

While the first three chapters are especially focused on Israel's relations with domesticated animals, and chapter four includes both domesticated and wild animals, chapter five shifts the focus further toward wild animals. Although the Bible's writers lived more closely with domesticated animals, they were also familiar with wild ones. Here I ask about the ways in which those writers interpreted wild animals through what I call, borrowing from the sociologist Adrian Franklin, the Bible's "zoological gaze." It may actually be more appropriate to refer to the Bible's "zoological gazes," since various biblical texts see wild animals in different ways. A number of these texts understand wild animals as threatening, both literally and as symbols for other threatening forces and situations. Some texts call attention instead to more positive qualities. Many references to wild animals also shed light on the Bible's views about God, however; and these references can be either threatening or reassuring, depending on the context. A few of these texts, such as Psalm 104 or Job 38–41, also indicate that God has direct relationships with wild animals, independent of God's relationships with humans.

This conversation leads then in the following chapter to some reflection on the relevance for biblical interpretation of the idea, articulated by several scholars of religious studies, that animals might be considered religious or theological "subjects" rather than "objects." In recent years, a number of primatologists, including Barbara King, Frans de Waal, and Jane Goodall, have made intriguing observations about the possible presence among animals of building blocks for morality, empathy, grief, meaning-making, altruism, justice, and even, in Goodall's case, "spirituality." Although I do not attempt to make empirical claims about animal morality or religion, I do suggest in chapter 6 that, as strange as such claims may seem to our modern sensibilities, parts of the Hebrew Bible already gesture in a similar direction. When the Psalms and other texts represent animals and other elements of nature as subjects of praise for God, it is easy to dismiss such language as nothing more than an enthusiastic use of metaphor. Yet such quick dismissal may fail to take seriously the biblical notion that God does "save human and animal" (Ps. 36:6), and judges them both as well. Pulling together references from several different biblical texts and contemporary scholars, and reading the psalmists and the primatologists as perhaps having more shared interests than one might initially think, I propose reimagining biblical religion as a phenomenon that did, in certain respects at least, include animals as well as humans within its purview.

A concluding chapter then turns to the problem of reading ancient texts from the Hebrew Bible in a modern world that is facing dramatic species extinctions. The environmental ethicist Holmes Rolston III once referred to Noah's ark as "the first Endangered Species Project."[44] Whereas Rolston was well aware of tensions between science and religion and navigated them admirably, I take up his brief engagement with the story of Noah and other texts from the Hebrew Bible primarily as a challenge to reimagine the role of biblical interpretation in an age of extinction. Scientists tell us that extinctions have always been a part of life, but that they are increasing rapidly as both direct and indirect consequences of human actions. While I make no attempt to correlate ancient religion with modern evolutionary science, which the writers of the Bible could not have known, I do reframe such tales from Genesis as those of Creation, the Flood, and Noah's ark with prophetic texts such as Jeremiah

12:4 and Hosea 4:3 that also understand the disappearance of animals and plants as consequences of human activities. Noting the arguments of Thom van Dooren and Donna Haraway that species extinctions and other environmental threats compel us to learn to tell new stories, or retell old stories in new ways, I offer in conclusion a retelling of the Bible's story of animal life that may be more useful for our contemporary context than some of the stories we have told about the Bible and its animals in the past. By reading several texts together in dialogue with contemporary concerns about species extinctions, I hope to suggest that, even though the Bible cannot solve our contemporary ecological problems, it may underscore our responsibility for the survival or destruction of other species.

The Hebrew Bible itself recognizes that thinking about animals is a wise and worthy pursuit. Solomon, before getting himself into trouble with the biblical storytellers, receives from God wisdom and discernment as vast as "the sand on the seashore" (1 Kgs 4:29 [Hebrew 5:9]). And what does this wisdom and discernment entail? Among other things, Solomon "spoke about trees, from the cedar that is in Lebanon to the hyssop that comes out of the wall. He would speak about animals, and birds, and creeping things, and fish" (1 Kgs 4:33 [Hebrew 5:13]). When one hears about religion today, and particularly religion influenced by biblical traditions, one seldom hears about Solomon's interest in "animals, and birds, and creeping things, and fish." In his excellent study *The Question of the Animal and Religion*, however, Aaron Gross makes a strong case that "attending to" animals is a crucial practice for both scholars and practitioners of religion.[45] I hope to suggest here that "attending to" animals is crucial for biblical studies as well, as it was already for Solomon; and that such attention will benefit from interdisciplinary engagement with contemporary animal studies. This is an invitation, then, to attend to the Bible's animals in dialogue with animal studies.

1

Israel's Companion Species and the Creation of Bibles

Some of the Dead Sea Scrolls consist of papyrus, a plant-based writing surface, and at least one is metal. Most of them, however, are parchment, made of animal skins. In 2001, using new technology, a team of researchers analyzed DNA from the lengthy Temple Scroll and other scroll fragments.[1] The Temple Scroll and several of the other fragments were found to derive from domestic goatskins, and other pieces from the skin of the Nubian ibex, one of the goat's wild relatives. The researchers list cave numbers, but apart from the Temple Scroll, they give no indication of the literary contents of the scrolls from which fragments were analyzed. Given the large percentage of scrolls that contain biblical material, however, it seems safe to conclude that the scribes who wrote Dead Sea Scrolls chose to preserve biblical texts on the skins of goats and ibexes.

Scholars have long known that biblical literature and other ancient texts were preserved on animal skins. Famous biblical manuscripts, such as the Alexandrinus, Sinaiticus, Vaticanus, and Aleppo codices, are all made from parchment. Their animal origins are still apparent from the presence of such features as hair follicle patterns, which, quite apart from DNA analysis, sometimes make it possible to determine the species from which a piece of parchment was created.[2] Multiple rabbinic sources also discuss the preparation and use of animal skins in the creation of Torah scrolls.[3] Given the popularity of parchment as an ancient writing surface, it is hardly surprising that the scribes who produced biblical texts utilized them.

At least one biblical scholar has proposed a connection between the use of parchment and the process of canonizing biblical texts. Menahem Haran has noted that, in Egypt, where papyrus appears to have been more popular than parchment, "skins were retained for works of particular importance or of special use, such as collections of laws, records which were intended to be preserved for a long period of time, or particular books which were put on display in temples."[4] Parchment lasts longer than papyrus and was thus deemed more suitable for documents intended to survive. Haran suggests that similar practices are likely to have been followed in pre-exilic Israel, when most written materials, including early versions of biblical texts, were probably recorded on papyrus. By the time of the Talmud, however, the use of skins for the production of Torah scrolls was required. Haran argues that this transition from papyrus to parchment is likely to have taken place during the Second Temple period, as first the Torah and then other texts gradually came to be regarded as holy books. The development of Judaism into a religion that consulted an identifiable set of writings in order to guide communal life necessitated the selection of writing materials that could withstand the passage of time, allowing scrolls of significant books to be passed down and read by future generations. Parchment met this need, and became the preferred writing surface for books that were increasingly granted a central religious role. Thus the processes that we call canonization correlate with a growing use of animal skins. What we now call the Bible was literally created from animal skins, and the religions that relied upon it drew their life, in part, from the bodies of dead animals.

How many goats, how many ibexes, how many sheep, cattle, and other animals whose skins were used for parchment provided the material conditions for the survival of Judaism and Christianity as text-based religious traditions? There is, of course, no way to answer that question. The question itself, however, points toward a need to take more seriously the relationships between biblical literature and animals. For it underscores the possibility that neither the books of the Hebrew Bible, nor Judaism and Christianity as religions based in part on interpretations of the Bible, would have taken the forms they did without the presence of animals, interacting with humans in specific times and places. We may even wonder whether this association between animal skins and biblical texts helps us understand, in part, the appearance of animal figures and human–animal hybrids in biblical manuscripts across the centuries, to which Giorgio Agamben draws attention at the beginning of *The Open: Man and Animal*.[5] The Bible in the form in which we know it is a product of our contextualized relations with particular species of animals. They do not intrude upon the Bible, but made it possible.

The significance of goatskins for the construction of the Hebrew Bible is not limited to their use as a writing surface. In Genesis 27, Rebekah instructs her son Jacob to "Go to the flock, and get me from there two young goats" (27:9).[6] From these goats she makes food for her husband and Jacob's father, Isaac. Because Jacob is "smooth" while his brother Esau is "hairy," Rebekah famously takes another step. After dressing Jacob in Esau's clothing, "she put the skins of the young goats on his hands and on the smooth parts of his neck" (27:16). When Isaac feels the hair on Jacob's hands, eats the goat dish, drinks wine, and smells the clothes on his son, Isaac blesses Jacob thinking that Jacob is Esau. Both Jacob and Rebekah play active roles in tricking Isaac. But the trick's success depends, crucially, on the bodies of young goats. Without the goat parts that his mother cooks for food, or the goatskins and hair that are attached to his body, Jacob would not receive Isaac's blessing. Jacob's name, of course, is subsequently changed to Israel (32:28 [Hebrew 32:29]; 35:10), an indication of his status as the primary legendary ancestor of, and a point of symbolic identification for, the Israelites. One might conclude, then, that goatskins not only made possible the Hebrew Bible as a material object to be preserved and passed down. They also facilitated the symbolic creation of Israel, as a people whose flourishing is grounded in part in a tradition that their ancestor Jacob/Israel and his clever mother used goatskins to secure a blessing. We might even say that the narrative inscribed on animal skins acknowledges in its content that animals were necessary for the creation of the people whose story the skins preserve.

Rebekah's use of goatskins to secure the blessing of Israel seems to confirm the relevance for biblical interpretation of Aaron Gross's observation that "human communities everywhere imagine themselves—their subjectivity, their ethics, their ancestry—with and through animals."[7]

Gross makes this point in the process of arguing for the importance of contemporary interdisciplinary animal studies and of what he calls a "multifaceted, critical 'animal hermeneutics.'" As explicated by Gross, such a hermeneutics underscores the "basic observation that *across time and across cultures humans imagine themselves through animal others*" (5; emphasis his). To be sure, distinctions between humans and other animals are constructed in many different ways; and "even within a given time and place, multiple understandings of the human/animal operate in relation to and competition with one another" (11). Yet the human tendency to conceptualize identity and otherness in relation to nonhuman animals is extremely widespread and goes back far in history. If animals "invariably play a decisive role in human self-conception," as Gross suggests (8), then we should expect to find them playing such a role in the Hebrew Bible.

In this chapter, then, I want to consider in more detail the story of Jacob in Genesis as well as several related texts. The story of Jacob is an ideal object for reflection on Israel's "self-conception," whether one is interested in animals or not. After all, as noted above, Jacob is given the name "Israel" in both Genesis 32:28 (Hebrew 32:29) and 35:10. The new appellation makes Jacob the primary legendary ancestor of the Israelites and what biblical scholars call their "eponymous" ancestor, that is, the ancestor carrying Israel's name. His sons and two of his grandsons are also understood as eponymous ancestors of the tribes who collectively constitute Israel as a people, and the story of the births of those sons to four women in Genesis 30 has long been read as a narrative representation of imagined relations among those tribes. So, too, his relationship with his brother Esau may shed light on the ways in which the Israelites imagined their relations with the Edomites, said to be descendants of Esau.

Because animals appear multiple times in Jacob's story, however, it also serves as a useful text with which to begin exploring the relevance of animal studies for biblical interpretation. For as noted in the Introduction, animal studies has emerged as an exciting area of interdisciplinary study across the contemporary academy, yet has barely begun to be taken into account by biblical scholars. Thus, after briefly reviewing several elements of Jacob's story in order to highlight the presence of animals in it, I will summarize three emphases found in contemporary animal studies that in my view help us make sense of that story. These emphases are (1) the constitutive importance of what Donna Haraway calls "companion species," including in Israel's case goats and sheep; (2) the instability of the human/animal binary opposition, emphasized by numerous thinkers including Jacques Derrida and Matthew Calarco; and (3) associations between species difference and differences among humans, particularly, in the case of biblical literature, gender and ethnic differences and the identification of some humans as slaves. Although the story of Jacob provides my primary textual focus here, the elements of animal studies that are utilized in this chapter for the interpretation of Jacob's story also play a role in several of the chapters that follow.

Animals in the Jacob Story

Early in Jacob's story, his elder brother Esau is said to be "red" from birth, "all of him like a hairy mantle" (Gen. 25:25). He is characterized by excessive hairiness. As Susan Niditch has shown, male hairiness has connotations in biblical literature that are often positive in context, including an association between hairiness and manhood.[8] Such hairiness might also associate Esau with animals, however, or in any case mammals, who generally have more hair than the hairiest of men. In fact, Esau's hairiness is sometimes used by scholars to place him in the folk tradition of "wild men," who, like Enkidu in the Mesopotamian story of Gilgamesh, are closely associated with animals.[9] This association with animals is strengthened by Esau's characterization as "a man who knows hunting, a man of the field" (25:27). Although "wild men" such as Enkidu may protect animals from hunters, Esau is located where animals are, and he knows how to find them. Jacob, by contrast, is found among the tents (25:27); and in chapter 27, Jacob explicitly refers to himself as "a smooth man" in distinction from Esau, described as "a hairy man" (27:11).

In chapter 27, however, after Esau goes out to hunt game for his father in order to receive Isaac's blessing, Rebekah proves to be skilled in her use of animals as well. As we have seen, she instructs Jacob to "Go to the flock, and get me from there two young goats" (27:9). From the goats she makes food for Isaac and the skin coverings that she places on Jacob's hands and neck to make him feel like his hairy brother (27:16). The trick's success depends on the bodies of goats, as noted above; but it also relies upon some similarity between goatskins and the hairy skin of Esau. Without the goat parts that his mother cooks for food, or the goatskins and hair that are attached to his body, Jacob would not receive Isaac's blessing.

The presence of animals thus structures Jacob's story, and hence this story of Israel's origins and identity, from the beginning. And animals recur throughout Jacob's story. In chapter 29, his first encounter with Rachel involves flocks that she tends for her father Laban, who is Jacob's maternal uncle. Jacob rolls a stone from off a well in order to allow Rachel's animals to drink. Jacob reminds Laban in 30:25–30 that the work Jacob has done to acquire Laban's daughters, Leah and Rachel, includes tending Laban's livestock, which flourish under Jacob's care. He continues working for his uncle as part of a deal that allows Jacob to keep "all the sheep that are speckled or spotted and all the sheep that are black among the lambs and all the spotted or speckled among the goats" (30:32). Though Laban attempts to hide such animals, the text describes in some detail how Jacob, through a kind of magic, manipulates the breeding of goats and sheep to increase the number of animals received as wages (30:37–42). Jacob has apparently inherited his mother's skill at using animals to trick fathers and achieve desired goals. By the end of the chapter, Jacob has not only amassed "great flocks" of sheep and goats, but also "female slaves and male slaves and camels and donkeys" (30:43).

In chapter 31, Jacob calls Rachel and Leah to join him in a field where his flock is. There he notes how God increased his livestock by causing speckled animals to be born when Laban pays in speckled animals, and striped animals to be born when Laban pays in striped animals. He then recounts a dream about male goats mounting other goats. God's messenger implies in the dream that God caused striped, speckled, and spotted male goats to breed, to Jacob's benefit. After Jacob departs for Canaan, Laban chides him for sneaking away with Laban's daughters and accuses him of stealing Laban's household gods, which are hidden in Rachel's camel saddle. When the gods are not found, Jacob gives a speech about the twenty years he spent tending Laban's flocks and assuming the costs when sheep or goats were taken by wild animals. As Jacob notes, "I served you fourteen years for your two daughters and six years for your flock" (31:41). In the next chapter, Jacob attempts to defuse Esau's anger with a gift of "two hundred female goats and twenty male goats, two hundred ewes and twenty rams, thirty nursing camels and their offspring, forty cows and ten bulls, twenty she-asses and ten he-asses" (32:14–15). If animals played a role in the original schism between Jacob and Esau, now Jacob hopes that animals can resolve the conflict. The chapter concludes with Jacob's wrestling match with a figure who initially appears to be a man but actually is nonhuman. When this figure cannot win the match, he blesses Jacob and names him "Israel" (32:28 [Hebrew 32:29]). The narrator notes, however, that because Jacob has been struck on the thigh, "the sons of Israel" will not eat certain sinew meats from the thighs of their animals (32:32).

After Jacob persuades his brother to accept the gifts of animals, he also notes that he needs to travel more slowly than Esau so as not to overtax either his many children or his own remaining "flocks and herds, which are nursing" (33:13), in other words, which have many young of their own. When he arrives eventually at Succoth, which means "booths" or "sheds," he "made booths for his cattle" (33:17), booths that give Succoth its name. Subsequently he travels to Shechem, where he buys land from Hamor, whose name means "ass" or "donkey." This purchase sets the stage for the sexual shaming of Jacob's daughter Dinah by Hamor's son, Shechem, which takes place while Jacob's sons "were with the cattle in the field" (34:5).[10] Jacob's sons avenge their sister's humiliation by persuading the men of Shechem to be circumcised as a step toward alliance. As part of this alliance, the sons of Jacob note, "we will give our daughters to you, and we will take your daughters for ourselves" (34:16). When Hamor and Shechem repeat this offer to the men of their city, they add that "all their cattle and their property and all their animals" will also move between the two groups of men, along with daughters, as part of the alliance (34:23). The offer is apparently a ruse, and Dinah's brothers Simeon and Levi kill the men of Shechem after they are circumcised, when they are in too much pain to fight. As a consequence, Jacob's sons "took their flocks and their herds and their donkeys, and whatever was in the city and whatever was in the field" (34:28). As with the story of their father, so also in this tale of Jacob's sons, we see women and animals referred to together as objects exchanged or taken between men.

Other animals appear in the story of Jacob and, later, in the stories of his sons, especially Joseph. But even this brief summary of a few chapters should indicate how common animals are in the story of Israel's origins. Israel's narrative emergence is inextricably intertwined with domesticated animals in particular, especially goats and sheep, but also cattle, donkeys, and camels.

Re-reading with an Animal Hermeneutics

Biblical scholars usually integrate these animals into the conventional reading strategies of biblical studies. One can, for example, find discussions of the historical role of small-cattle herding in both commentaries and studies of Israel's social world.[11] I want to suggest, however, that our interpretation of Jacob's story and other biblical texts that deal with animals may be enriched if we reexamine them as well from the perspective of an animal hermeneutics. In addition to Gross's observation about the roles animals play in human self-understanding, I note here three emphases from contemporary animal studies that are also useful for biblical interpretation: (1) the constitutive importance of companion species for human history and culture, (2) the instability of the human–animal binary, and (3) the ubiquitous association between species difference and differences among humans, particularly, in the case of this text, gender and ethnic differences and the designation of some humans as slaves. Though the emphases are interrelated, I take each in turn, summarizing a few points made in animal studies while returning to Jacob's story and other texts throughout to indicate the potential relevance for biblical interpretation.[12]

Companion Species: The phrase "companion species" is most closely associated with feminist cultural theorist and biologist Donna Haraway. As explicated by Haraway, "companion species" include, but are not identical to, "companion animals," those individual animals (such as pets) with whom many humans live. The notion of companion species is used in a more comprehensive sense to analyze what Haraway calls "co-constitutive human relationships with other critters."[13] Thus it encompasses a wider range of types of interactions among humans, other animals, and plants than simply the relationships between humans and individual pets. Haraway notes that human nature and human cultures do not preexist such interactions with other species. Individually and collectively, humans always "become who they are" with other living and non-living entities in particular "situated histories, situated naturecultures" (25). As the neologism "naturecultures" indicates, Haraway's understanding of companion species calls into question dichotomizing oppositions between "culture" and "nature," as well as associated oppositions between "human" and "animal," "living" and "non-living," or, to cite again that opposition beloved by twentieth-century biblical scholarship, "history" and "nature." Against tendencies to understand human existence independently of other living beings and material circumstances, Haraway argues that we are always "entangled" with other "critters" in specific "contact zones." Haraway takes the phrase "contact zone" from canine agility training; but she notes that it occurs also in postcolonial studies, acknowledging thereby that power relations and complex histories of conflict between humans structure companion species contact zones.

Although engaged with critical theory, Haraway's analyses of companion species relationships are usually developed around concrete cases. Starting from specific examples of species interaction (this training dog with this woman, these herding dogs with these sheep, these sheep with these tribes as well as their colonizers, and so forth) in particular contact zones, she explores such interactions in ways that make animals agents of history, active participants worthy of sustained attention rather than simply objects in the "background" or "context." While Haraway is especially interested in interactions between humans and dogs, she also gives attention to other companion species, including other domesticated animals such as sheep and chickens; and to the histories of labor, economy, technology, geography, migration, colonialism, ethnic relations, gender relations, and so forth, that shape the contact zones in which humans and our companion species co-evolve. Significantly for my purposes, Haraway includes novels, photographs, and other forms of symbolic representation among the sites that are useful for analyzing companion species relations. Thus, while she shows little interest in biblical literature, one could easily conclude from Haraway's work that biblical texts, too, with their many references to animals and plants, can be interpreted as products of co-constitutive companion species relationships that "entangled" the writers of the Bible in the contact zones that we more often refer to as the Bible's ancient contexts.

Now it is not difficult to recognize that the goats and sheep populating Jacob's story and other biblical texts could be considered examples of "companion species" in Haraway's sense. Their presence testifies to the origins of biblical literature in the "situated naturecultures" of the ancient Levant, where, as histories of domestication and zooarchaeological evidence have shown, the herding of goats and sheep was crucial for human livelihood long before the emergence of Israelites as well as during the periods in which biblical literature was being written.[14] After dogs, goats and then sheep appear to have been the earliest animals domesticated in the ancient Near East. Indeed, the bones of goats and sheep generally make up the largest number of bones found in archaeological sites, where animal bones are usually more numerous than any other type of archaeological artifact except pottery pieces. The third largest group of animals whose bones are found at most archaeological sites are cattle, which require more water and pasturage than sheep and goats (hence their smaller numbers) but are prized for their ability to plow and pull heavy loads.

When readers of the Bible encounter such Hebrew words as those for "flock" and "shepherd," they may imagine primarily flocks of sheep. But biblical "flocks" included both goats and sheep, with sheep outnumbering goats in some places but not others. These mixed flocks allowed herders to maximize available pasturage, since goats eat a wider range of plants than sheep. Because goats are also hardier than sheep, and diseases that affect one species may not affect the other, herding both goats and sheep provides a kind of risk-management strategy. The fact that sheep bones still outnumber goat bones at many sites is sometimes taken as an indication that extra sheep were raised for trade in an ancient market economy; but the zooarchaeologist Aharon Sasson argues that fluctuations in relative numbers of goats and sheep more likely result from a subsistence strategy in which sheep were prized for their wool, while goats, being able to survive harsher conditions, provided more herd security.[15] In either case, the two species together were used for milk, wool, skins, tools made from bones or horns, and meat. Meat made up a smaller proportion of the average diet in ancient Israel than it does today, though the amount of meat consumed likely differed from place to place and between social strata. Most of the goats and sheep killed for meat were probably young males, who do not contribute milk, reach a good size within two or three years, and are not needed in large numbers for reproduction within the herd. Though older animals were probably also eaten when they were no longer useful for other purposes, the tendency to eat young animals may shed light on the fact that Rebekah explicitly asks Jacob to bring two "kids" for Isaac's food (Gen. 27:9; cf. 38:17; Judg. 13:19).

The constant presence of sheep and goats in Israel's story need not be seen as indicating that the Israelites associated themselves originally with rural pastoral nomadism rather than village or city life, as some scholars claimed in the past. The herding of flocks took place in urban, village, rural, and nomadic or semi-nomadic contexts throughout Israel, as in the larger ancient Near East; and pastoral nomads interacted with farmers, sometimes participating in farming themselves. Thus, in spite of the fact that biblical texts in their written forms were probably produced in urban contexts, the earliest authors and audiences for biblical traditions would certainly have been familiar with the realities of living alongside sheep and goats. This familiarity can be seen not only in the recurring references to the animals and their flocks, but also in textual details that provide evidence of knowledge about animal lives. For example, while the growth of Jacob's flocks is attributed in Genesis 30:37–43 to a kind of magic, the dream he recounts to Leah and Rachel in 31:10–13 betrays an awareness of livestock breeding that we today associate with genetics. If, as Jacob's dream indicates, the striped, speckled, and spotted male animals mount the female animals more often than the other males in Laban's flock do, the offspring produced are more likely to be striped, speckled, and spotted as well, and so to belong to Jacob rather than Laban according to the bargain they have made. This account of the multiplication of Jacob's goats and sheep assumes a pre-scientific awareness of animal reproduction that would surely have been common among people who lived alongside goats and sheep.

By associating flocks with Jacob's blessing and the growth of Jacob's household, Genesis allows us to understand these animals as an integral part of Israel's "becoming who they are," to borrow Haraway's language. Indeed, biblical narratives also associate shepherding with other, more distant, ancestors such as Abraham (e.g., Gen. 12:16; 13:2, 5–8; 20:14; 21:25–30) and revered leaders such as Moses (Exod. 3:1) and David (1 Sam. 16:11, 19; 17:15, 20, 28, 34–37). In the latter two cases, such characterizations resonate with ancient Near Eastern representations of political leaders as shepherds. But the literary use of animals to emphasize the scope of Jacob's blessing, and probably his prestige, is apparent from the large numbers of animals that Jacob is able to give Esau as a gift. As noted above, according to Genesis 32:14–15 Jacob gave Esau "two hundred female goats and twenty male goats, two hundred ewes and twenty rams, thirty nursing camels and their offspring, forty cows and ten bulls, twenty she-asses and ten he-asses" (32:14–15); and he still has numerous animals of his own to care for in chapter 33 (and to be desired by the men of Shechem in chapter 34). The mixing of species in this gift may reflect an accurate knowledge of the tendency of pastoralists to herd various types of animals as a risk-management strategy.[16] But the total number of animals owned by Jacob seems unrealistically large in comparison, for example, to zooarchaeological estimates of the number of animals per person that are likely to have lived in any one village in ancient Israel, which vary from less than one animal per person to just more than three (mostly goats and sheep, with some cattle).[17] Although actual numbers are difficult to calculate and surely varied from place to place, such an estimate highlights by contrast the large size of Jacob's flocks and herds. References to large herds are explicitly used in other texts to illustrate the extraordinary wealth of male characters, including Nabal, the "great man" who in 1 Samuel 25:2 has "three thousand sheep and a thousand goats." But Jacob's many animals also signify his blessing and—in tension with his earlier characterization as a trickster—his generosity to such potential enemies as the Edomites.

Moreover, the proliferation of Jacob's sheep, goats, and other animals is narratively tied to the struggle between Leah and Rachel that results in the proliferation of Jacob's sons. Both Jacob and Laban link Jacob's acquisition of Laban's daughters to Jacob's acquisition of livestock (Gen. 31:41–43). If these daughters are subsequently understood to have "built up the house of Israel," in the words of Ruth 4:11, so too the reproduction of Jacob's animals represents Israel's expansion. The blessing of Israel is signified narratively by the propagation of both Israel's children and Israel's companion species. In Gen. 33:13, Jacob even expresses concern in a single verse for both his children and his nursing animals. The generation of human offspring and animal offspring are both considered signs of the fertility that is given by God in the Bible, along with the successful growth of crops. As Moses argues in Deuteronomy 7:14, if the Israelites obey the stipulations of God's covenant, "there will not be sterility or barrenness among you or among your animals."

Given how inextricably intertwined the narrated lives of Israelite ancestors are with their companion species, it is unsurprising that biblical writers also found in relationships with sheep and goats a rich resource for political and religious imagery. Like other ancient texts, biblical literature utilizes the language of shepherding and flocks to refer to both human leaders and God, on the one hand, and the people they lead, on the other hand. This imagery, discussed further in chapter 3, is perhaps best known from its use in Psalm 23; but it can be found in many biblical texts.[18] The consequent impact of specific species of animals—flocks of sheep and goats—on Western literary and religious thought is considerable. We only have to imagine how differently Judaism and Christianity might have looked if the cross-species relationships used to represent relationships between humans and God involved elephants and mahouts, for example, rather than flocks and shepherds. And as we shall see in chapter 3, this shepherding imagery may have influenced the religious practices of the Israelites by informing their understanding of the ritual of sacrifice, a ritual that ultimately would shape not only post-biblical Judaism but also Christianity. Goats and sheep are thus "co-constitutive" partners in the creation of Israelite religion as well as Israelite identity. Without goats and sheep, Israel's story as we have it, and the religions grounded in that story, would not exist.

Destabilizing the Human–Animal Binary: When the Bible uses herding images to represent God or political leaders as shepherds, the logic of its symbolism puts human beings in the positions of sheep and goats. Rather than simply placing animals alongside Israel in pastoral scenes, it takes advantage of the familiarity that the Israelites had with their subordinate companion species to represent the Israelites themselves as animals, subordinated to a divine or political lord. The differences between the Israelites and the animals they lived with are downplayed while similarities are highlighted: all of them are cared for by some other entity. Beyond herding symbolism, moreover, the animals of the Israelites are sometimes included among the people in biblical literature, as, for example, when

Israelite children and animals are spared by God in Egypt while Egyptian children and animals are killed (Exod. 11:4–7; 12:12, 29–32). In that story, which I return to in the next chapter, a clear line is drawn between the Israelites, human *and* animal, and the Egyptians, human *and* animal; but animals belong to both groups of people.

The firmness of the distinction between human and animal might seem self-evident to most readers of the Bible. Indeed, it has served as a foundational contrast for most of Western culture. Yet as Matthew Calarco notes, "One of the defining characteristics of our age is the radical breakdown of the human/animal distinction."[19] As noted in the Introduction, many scholars associated with animal studies, including Haraway and Calarco, critically interrogate the particular types of distinctions we routinely make between humans and other animals and the effects that these distinctions have on our treatment of nonhuman life. Such interrogation may call attention to ways in which distinctions between humans and animals are not only asserted but also transgressed or destabilized in various cultural practices, including literature and religion.

One influential thinker whose work raises questions about the ways in which we draw boundaries between humans and animals is Jacques Derrida. Derrida's writings have already served as valuable resources for many biblical scholars and other scholars of religion, even apart from his attention to animal questions.[20] Thus his approach to what he calls "the question of the animal," which has received significant attention from animal studies scholars, may prove useful for a study of biblical interpretation and animal studies as well. Indeed, while Derrida's exploration of animal issues is most often focused on modern philosophical and literary texts, he also turns to the biblical book of Genesis at several points in his influential lectures published as *The Animal That Therefore I Am*, where he reads such texts as the stories of Adam and Eve and of Cain and Abel.[21]

In a number of essays, lectures, and interviews, Derrida analyzes the ways in which Western philosophical and literary traditions attempt to draw a dogmatic line between "man" and "animal" in order to define the properly human. Like other thinkers associated with animal studies, Derrida clearly finds many of these attempts problematic. After all, the identification of specific characteristics that are supposed to distinguish humans from all animals has proven to be increasingly dubious as our scientific knowledge of other animals has increased. Yet Derrida's critique of attempts to draw a clear line between "man" and "animal" does not entail, as it does for some thinkers, the elimination of differences between humans and other animals. He emphasizes instead the multiple differences that exist among diverse types of animals, which are both similar and dissimilar to humans in many different ways. To examine the relationships between humans and animals by comparing us carefully with great apes, who share so much of our genetic identity, or dogs, who share a history of domestication and co-evolution with us that is thousands of years old, is an altogether different enterprise than a comparison between, say, humans and snakes, or humans and bats, or for that matter snakes and bats. Close attention to the multiple modes of life found among non-human animals thus has the paradoxical effect of pluralizing the category of "animal" while simultaneously destabilizing the singular boundary constructed between humans and all other animals. Once one begins to examine the particular characteristics of a wide range of living creatures, routine appeals to such traditional criteria as language, self-consciousness or reason no longer lead so easily to absolute distinctions between "the human" as such, and "the animal" as such. As Derrida puts it, "there is not one opposition" between the human and the animal. Rather "there are, between different organizational structures of the living being, many fractures, heterogeneities, differential structures."[22] Derrida's goal therefore is not to propose "some homogeneous continuity" between humans and other animals.[23] Instead of simply "effacing" the line between human and animal, Derrida is interested "in multiplying its figures, in complicating, thickening, delinearizing, folding, and dividing the line precisely by making it increase and multiply" (29). (And we may hear in that phrase, "increase and multiply," an allusion to God's commands to living creatures in Genesis 1:22, 28.) What we have to reckon with is not a single boundary between humans and animals, but rather "a heterogeneous multiplicity of the living" (31), a wide range of similarities and differences that are construed in many ways by different cultures, including those that gave us the Bible.

Derrida's work also engages ethical questions about violence carried out routinely against other animals. The attempt to establish a clear boundary between humans and animals provides one of the foundations for the anthropocentrism and human exceptionalism that fuel and justify such violence: because we assume that we are absolutely unlike them, we assert our right to dominate them. But rather than focusing solely on politics and activism to address this violence, Derrida's work calls our attention to places in which our traditions, including biblical traditions, assume and construct human exceptionalism, for example, by permitting the killing of animals (or what Derrida calls "a place left open . . . for a noncriminal putting to death").[24] At the same time, and paradoxically, Derrida notes the ways in which our traditions blur the lines between other animals and *some* humans, for example, by permitting the mistreatment of humans who, being considered less than properly human, are animalized. The distinctions we make between humans and other animals are widespread and ethically fraught, but also multiple and contradictory.

I will return to Derrida's work and some of its implications below and in subsequent chapters. Here, though, I want to note that the book of Genesis combines certain dynamics that resonate with Derrida's reflections. These dynamics consist of, on the one hand, making distinctions between humans and animals in ways that undergird the domination of animals by humans; and, on the other hand, simultaneously undermining, destabilizing, or pluralizing distinctions between humans and animals. Earlier in the book than the stories of Jacob, both of these dynamics are at work, for example, in the Genesis creation accounts, accounts that clearly hold Derrida's interest in *The Animal That Therefore I Am*.

Both creation accounts in Genesis seem at various points to make a clear distinction between humans and animals. In the priestly creation account in 1:1–2:4a, humans are created after all the animals, and separately from them. Famously, humans alone are said to be created "in the image of God" (1:27); and after blessing them, God tells the humans, "Be fruitful and multiply and fill the earth and subdue it. Rule over the fish of the sea, and the birds of the skies, and every living creature that moves on the earth" (1:28). These verses have received a great deal of attention in recent years as readers have debated the implications of divinely mandated rule over the earth: Should we read this passage in terms of domination, or something closer to care and stewardship? Even interpreters who wish to promote an ecological reading of the Bible adopt a range of positions about this question. But however one understands the implications of human rule, the text clearly makes a distinction between humans and the animals who are in some way subordinated to humans. In the separate so-called Yahwist creation account (2:4b–3:24), nothing is said about human dominion over animals. Nevertheless, the first human, who in this story is created before the animals rather than after them, is given responsibility for giving them names. It is also humans rather than animals who are said to gain knowledge of good and evil and thereby become like gods (3:22). Moreover, the story of Cain and Abel that follows immediately after this tale and continues the Yahwist creation account assumes that humans can sacrifice animals, and that God finds these sacrifices pleasing. It is therefore easy to see how so many readers come away from these stories concluding that the boundary between humans and animals has been secured.

Yet things are not as simple as they initially appear. Although humans are created separately from, and after, animals in Genesis 1, they are nevertheless created on the same sixth day of creation as "living souls of every kind, animals and creeping things and living creatures of the earth of every kind" (1:24). I have intentionally included the word "souls" in my translation at this point to indicate the reference in Hebrew, in both 1:24 and 1:25, to the animals' *nephesh*, a word that has often been translated as "soul" when applied to the humans who, elsewhere in the Bible, also have one. Alternative English translations for *nephesh* are preferable to avoid implications of disembodiment that are sometimes associated with the word "soul" (we might refer simply to "living being"), but the crucial point to recognize here is that both humans and other animals are created in the Hebrew Bible as or with *nephesh*. In addition, plants are explicitly given as food not only to humans, but also to animals, birds, and creeping things, everything "which has in it living *nephesh*" (1:30). And all of these creatures, including the humans, are deemed "very good" by God (1:31). Thus the distinction between humans and other living things is not absolute: humans are different from the animals in some ways but similar in others, as indicated by shared substance and shared food sources. Even as the line between humans and animals is blurred, moreover, the text pluralizes animal life. The animals created on the sixth day are not referred to as a single category, "the animals," but as animals, creeping things, and living things, sometimes understood as "cattle and creeping things and wild animals" (NRSV) or even "cattle, wild animals and reptiles."[25] In addition, some animals are created on the fifth day rather than the sixth, specifically "the great sea monsters and every living *nephesh* that moves, with which the waters swarm, of every kind, and winged birds of every kind" (1:21). Rather than a homogeneous category of "animals," the text shows us multiple types of living creatures, a "heterogeneous multiplicity of the living," to recall Derrida's phrase, all created by God and considered "good" (1:21). These creatures, like the humans (1:28), are commanded to "increase [literally, "be fruitful"] and multiply," filling the seas and the skies with diverse forms of life that dwell in multiple God-given habitats (the waters, the skies, the earth).

In the Yahwist account, too, distinctions between humans and animals are complex. In this story of creation, God initially creates only a first human, the *adam*, from the *adamah*, traditionally translated as "ground" but probably understood better as "arable land" or "fertile soil."[26] This creature becomes a "living *nephesh*" when God breathers into it "the breath of life" (2:7). Only after creating the human does God seem to decide that "It is not good for the human to be alone" (2:18). But at this point, rather than immediately creating another human, God creates "every living creature of the field and every bird of the sky," using as substance the same soil (*adamah*) that earlier was used to create the human as a "living *nephesh*" (2:7). God then brings these new breathing creatures (cf. Gen. 6:17; 7:15; Ps. 104:29–30) to the human "to see what he would call it," and every "living *nephesh*" receives its name (2:19). God subsequently recognizes that the human needs a partner that corresponds more closely to it than these other creatures do, and so creates a second human from the first, resulting in both woman and man. But the woman, too, is given a name by the *adam*, as the animals were previously (Gen. 3:20; cf. 2:23). A specific animal, the snake, talks as the humans do and receives a punishment with them. Yet the snake also knows things about God that the humans do not know, truthfully reporting to the woman that they will not die on the day they eat fruit from the tree in the garden (3:4). The snake is aware that God is actually concerned that the humans will become like gods (3:5), a fact that God, represented more anthropomorphically in this story than in Genesis 1, subsequently confirms when deciding that the humans need to be removed from the garden (3:22). The story can therefore be read not simply as complicating the similarities and differences between humans and animals, but also as complicating the similarities and differences among humans, animals, and God.

Thus, in spite of the fact that the creation narratives are often read as emphasizing the construction of a firm boundary between humans and animals and justifying the domination of the latter by the former, a careful reexamination also supports a more complicated reading. There are, to be sure, elements that appear to accept the use of animal bodies for human benefit, such as God's provision of animal skins to Adam and Eve for clothing (3:21), which Robert Seesengood refers to as "the first murder in the biblical text."[27] But there are enough competing motifs in Genesis 1–3 that writers interested in developing a kind of liberation theology for animals have also found resources even in these stories.[28] Here I am less interested in arguing that the creation texts are, or are not, inherently liberating or oppressive for animals than I am in making a different point. While distinctions between humans and animals are clearly made in these texts, those same distinctions are also undermined or blurred by other features of the stories. As in the case of debates about the Bible's views on gender and sexuality, so also in the case of relationships among humans, animals, and God, the biblical creation accounts are complex and contradictory enough that readers can construe them in many different ways, by emphasizing some textual elements rather than others. Our interpretations of them are performative accounts: they generate different versions of "what the Bible says" about animals.[29]

And what do we find, when we bring these issues back to the story of Jacob? Both Isaac's request to Esau for game (27:3–4) and Rebekah's request to Jacob for goats (27:9–10) assume, as numerous texts do, that animals can be slaughtered for meat. Rebekah's use of animal skins to trick her husband, which replicates an activity first carried out in biblical narrative by God (who clothes Adam and Eve in animal skins), assumes that animal bodies can be used for other human purposes as well. Such assumptions surely reinforce the boundary between humans and at least some animals. Yet this boundary is also disturbed by the storyline. Isaac, having lost his sight, relies in part upon that sense more closely associated with other mammals than with humans: the sense of smell, which he uses to identify the clothes of Esau that Jacob wears. More significantly, Isaac is successfully tricked by the hairy goatskins that Rebekah places on Jacob's hands and neck. Jacob wears the skins of animals, yet Rebekah's trick is effective only because those skins feel sufficiently like the skin of Esau to fool the father who loves him. Goats may differ from humans in many ways, but the story recognizes that differences between goats and hirsute humans are not absolute. Although Isaac may desire the meat of animal bodies, the skin of certain humans and the skin of certain animals are, for carnivorous Isaac, impossible to distinguish.

The Hermeneutics of "Carnophallogocentrism": The boundary between human and animal does not simply provide a rationale for the human exploitation of other creatures. It can also be used to distinguish those humans thought to fall closer to, and those humans thought to fall further from, an assumed norm for the properly human. The use of animal images to represent other humans is not inherently negative, as is clear, for example, from lion symbolism, which is used in both positive and negative ways in the Hebrew Bible and elsewhere in the ancient Near East.[30] But some humans and groups of humans are associated with animals more often than others, and frequently in ways that either stigmatize humans deemed insufficiently human or underscore their subordinate status. Since violence against the other-than-human is sanctioned by such practices as killing animals for food or subjecting them to labor, then in the words of Cary Wolfe the "discourse of species will always be available for use by some humans against other humans as well, to countenance violence against the social other of *whatever* species—or gender, or race, or class, or sexual difference."[31] If animals can be mistreated or killed with impunity, and if humans can be animalized, then a careful analysis of the ways in which animal difference is construed may be crucial for grappling with the ethical implications of differences among, and violence between, humans.

Derrida's neologism "carnophallogocentrism" was coined partly to suggest that the exclusion of animals from ethical consideration cannot be separated from the exclusion of other humans from subjectivity and ethics, including women (note how "carnophallogocentrim" builds upon the better-known term "phallogocentrism"), feminized men (Derrida makes an explicit reference to homosexuality in this context), and other men deemed less than human on the basis of, for example, race, ethnicity, nation, class or religion.[32] Although Derrida's comments on carnophallogocentrism are especially focused on modernity, his engagement with biblical literature in his animal writings indicates that biblical scholars, too, may find it useful to ask how women and some men are associated with edible animals in biblical literature.

How are animal difference and sexual difference associated in Jacob's story? At the beginning of the story, Esau is associated with signifiers of masculinity, especially body hair, hunting, and his father's favor. Jacob, his mother's favorite, is associated rather with tents and smoothness. He is arguably the more "effeminate" man, who masquerades as his manly brother by wearing animal skins and clothes that smell like the field.[33] Here animalization appears to be linked to manhood. Yet two forms of animalized manhood actually appear in Jacob's story. If Esau is associated with masculinity and wild animals, Jacob is associated with women and domesticated animals. Indeed, Niditch proposes "domesticated man" as a possible translation for the description of Jacob (*ish tam*) that contrasts with that of Esau in 25:27. The contrast reminds us of the distinction between wild and domesticated that partly structures the Hebrew Bible's conceptualization of animals in other texts, but here it has gendered connotations. Jacob initially represents a kind of "subordinate masculinity."[34]

As Jacob's story progresses, he is increasingly characterized in ways that conform more readily to conventions for masculinity. An association between domesticated animals and women becomes more apparent, however. Rachel, whose name means "ewe," first appears "coming with the flock" (Gen. 29:6). Though meanings for the names Leah and Rebekah are more obscure, "cow" is sometimes given as a possibility for each.[35] As we have seen, a parallel is created between Jacob's work for Leah and Rachel, who bear his children together with their slave women Bilhah and Zilpah; and his work for the goats and sheep who become his animals and give birth to animals for him. In Jacob's words, "I served you fourteen years for your two daughters and six years for your flock" (31:41).

This association between women and animals as objects acquired by men appears in other texts as well. Already in Genesis 2:18–22, God creates the woman only after noticing, apparently, that the animals are insufficient companions for the human. Even then, the man names the woman as he has previously named the animals (2:23; 3:20), perhaps indicating the man's domination of both women and animals.[36] Exodus 20:17 uses masculine linguistic forms to warn a male audience that "You will not covet the house of your neighbor. You will not covet the woman of your neighbor, or his male slave, or his female slave, or his ox, or his donkey, or anything that belongs to your neighbor." This prohibition lists things belonging to one male Israelite that another male Israelite might be tempted to desire, including women, slaves, and animals. On the basis of this and other legal texts, Danna Nolan Fewell and David Gunn note that "well-to-do male heads of households . . . are the Subject the law is constructing. Everyone else is presented as Other."[37] Because Fewell and Gunn are writing about gender, they focus on the exclusion of women in particular from this construction of the Subject of biblical law. But the appearance of animals alongside women and slaves in this passage could be taken as a biblical illustration of the argument made by Derrida, as well as by certain ecofeminist writers, that exclusions of gender *and species* are constitutive of Western subjectivity and culture.[38] Women and animals are placed together in a shared category of biblical objects.

Thus we should not be surprised when, in 2 Samuel 12, the prophet Nathan represents Bathsheba (*bat-sheva*) as a small female lamb who is loved like a daughter (*bat*) by the poor man who owns her. The poor man's lamb is said to "lie on his bosom" (12:3), language that implies some intimate relationship. Yet a rich man, not wishing to use his own flocks and herds to feed a traveler, steals the poor man's lamb and feeds it to a guest. As Nathan makes clear, this rich man represents David, who has stolen another man's woman rather than being content with the women God gave him. The lamb beloved like a daughter (*bat*) who is taken and served as food represents *bat-sheva*, the woman taken by David for sex. A woman as sexual object is represented symbolically as an edible animal. Thus David's story is characterized by what Derrida calls not only "carnophallogocentrism" but also "carnivorous virility,"[39] where a man's authority to consume a woman sexually and a man's authority to slaughter an animal for meat form background assumptions against which the behavior of Israel's king is evaluated.

The fate of Bathsheba is perhaps less troubling than those of other women who are animalized in biblical narrative, including the Daughter of Jephthah, whose sacrifice in Judges 11 puts her in the position of an animal, and the young woman in Judges 19, whose dismembered body is used to send a message that parallels a message sent by Saul with the butchered bodies of cattle (1 Sam. 11:5–7). Together with such texts, the story of Jacob's labor for women and animals underscores the presence in the Bible of what the philosopher Kelly Oliver calls an "intimate association between animal difference and sexual difference."[40]

But the association of animal difference with other types of human difference goes beyond matters of sexual difference in the story of Jacob. When Genesis 30:43 remarks upon Jacob's wealth, the narrator does not simply refer to flocks of sheep and goats, donkeys, and camels. We are also told that Jacob acquired female and male slaves. Here, too, a parallel can be drawn between the narrative of Genesis and legal texts, since Exodus 20:17 also refers to male and female slaves as one man's property that another man might covet. Both texts put domesticated animals and human slaves in a shared category of objects subordinated to heads of households, making thereby an association between animals and slaves that can be found from the ancient world (articulated explicitly, e.g., by Aristotle) to modernity.[41] This association is not always distinct from the association between animals and women, as is intimated by the scene in which Rachel and Leah give their slave women, Bilhah and Zilpah, to Jacob for breeding purposes (Gen. 30:1–13).

Moreover, biblical literature articulates animal difference and gender difference with ethnic difference. The story of Jacob, who represents Israel, and Esau, who represents Edom, is one of several Genesis narratives that use family tales to navigate relationships between the Israelites and their ethnic neighbors in the Persian period.[42] The gendered animalization involved in the distinction between a more manly but wild Esau, and a less manly but clever and domesticated Jacob, may fit into a larger pattern of deploying animal associations when talking about Israel's ethnic others. Ishmael, too, who is also considered a legendary ancestor of some of Israel's neighbors, is compared to a "wild ass" in Genesis 16:12. Since the comparison is followed immediately by a reference to recurring conflicts between Ishmaelites and their "brothers," presumably including the Israelites, the point of the comparison seems to be that Ishmael's descendants prefer to live alone and in disharmony with others. More disturbing animal images are also used for Israel's ethnic others, as in Ezekiel 23:19–21, where Israel's tendency to make alliances with Egypt is condemned with the rhetorical claim that Israel sought as her lovers Egyptians who had penises like donkeys and emissions like horses. The Israelites did not only use animals to "imagine themselves," as Gross puts it. They also used animals to imagine the non-Israelites with whom they had to live.

Conclusion

I have been able to give only a sketch here of some of the emphases found in contemporary animal studies. Nearly all of the issues raised above will recur in the chapters that follow, however; and several additional points made by scholars working in animal studies will emerge as well. Other biblical texts, beyond those referred to here, will also be considered; and some of the texts I have referred to here will be considered again in different contexts. But I hope this discussion, admittedly brief, at least suggests that biblical scholars and other readers may find it useful to engage animal studies when interpreting the Hebrew Bible.

Although the Bible is surely one of the most frequently read texts in history, it is doubtful that most of its readers give much thought to the animals found in it. Even fewer are likely to reflect on the actual animals who lived alongside the writers of biblical literature, or the earliest scribes who put its pieces together and treated it in ways that turned it into such an influential collection. Yet the fact that we have a Bible at all is due in part to the existence of animals, including specific species such as goats, who provided not only significant elements of content and nourishment for its writers but also parchment for its survival and transmission. We owe those animals at least our close attention to the literary animals who populate the traditions inscribed on their skins.

2

Tracking the Dogs of Exodus

In chapter 1, I suggest that goats and sheep were what Donna Haraway calls "companion species" for the Israelites, whose lives, and those of their neighbors, were shaped in significant ways by their interactions with these and other animals. If the Israelites cared for goats and sheep, these likewise made possible both the material survival of the Israelites and their culture, including their religious traditions and practices. Goats and sheep clearly left their footprints—and their skins—on the Bible, and on the religions that use it.

Although sheep and goats played a constitutive role in the formation of the Bible, most readers of the Bible today have much less familiarity with them than did the Israelites. To be sure, goats and sheep are still important for the livelihood of many people around the world. Even in the industrial West, our lives are often entangled with them. Westerners often wear woolen clothes or eat goat cheese or lamb. On a regular basis, however, most of us have little direct contact with live sheep or goats.

In contrast, many of us interact regularly with dogs and cats. In the United States alone, 83.3 million dogs are estimated to have been living with humans in 2014, and 77.8 million in 2015.[1] Domestic cats numbered an estimated 95.6 million in 2013–14 and 85.8 million in 2014–15.[2] Not surprisingly, both species play influential roles in contemporary animal studies. In *The Animal That Therefore I Am*, Derrida develops his ruminations on "the question of the animal" by reflecting on, among other things, his unsettling experience of being naked under the gaze of his female cat.

Haraway places more emphasis on human interactions with dogs, including her own, in her explication of companion species relationships.[3]

Haraway is certainly not alone in creating a new academic literature on dogs. Although the formal study of dogs attracted little attention from scholars for many years, today there exist numerous studies of their behavior, their histories of domestication and interaction with humans, and their roles in human culture.[4] The combination of unusual abilities (such as an exceptional sense of smell) that dogs share with their canid relatives, and a sensitivity to human behavior unmatched even by our great ape relatives, fascinates animal behaviorists, cultural theorists, and the wider public. There is widespread agreement that dogs were the first animals domesticated by humans. While considerable debate remains about the processes that led to the evolution of dogs from wolves, a growing number of writers follow Stephen Budiansky in arguing that dogs should be understood as active agents in those processes, and not simply objects of human activity.[5] Laura Hobgood-Oster goes so far as to suggest that dogs and humans domesticated one another.[6] Strikingly, some of the earliest evidence for the long relationship between dogs and humans comes from the bones of dogs who were buried intentionally, sometimes with humans, at numerous sites around the world. The oldest of these burials discovered to date, found at an archaeological site near Bonn, Germany (the "Bonn-Oberkassel dog"), is believed to be 14,000 years old and is considered by some scholars "the oldest securely established dog specimen known in the world."[7] Given this long history of association between dogs and humans, it is hardly surprising that dogs have also played important roles in literature and other arts, from Argos, the faithful hound in Homer's *Odyssey* who recognizes Odysseus on his return home, to the numerous dogs who roam through visual and written representations of Christian saints across the centuries,[8] to modern literary dogs found in such famous works as Jack London's *Call of the Wild*, Virginia Woolf's *Flush*, or J. M. Coetzee's *Disgrace*.

Evidence for dogs can also be found in the geographical areas associated with Israel and the ancient Near East. One of the earliest examples of a dog buried with a human comes from Ein Mallaha, a Natufian (pre-agricultural) site discovered in the northern section of what is now Israel that is estimated to be between 10,000 and 12,000 years old. The excavation there of an elderly human skeleton with one of its hands resting on the skeleton of a puppy has been interpreted as "proof that an affectionate rather than gastronomic relationship existed between [the puppy] and the buried person."[9] Two more dogs were discovered buried with humans at another Natufian site, Hayonim Terrace, further to the west.[10] Although Natufian dog burials are far too old to shed much light on the Bible, dog burials are attested from later periods as well. Most famous perhaps, and more relevant to the period in which the Hebrew Bible was written, are the hundreds of dogs buried at Persian-period Ashkelon during the fifth century BCE.[11] This unusual discovery perplexes scholars, who call it a "conundrum,"[12] but other dog burials in smaller numbers have also been discovered both nearby (e.g., at Ashdod) and across the ancient Near East, in addition to the many mummified dog remains from Egypt. Indeed, as the anthropologist Darcy Morey emphasizes, the ancient Near Eastern burials are part of a global phenomenon, in which dogs have been buried, sometimes alone and sometimes together with humans, in many different times and places.[13]

In addition to dog bones, both written and iconographic sources testify to the presence of dogs in ancient Near Eastern and Mediterranean societies. Some of these sources are mundane, such as the appearance of dogs alongside other animals in proverbs and folk parables.[14] Other sources, however, deal with matters that are clearly more religious. Thus discussions of ancient canine sources frequently emphasize the association of dogs with the Mesopotamian healing goddess Gula-Ninisina, who is represented pictorially with dogs and sometimes even in the form of a dog.[15] This association between dogs and healing, which also appears in connection with other ancient figures such as Asclepius in Greece, is sometimes said to have been motivated by recognition of the healing powers of a dog licking wounds.[16] At a temple to Gula in Isin, archaeologists found dog figurines, dog plaques, and more than thirty skeletons of actual dogs of varying ages, leading Barbara Böck to "imagine that the adult dogs were meant to lick the wounds of sick people while the puppies were used as sucking animals."[17] Reflecting on ancient Near Eastern dog burials, "puppy rituals,"[18] and related phenomena, Morey goes so far as to speak of "the perception of dogs as possessing spiritual qualities."[19] Scholars writing on animals and religion are willing to trace that perception of dogs into other periods and contexts as well.[20]

In contrast to all of this, when one turns to the literature on dogs in the Hebrew Bible and early Judaism, one encounters a very different picture. In 1960, D. Winton Thomas published an influential article on the dog in the Bible and the ancient Near East that repeatedly emphasized the Bible's negative understanding of the dog as a "vile and contemptible animal . . . the scavenger *par excellence*" (414), "a vile, contemptible animal" (417), "an animal held in general contempt" (418), "the most ignoble and contemptible of animals" (424), and "a contemptible animal" (426).[21] Notwithstanding this strong, repetitive language, Thomas did acknowledge more positive connotations of dogs in the ancient Near East, particularly where dogs symbolize faithful human servants of both humans and deities. Thus his closing sentence refers to "that lowly animal, the dog, despised and generally wretched, yet . . . in religious circles, in prayer and worship, not without honour" (427). In spite of this gesture toward positive ways of understanding the dog, most subsequent commentators on biblical references to dogs have followed Thomas in characterizing them primarily negatively. Thus the Bible's dogs are said by scholars to be "regarded with particular disgust because of their unique status as urban carnivores," "the most despised of all creatures," an "indiscriminate, blood-thirsty scavenger," a "detested predator," and "a worthless creature."[22] They "were not afforded a great deal of respect or affection in Israelite or Judahite society," held a "contemptible status" in the ancient Near East, and were viewed with "disdain."[23] They are supposedly "always spoken of in contempt" in the Bible, and generate "bad connotations" and "ill feelings."[24] The Bible, we are told, has an "antipathy towards canines" and a "negative/suspicious approach to dogs."[25] This negative attitude has even been associated with monotheism in particular.[26] Some commentators who emphasize negative attitudes toward dogs do follow Thomas in acknowledging that other attitudes exist. Given the Bible's supposed derision, however, one might find it surprising that readers of the Bible have anything to do with dogs at all.

Geoffrey Miller has recently argued that this consensus about the negative perception of dogs in the Hebrew Bible is exaggerated. Miller emphasizes several important working roles played by dogs in the ancient world, including as hunters, sheepdogs, guard dogs, and possibly companions. Biblical literature indicates that some of these roles were known in Israel as well (e.g., Job 30:1; Isa. 56:10). Noting that such biblical references to dogs are simply neutral rather than negative, Miller also calls attention to more positive references. Without denying the existence of "a few Old Testament passages that clearly portray dogs in a negative manner," his article presents a more nuanced picture than most discussions of the Bible's dogs.[27]

Like Miller, I am skeptical about reducing the Bible's dogs to "vile" and "contemptible" animals. But here I take a somewhat different approach to them. Although I return below to several of the texts and interpretive issues that Miller, Thomas, and others discuss, I want to turn first to a provocative short essay by Emmanuel Levinas, titled "The Name of a Dog, or Natural Rights."[28] Many writers associated with animal studies have discussed "The Name of a Dog." Yet only a few give attention to two references to dogs in Exodus (one found in narrative, and one found in legal literature) that Levinas, following certain rabbinic sources, engages. By reading these texts together, as Levinas and his rabbinic sources do, and reading them in relation to other texts from Exodus that stand alongside them, I hope to highlight some of the complexities involved in the Bible's attitudes toward animals.[29]

Levinas and the Dogs of Exodus

Levinas opens "The Name of a Dog" with the first of two quotations from Exodus, specifically, Exodus 22:31 (Hebrew 22:30): "You shall be people consecrated to me; therefore you shall not eat any meat that is mangled by beasts in the field; you shall throw it to the dogs."[30] Taking this commandment as his point of departure, Levinas moves quickly through a paragraph that references meat-eating, Adam's vegetarianism (with a suggestion that humans were created vegetarian), hunting, and a kind of comparison between "the horrors of war" and "the butchery that every day claims our 'consecrated' mouths" before exclaiming, "But enough of this theology! It is the dog mentioned at the end of the verse that I am especially interested in. I am thinking of Bobby" (151). Rather than telling us immediately who "Bobby" is, however, Levinas next works his way through several figures of speech that he calls "allegories"—"a dog's life," "raining cats and dogs," the "wolf" that hides under "dogged faithfulness," and so on—only to arrive at another passage from Exodus.

For as Levinas notes, Jewish tradition interprets the reference to dogs eating meat in Exodus 22 by recalling other dogs in Exodus 11. There Moses, recounting a word from God, speaks to the Israelites about the night of the last plague, a night when the firstborn shall die throughout Egypt. Although there will be much wailing in Egypt on that night, Moses tells the Israelites in 11:6 that "not a dog shall growl at any of the Israelites—not at people, not at animals—so that you may know that the LORD makes a distinction between Egypt and Israel" (11:6). As Levinas observes, certain Jewish texts find in this verse in chapter 11 a rationale for giving torn flesh to dogs in Exodus 22. According to this tradition, the carrion in Exodus 22 is God's reward to the dogs for having held their tongues in Exodus 11. Though Levinas does not cite specific sources for this tradition, it can be found among other places in the Mekhilta of Rabbi Ishmael, which, commenting on the meat that is thrown to dogs in Exodus 22, states: "This is to teach you that the Holy One, blessed be He, does not withhold the reward of any creature. It is said, 'But against any of the children of Israel shall not a dog whet his tongue' (Ex. 11.7). Said the Holy One, blessed be He: Give him his reward."[31] Using this interpretation as a way to shift his focus from the dogs of Exodus 22 to the dogs of Exodus 11, Levinas notes that the dogs' silent recognition of the Israelites takes place just as the Israelites are being freed from Egyptian bondage. This is the moment, according to Exodus, that "not a dog shall growl." By holding their tongues, the dogs mark the liberation of Israelite slaves. And here, Levinas observes, we see what it means to say that dogs are the friends of humanity. For "with neither ethics nor *logos*, the dog will attest to the dignity of its person" (152).

This reference to the dog who attests to human dignity serves as an important transition in the short piece by Levinas. For it is only after his meditation on Exodus 11 that Levinas turns to another dog who attested to human dignity when Levinas finally introduces us to Bobby, the friend of whom he has been "thinking." The setting for this introduction is another scene of bondage. In a Nazi camp for Jewish prisoners of war, Levinas and his fellows are being dehumanized. In the eyes of the Germans, Levinas says, "We were subhuman, a gang of apes" (153). And yet in this desolate location, where it was easy to forget "our essence as thinking creatures," for several weeks "a wandering dog entered our lives":

One day he came to meet this rabble as we returned under guard from work. . . . [W]e called him Bobby, an exotic name, as one does with a cherished dog. He would appear at morning assembly and was waiting for us as we returned, jumping up and down and barking in delight. For him there was no doubt that we were men.

Levinas draws a contrast between Bobby the dog and the German masters. But the contrast, ironically, makes Bobby seem humane, and the Germans more beastly. The distinction between humans and animals becomes, here, rhetorically complex: If the Nazis dehumanize their Jewish prisoners by treating them like animals ("We were subhuman, a gang of apes"), this animal happily and perceptively recognizes those prisoners as human ("For him there was no doubt that we were men"). Like the dogs of Exodus 11, according to the interpretation of Levinas, Bobby "attests to the dignity" of humans in captivity. Thus Levinas concludes:

This dog was the last Kantian in Nazi Germany, without the brain needed to universalize maxims and drives. He was a descendant of the dogs of Egypt. And his friendly growling, his animal faith, was born from the silence of his forefathers on the banks of the Nile. (153)

So this extraordinary little essay with a dog in its title, which opens with one reference to dogs in Exodus 22, closes with a reference to other dogs in Exodus 11.

Discussions of animals are rare enough in Levinas's work that Derrida refers to this essay at one point as "a sort of hapax."[32] A hapax, of course, or hapax legomenon, is in the language of textual scholarship a word that appears in a work or corpus only once. In context, Derrida clearly implies that the attention Levinas gives to animals here does not recur in his work. And partly because of its unusual focus, "The Name of a Dog" has been the object of numerous other readings that reflect upon the possible implications or limitations of Levinasian thought for contemporary animal ethics.[33] Such readings necessarily wrestle with paradox in this piece by Levinas. For what should one do with a canine Kantian who nevertheless lacks "the brain needed to universalize maxims and drives"? How should one respond to a piece that juxtaposes the violence of humans against animals, the violence of animals against animals, and the violence of humans against humans, all in the troubling context of the Shoah? And what, if anything, does this piece tell us about the possibilities for a different approach to animal ethics, an approach that might allow us to see the "face" of our animal others?

Not surprisingly, readers of Levinas have been unable to reach agreement about these questions. The diverse readings of such a short piece seem, in fact, to be grounded in divergent currents at work within the essay itself. As David Clark observes, "The enigma of the animal evokes contradictory thoughts and feelings in Levinas."[34] The rhetorical drift of "The Name of a Dog" moves from a reflection on eating animals, a reflection that evokes "the horrors of war" and the carnivorous "butchery" that could "make you a vegetarian again," to the horrors of a war camp for Jewish prisoners who are reduced by the Nazis to "beings entrapped in their species . . . beings without language," beings whose attempts to express themselves are treated as nothing more than "monkey talk."[35] Reflecting on this movement, it is hard to disagree with John Llewelyn when he notes that Levinas here "all but proposes an analogy between the unspeakable human Holocaust and the unspoken animal one."[36] As if to keep that controversial analogy in check, however, Levinas also gestures clearly toward distinctions between humans and animals: Bobby may be a Kantian, but he lacks "the brain needed to universalize maxims and drives," the brain, that is, of a rational, dutiful humanity. We do well to remember the context for Levinas's refusal, here, to obliterate altogether distinctions between humans and other animals, even if such distinctions are destabilized elsewhere in his essay. The racism of the Nazi regime, which turned Levinas and his fellows into a "gang of apes" reduced to "monkey talk," serves as a stark reminder that, in Clark's words, "the animalization of human beings leads directly to . . . horrific consequences."[37] And yet, the moving invocation of this dog Bobby, of whom Levinas has been thinking all these years, and who, with "animal faith" and "friendly growling," recognizes humanity in the faces of the prisoners, suggests to many readers that Levinas comes tantalizingly close in this essay to breaking out of his self-professed agnosticism about the extent to which an animal has "the right to be called 'face.'"[38]

Ultimately, most readers of the essay, including Derrida, conclude that Levinas remains penned in by an anthropocentric ethics that relies upon a clear distinction between humans and animals, a distinction that excludes animals from serious ethical consideration by Levinas himself.

Such readers adopt different positions, however, about the ease with which, or whether, Levinas's ethical framework could be extended in such a way as to make room for our responsibility for other animals. But it is striking to note that, even as their responses diverge from one another both in their styles of reading and in their conclusions about Levinas and animal ethics, most commentators on "The Name of a Dog" share one characteristic that cannot fail to catch the attention of the biblical scholar. They generally show far more interest in Bobby than in the unnamed dogs of Exodus who both open and close Bobby's tale.[39]

Of course, if readers of Levinas who are interested in animal ethics seem disinclined to follow Levinas and his dogs down the path toward biblical interpretation, biblical scholars have not done much to lure them there. Indeed, it is striking to note that commentaries on Exodus sometimes discuss the verses in which dogs appear without referring explicitly to dogs at all.[40]

In modern scholarship, moreover, the dogs of Exodus 11 and the dogs of Exodus 22 are, for methodological reasons, seldom placed in relation to one another as they are by Levinas. After all, the dogs of Exodus 11 appear in the narrative account of the Israelite exodus from Egypt. The dogs of Exodus 22, on the other hand, show up in legal material comprising the book's latter half, material that is assumed by scholars (no doubt correctly) to have originated independently of the narrative framework within which it has been placed. Apart from the fact that these two passages provide us with the only two references to dogs in the book of Exodus, they seem to have little in common.

But what might we find if we pursue the path taken by Levinas when, following Jewish tradition, he links these two sets of dogs, and hence different sets of texts, in Exodus to one another? Instead of asking whether the philosophy of Levinas offers a sufficient framework for handling the question of the animal, I am more interested here in taking a cue from a passing comment by Derrida, who, immediately after quoting a reference by Levinas to the dogs of Exodus, remarks that "there would be much to say concerning this allusion to Egypt."[41] Derrida himself then says relatively little about it. But if Clark observes, toward the end of his moving essay on "The Last Kantian in Nazi Germany," that the dog Bobby "traces and retraces the oppositional limits that configure the human and the animal" (193), perhaps the dogs of Exodus, who according to Levinas are Bobby's silent ancestors, can point us toward certain biblical ways of dealing with, and sometimes complicating, those same "oppositional limits."

Following the Dogs of Exodus Across Boundaries

The verse from Exodus 22 with which Levinas opens his essay is included among the texts that, as noted above, are often taken as implying a negative view of dogs. Many of these passages fall into two general categories. Several texts use canine references rhetorically to insult human beings by comparing them to dogs or, in some cases, dead dogs (e.g., 1 Sam. 23:14; 2 Sam. 3:8; 9:8; 16:9; Ps. 22:16, 20; 59:6; Prov. 26:11; Isa. 56:10–11). Yet cross-cultural evidence, including evidence from modern Western societies, demonstrates that the use of canine references as insults ("dog," "bitch," etc.) frequently coexists with affection toward actual dogs.[42] Passages in which biblical characters refer to *themselves* as dogs in a self-deprecating fashion may shed light on connotations of this category of texts that are not always made explicit. In 2 Kings 8:12, Elisha predicts that Hazael, an official under the Syrian king, will eventually lead a devastating military campaign against Israel. Hazael, however, protests in 8:13 that he is only "your servant, a dog." The parallel here between "servant" and "dog" fits into a series of ancient Near Eastern references in which subordinates use these terms to underscore their deference to social superiors.[43] In the hierarchical societies of the ancient Near East, including Israel, such deference need not be understood as contemptible groveling. It might well be understood as loyal service, for which dogs were exemplars. Referring to oneself as "your servant, a dog" serves to underscore one's appropriate deference to a figure who, officially at least, deserves respect or obedience. The rhetorical use of "dog" as an insult, then, may simply be a function of this same set of connotations, seen from the perspective of one who wishes to assert dominance rather than subordinate service. A character such as Goliath (1 Sam. 17:43) may protest at the implication that he is being treated as a dog, not because dogs were considered contemptible as is often claimed, but rather because he believes his position of power and strength is not appropriately acknowledged by his assumed inferior, David. The submission of dogs to humans, a constitutive feature of their domestication, may on occasion lead to contempt; but since this same submission manifests itself in both positive and negative ways, depending on context, it is probably more appropriate to speak of "ambivalence" than disgust.⁴⁴ The faithful service of a dog inspires both admiration and discomfort. Indeed, biblical ambivalence toward dogs may not be radically different from ambivalence toward the many status hierarchies that shaped ancient human societies, hierarchies that are sometimes critiqued but often affirmed in biblical literature.

In other texts, however, including Exodus 22, commentators derive negative connotations from the fact that dogs eat food that humans will not eat. In a number of these passages, dogs eat human flesh or drink human blood (e.g., 1 Kgs 16:4; 21:19, 23–24; 22:38; 2 Kgs 9:10, 35–37; Ps. 68:22–23; cf. Jer. 15:3). The specification of blood in several of these passages is worth underscoring. The Hebrew Bible famously prohibits the human ingestion of blood, in which the "life" (*nephesh*) of living creatures was thought to reside (e.g., Lev. 17:10–16). Any negative connotations associated with dogs as creatures who not only eat human bodies but drink human blood may have been intensified by such a prohibition. More important for my purposes, we see from these references that the dogs' search for food across biblical literature blurs the boundary between humans and other creatures. For it exposes the fact that human bodies and the bodies of other animals are equally edible meat for carnivores.

The dogs in Exodus 22, however, are not eating human meat, but rather meat that humans should not eat, meat that has apparently been killed by other animals and is now given to the dogs. What sorts of dogs are imagined here? Are they feral scavengers, comparable to the ubiquitous "village dogs" discussed by Raymond and Lorna Coppinger?⁴⁵ In that case, we might imagine them to be similar to the dogs that eat Jezebel (2 Kgs 9:10, 35–37) or that the Psalmist has in mind when comparing enemies to packs of dogs roaming about a city (Ps. 59: 6, 14 [Hebrew 59:7, 15]. Or is it the case, as some scholars suggest, that since the meat these dogs are given comes from an animal that has been torn "in the field," the dogs referred to here are more likely to be herding or guard dogs, comparable to "the dogs of my flock" Job refers to in Job 30:1?⁴⁶ It is difficult to answer this question with certainty, but it is worth noting that "flocks" are referred to explicitly in Exodus 22:30 (Hebrew 22:29), just prior to the appearance of dogs in 22:31 (Hebrew 22:30).

In either case, as Walter Houston notes, the dogs in Exodus 22 serve what was likely one of their common functions as scavengers who "get rid of unclean and uneatable refuse." Though this function can inspire disgust, it is also extremely useful. Yet it "puts them into an ideologically ambiguous position."[47] On the one hand, the willingness of dogs to eat corpses (human and otherwise) differentiates them from other domestic animals, and appears to place them closer to wild animals, which in the Hebrew Bible are sometimes conceptualized separately from domesticated animals. On the other hand, dogs are certainly not wild animals but domesticated ones, with "the longest history of human domestication of any animal by several thousand years."[48] They have evolved in complex relationships with human beings, over many centuries, and under circumstances that, as noted earlier, are still being debated. They are often found inside rather than outside human communities; but they are also frequently found just on the boundaries of those communities, as in the case of the Coppingers' "village dogs." Thus dogs exist in an unusual space of their own, a fact that inspires ambivalence toward them in many cultures, including cultures in which they are highly prized.[49] Their unusual position leads Houston to refer to dogs as "anomalous" animals in the sense given to that word by Mary Douglas: their actions and locations confound the boundaries and categories that we most often use to make sense of our world.[50] In Exodus 22, it is, precisely, dogs who eat meat killed by wild animals, dogs in distinction from wild animals, but dogs also in distinction from either human beings (who live in proximity to the dogs but do not eat the meat in question) or other domesticated animals (who for the most part do not eat meat at all). We thus see here that the category of "animal" is differentiated within the Hebrew Bible in several respects: there are domesticated animals, there are wild animals, but there are also dogs, who do not fit neatly into either category.

Recognition of the unusual status of dogs may help us understand one biblical reference to them that has been especially controversial. Deuteronomy 23:18 (Hebrew 23:19) stipulates: "You will not bring the fee of a prostitute or the hire of a dog to the house of YHWH your God for any vow. For both of them are abhorrent to YHWH your God." At one time, the term "dog" was understood here to refer to a male prostitute. This interpretation rested not simply on the inclusion of both dog and prostitute in this verse, but also on the appearance of the Hebrew terms *qedeshah* and *qadesh* in the previous verse. The latter terms were at one time believed to refer to female and male cult prostitutes. In recent years, however, older assumptions about the existence of cultic prostitution have increasingly been called into question.[51] Partly as a consequence, some scholars now consider it more likely that the term "dog" in Deuteronomy 23:18 (Hebrew 23:19) does "actually refer to a canine," in Elaine Goodfriend's words.[52] As Goodfriend notes, this interpretation is consistent with traditional Jewish readings. But why, then, would a payment received for a dog be deemed unacceptable in the temple? Goodfriend emphasizes the association between dogs and consumption of blood. Other scholars suggest that a cultic use of dogs among Israel's neighbors, possibly associated with the dog burials at Ashkelon, may explain the Deuteronomic prohibition.[53] But perhaps dogs and prostitutes are associated with one another in Deuteronomy and elsewhere (e.g., 1 Kgs 22:38) because both of them inhabit liminal social spaces. As Phyllis Bird points out, the prostitute in the Hebrew Bible and the ancient Near East is also a figure who generates considerable ambivalence.[54] She plays positive roles in some sources (as, e.g., in Gen. 38, Josh. 2, and the Epic of Gilgamesh), but exists on the margins of society, which sometimes stigmatizes her. Both the prostitute and the dog provide valued services (from the perspectives of those who gave us the texts) while acting in ways that create discomfort and, sometimes, disdain. Their presence is desired even as they threaten the propriety of social boundaries. The ambivalence each of them produces may explain why they are associated with one another in Deuteronomy and 1 Kings.

Exodus 22, however, does not explicitly say anything negative about dogs. The meat that is given to them there is usually understood as food fit only for a dog. Yet the rhetoric of Levinas turns this meat into something positive, something to which the dogs have a "right." Levinas accomplishes this transvaluation by following his rabbinic sources, which, as noted above, interpret the meat in Exodus 22 as the dogs' reward for actions taken by other dogs, in Egypt, in Exodus 11. And meat is not the only reward that Jewish tradition gives to dogs for their ancestors' role in Exodus 11. During the Middle Ages, dog dung was frequently used in the process of turning animal skins into biblical scrolls, apparently to help soften the skins. This contribution to the Bible's material history reminds us that dogs, like the goats and other animals referred to in chapter 1, were co-constitutive partners in the Bible's production and survival. And according to one Jewish tradition, this honor of having their dung used in the production of holy scrolls was, like the meat in Exodus 22, given to dogs as a consequence for holding their tongues in Exodus 11.[55]

Such a jump between contexts is hardly unusual in rabbinic hermeneutics, and we might assume that the presence of dogs in both Exodus 22 and Exodus 11 is otherwise the only point of connection between the two chapters. If we follow the dogs' tracks through these sections of Exodus, however, and look carefully at the larger literary contexts for each verse, we start to notice other links as well, links that Levinas himself does not mention. And some of these links further complicate the ways in which humans are, and are not, differentiated from other animals in the Hebrew Bible.

The stipulation that carrion should be given to dogs is not actually located among the biblical laws on clean and unclean animals, laws that differentiate among animals in still other ways (see, e.g., Lev. 11:1–47; Deut. 14:3–21).[56] Animals do appear, however, in several of the laws that are found in this same section of Exodus, a section (21:1–23:33) often referred to as the "Covenant Code" or "Book of the Covenant." So, for example, in 23:4 we read that one should return a stray ox or donkey even if it belongs to one's enemy. In 23:5 we read that one should relieve a donkey lying under its burden even if it belongs to a person one hates. Several verses later, we find a commandment to let fields, vineyards, and olive orchards rest every seventh year, accompanied by a specification that poor Israelites and animals may both eat from the land during that year (23:11). The next commandment describes the seventh day as a day of rest not only for humans, but also for ox and donkey. Thus, concern for the well-being of others, which comes to expression in numerous laws from this section of Exodus, does not stop at the line between human and animal. Indeed, the concern for animal welfare may also resurface in 23:19 if one interprets the prohibition against boiling a young goat in its mother's milk in that verse, as some readers do, as being grounded in compassion for or humane treatment of animals.[57]

But if passages in Exodus 23 that seem to promote such compassion blur the line between humans and animals by including animals alongside humans as objects of concern, that line is blurred in a more unsettling way in the two verses that immediately precede the stipulation about giving food to dogs. For those verses specify that "you shall not delay to make offerings from the fullness of your harvest and from the outflow of your presses. The firstborn of your sons you shall give me. You shall do the same with your oxen and with your sheep; seven days it shall remain with its mother; on the eighth day you shall give it to me" (22:29–30, NRSV [Hebrew 22:28–29]). This is not the only place where Pentateuchal law requires the Israelites to offer firstborn sons along with firstborn animals and the first fruits of the field. In distinction from other passages, however, this chapter does not provide any means for substituting animal sacrifices in place of human ones. Thus it is possible to find in this chapter evidence that some Israelites considered child sacrifice acceptable to God. Indeed, several biblical scholars argue, on the basis of this passage and other evidence, that the prohibition on child sacrifice as something displeasing to Israel's god developed only over time, and unevenly, in the history of Israel.[58] Biblical literature as we have it thus speaks to both sides of this controversial issue: some texts condemn child sacrifice explicitly while others seem to allow it or even, as in Exodus 22, command it. Ezekiel 20:25–26 strangely tries to have it both ways, indicating that child sacrifice could be understood by a prophet who opposed it as having been required at some point by certain of God's commandments, perhaps the very ones from Exodus that we are reading, which, however, are in Ezekiel's rhetoric actually "laws that were not good," used by God to make Israel unclean and desolate. This strand of biblical thought therefore blurs the line between human and animal even at the point of sacrifice.

Derrida, in his discussion of "The Name of a Dog," calls attention to the fact that these verses, not quoted by Levinas, appear immediately prior to the biblical admonition to throw torn meat to the dogs.[59] Although Derrida doesn't elaborate on the significance of this contiguity, we may discern some of the implications of it when we recall that sacrifice has already appeared in his discussion of Levinas. For Derrida notes a few pages earlier that, in spite of the Levinasian emphasis on the biblical command "Thou shalt not kill," which Levinas associates with a prohibition on murder, Levinas restricts the scope of the command to "the face of the other, my neighbor, my brother, the human, or another human. Putting to death or sacrificing the animal, exploiting it to death . . . are not forbidden by 'Thou shalt not kill'" (110) in Levinasian ethics. We may also recall Derrida's reference a few pages earlier to "a war against the animal, *a sacrificial war* that is as old as Genesis" (101; my emphasis). The matter of sacrifice is also raised by Derrida in connection with Levinas and animals in "Eating Well," an interview with Jean-Luc Nancy where Derrida argues that the philosophies of Levinas and Heidegger "remain profound humanisms *to the extent that they do not sacrifice sacrifice*."[60] "Sacrifice," here, refers not simply to literal sacrifices but also to what Derrida calls the "sacrificial structure" of Western philosophical and religious discourses, in which one finds "a place left open . . . for a noncriminal putting to death." While the most obvious examples of this "noncriminal putting to death" involve animals, which, as Derrida, notes, Western culture permits to be killed, Derrida's discussion suggests that it may be difficult to restrict this "noncriminal putting to death" to animals without applying it to some humans (278). Both symbolically and literally, we put other humans to death all the time. And the Hebrew Bible, in spite of popular misconceptions to the contrary, does not consistently use sacrifice to draw a line between the permitted killing of animals and the forbidden killing of humans. Rather, biblical discourses of sacrifice such as that found in Exodus 22, which on its own can be read as permitting or even commanding the sacrifice of humans, highlight the difficulty of using the distinction between human and animal to define clearly the difference between sacrifice and murder.

Lines between human and animal are obscured, moreover, even in biblical passages where provision is made for the substitution of animals in place of firstborn humans as objects of sacrifice. Exodus 13:13 and 34:19–20, for example, allow the Israelites to substitute a sheep to redeem a firstborn human. Yet both passages also specify that the Israelites may substitute a sheep to redeem a firstborn donkey. In each case redemption of the donkey is mentioned before redemption of the human. The donkey's redemption is sometimes understood as a consequence of the donkey's unclean status; and although neither passage in Exodus gives this rationale for the substitution, a passage in Numbers 18:15 that refers to the redemption of "unclean animals" after a reference to the redemption of humans does make such an explanation plausible. Yet it is strange that the donkey alone of all unclean animals is singled out for redemption in Exodus, with no mention of its unclean status, in distinction, say, from Leviticus 27:27, which allows all unclean animals to be redeemed without mentioning the donkey or any other species in particular.[61] Whatever explanation we supply for these peculiarities, one effect of the substitution of a sheep for a donkey in Exodus is to set up a strange kind of equivalence in the book between human and donkey, which is differentiated as a consequence from other animals whose firstborn are not explicitly redeemed. The passages on sacrifice make divisions among animals while aligning some animals more closely with humans than others.

The reference to firstborn in Exodus 22:29–30 (Hebrew 22:28–29) also provides us with another link, in addition to the references to dogs, between this chapter, where dogs are given meat, and Exodus 11, where no dog will growl. For the book of Exodus itself explains the requirement to give the firstborn to God by referring back to the deliverance from Egypt. As Exodus 13 notes, when the Israelite children ask their parents about the reason for giving the firstborn, the Israelites should respond by recalling God's slaughter of "all the firstborn in the land of Egypt, from human firstborn to the firstborn of animals" (13:15). And this is precisely the event being foretold in Exodus 11's first reference to dogs. According to an oracle of God delivered by Moses, when the firstborn of all the Egyptians—humans and animals (11:5)—are killed, there will be a great cry in Egypt (11:6). But, the oracle continues, "not a dog shall growl at any of the Israelites—not at people, not at animals—so that you may know that the LORD makes a distinction between Egypt and Israel" (11:7, NRSV). Not only dogs, but also the deaths of firstborn, are shared by Exodus 11 and Exodus 22.

It is not actually certain that the dogs in Exodus 11 were understood originally to be refraining from growling, as Levinas and his sources assume. Most English translations, including NRSV, do read something like "no dog will growl"; and versions as old as the Septuagint and Targum understand the passage to refer to canine noisemaking. The passage refers literally in Hebrew, however, simply to actions made with the tongue. Some scholars suggest that these actions may be a kind of licking rather than growling or barking, perhaps implying the lapping of the blood of the dead.[62] Such an interpretation would be consistent with passages that refer to dogs eating dead humans or drinking their blood, though the language in such passages differs from the language used in Exodus 11. On the other hand, a similar expression in Joshua 10:21 (which represents humans rather than dogs moving their tongues) involves speech. Thus, in spite of ambiguities, there are grounds for concluding that Exodus 11 refers to growling or barking. Within some later Jewish traditions, in fact, these dogs were understood to be magical watchdogs belonging to the Egyptians, who would normally bark to alert the Egyptians but who are here silenced by Moses.[63] The appearance of these dogs on a night when mass death is taking place might be another example of a recurring cross-cultural representation of canines that, in the words of Susan McHugh, "positions the dog at the gateway of life and death."[64]

The point I wish to underscore here, however, is that the actions taken, or rather not taken, by these dogs cut across the boundary between animal and human. For the text is explicit about the fact that the dogs will not move their tongues against either human Israelites *or their animals* (11:7). The firstborn of all the animals associated with the Israelites shall live. By contrast, Moses specifies two verses earlier that every firstborn Egyptian will die, including their firstborn animals (11:5). Thus, there are humans and animals who die among the Egyptians, and humans and animals who live among the Israelites. God's actions for life and death transgress the division between humans and animals and are taken instead on the basis of a distinction between Egypt and Israel. And whatever they are or are not doing with their tongues, the dogs of Exodus, like God, recognize and act on the basis of this alternative distinction, which cuts across the species line.

Conclusion

If "the radical breakdown of the human/animal distinction" characterizes our era,[65] the instability of that distinction has been apparent, or should have been apparent, at least since Darwin demonstrated "fundamental continuities found among human beings and animals," as Calarco observes.[66] Yet Darwin's ideas had to contend in his own time with a widespread view of humanity's place in the world that assumed, partly on the basis of an interpretation of the Hebrew Bible, that a gulf existed between humanity and the rest of nature, including animals, who existed primarily for human benefit.[67] While Darwin's views are much more widely held today, it is still often assumed that the Bible works with a single, stable division between human and animal, such as the one that readers often find in Genesis 1. Yet it is not clear that biblical views about animals are at all stable or unified. While biblical texts do make distinctions between humans and animals, they also blur those distinctions, as I have suggested in this chapter (e.g., associating some humans with donkeys, associating other humans with animals that can be sacrificed, associating some animals with the poor, etc.). Moreover, biblical texts undermine the existence of any single category, "the animal," by pluralizing it (differentiating domestic animals from wild animals, dividing animals among ethnic groups of humans, distinguishing the clean from the unclean, treating certain animals such as dogs and donkeys in unusual ways, etc.). Written, as it was, prior to modern humanism, biblical literature fails to provide us with a clear picture of a unified human subject that can be distinguished easily from "the animal," as such. There may not exist a single "biblical view" of humans and animals at all. What we have in the Bible are, rather, to borrow words that Derrida applies to differences between species (including humans), "many fractures, heterogeneities, differential structures."[68] Close attention to the dogs of Exodus, and the passages in which they appear, offers us one way to begin exploring those heterogeneities.

The views found in the Hebrew Bible about specific species of animals, such as dogs, are also often more complex than simple statements made about them in the past allow. Although some references to dogs in both the Bible and rabbinic literature do have negative connotations, the interpretive tradition on which Levinas relies grants to dogs a more positive role. I would argue that it was able to do so, in part, because the Bible's own views are more nuanced than has often been acknowledged. Indeed, Heather McKay suggests in a compelling article on the Bible's horses and donkeys that our interpretations of biblical animals need to keep in mind the complexities of perspective, representation, and rhetorical distortion that feminist scholars have emphasized when analyzing biblical passages that refer to women.[69] Although this comparison is in several respects troubling, some biblical texts do associate women with animals. Thus we should read passages that refer to animals while keeping in mind, as we do when reading passages that refer to women or non-Israelites, that the attitudes found in any particular text cannot be assumed to represent the full range of views found in the Bible, and still less the range of views that probably existed in ancient Israel. Dogs and other animals are objects but not subjects of biblical representation, and references to them are shaped by the rhetorical goals of the passages in which they appear and the perspectives held by the specific human authors of those passages. While such passages do shed light on attitudes that some writers held toward animals in ancient Israel, we should be as cautious about the conclusions we draw from them as we would be when reading biblical rhetoric about humans whose social location differs from that of the male authors who were largely responsible for giving us biblical texts.

But let us return, finally, to the fact that the dogs of Exodus appear in a biblical book that, as Levinas notes, is often associated with human freedom. Today associations between Exodus and freedom are perhaps more difficult to make uncritically than they were at the time Levinas wrote his article. Limitations to the use of Exodus as a model for human liberation have been much discussed in recent years, including the close narrative link made in the Bible between the exodus of slaves from Egypt and the slaughter of Canaanites in conquest.[70] The Exodus narratives continue nonetheless to inspire many advocates for social justice. Yet the difficulties Levinas seems to have had in making room for animals in his ethics may be indicative of difficulties that others experience as well. Advocates for human freedom and social justice are, unfortunately, often skeptical about attempts to take seriously the question of the animal. Some of these skeptics recognize that animal rights and environmental activists are occasionally too cautious in their advocacy for human rights and welfare. But others simply adopt uncritically the anthropocentric assumption that matters of animal suffering and flourishing are too trivial to be taken seriously by advocates for justice.

Attention to the dogs of Exodus, however, and the passages associated with them, brings to light the fact that, whatever its limitations as a resource for modern liberation, the book of Exodus does not simplistically cordon off concerns for human welfare from concerns about animal welfare. Such concerns are inextricably intertwined with one another.

Animals and humans do die together as objects of sacrifice and slaughter. But animals and the poor are also juxtaposed as beneficiaries of prescribed agricultural practices, as we have seen. And in the Exodus narrative, the deliverance of the Israelites from Egypt itself involves animals. Those Israelite animals, against whom no dog moves its tongue, leave Egypt with the Israelite humans. Animals are already there in this paradigmatic story of liberation, already participating in the exodus of the Israelite slaves. Thus, attempts to work for their survival and welfare now may simply honor their presence among the Israelites then, as they walked together out of the house of bondage under the watchful eyes of the silent dogs of Exodus.

3

The Chimera of Biblical Sacrifice

"There was also the matter of a dead animal between Cain and Abel. And of a tamed, raised, and sacrificed animal."[1] These words introduce Derrida's brief reading of the story of Cain and Abel in *The Animal That Therefore I Am*. Derrida notes that "God prefers the sacrifice" of Abel's domesticated ("tamed, raised") animals over the agricultural offering brought by his brother. Derrida's comments draw our attention to Genesis 4, where, after Abel brings the firstborn of his flock to God and offers the fatty portions, God "gazed on Abel and on his offering, but on Cain and on his offering he did not gaze" (4:4–5). The biblical text does not actually explain God's preference for Abel's animal offering over Cain's offering of produce. This silence has led to centuries of speculative interpretation, beginning already in the ancient world and extending down to modern scholarship.[2] "Something seems to be missing here," Hermann Gunkel observes.[3] But one way of making sense of this obscure story is to read it as indicating a kind of divine fondness for the ritual killing of animals. In the words of Gerhard von Rad, "the sacrifice of blood was more pleasing to Yahweh."[4] Indeed, Abel's offering of animals appears in Genesis even prior to God's first explicit permission for humans to eat animals in Genesis 9:3. Readers have suggested as long ago as the Talmud that, before God gives Noah permission to eat animals in Genesis 9 (at a point where fear of humans on the part of animals is also introduced [9:2]), humans must have been vegetarian, living on the fruit of trees as God specifies in Genesis 2:16.[5] If Genesis is read this way, God's fondness for animal sacrifice actually precedes the consumption of animals by humans, who would presumably be raising animals for milk, wool, and other non-meat products. As W. Sibley Towner, in his commentary on the story of Cain and Abel, concludes after looking ahead to Genesis 8:21 (where God smells "the pleasing odor" of Noah's sacrifices), "the Lord apparently has always liked the smell of barbeque."[6]

This divine desire for the sight and smell of animal flesh has had a significant impact on biblical representations of animals. Many of the Bible's animals appear in the text primarily as objects of sacrifice. Thus if one is interested in engaging biblical literature in dialogue with animal studies, one has little choice about wading eventually into what Yvonne Sherwood calls the "massive, smoldering pile" of writings about sacrifice.[7] And this pile may not always smell as pleasing to us as Noah's pile of sacrificed animals, or the firstborn of Abel's flock, apparently smelled to God.

But how to proceed? Many biblical texts assume the value, and even the duty, of animal sacrifice. A significant number of these texts describe rituals associated with it, though the extent to which such descriptions correspond to actual historical practice is unclear. Yet surprisingly few biblical texts explicate the *meaning* of sacrifice in detail. Faced with this challenge, many biblical scholars obediently move through the paces of their disciplinary training, producing helpful if predictable lists of Hebrew and cognate terms for specific offerings, each of which can be glossed by a paraphrase of the circumstances associated with the offering in our ancient sources. A smaller number of readers, including Sherwood, have begun to reengage traditions about sacrifice in the wake of contemporary critical theories, including the writings of Derrida. And I will return, later in this chapter, to a very different approach taken by the Jewish Studies scholar Jonathan Klawans, who gives a more prominent role to the relationships that Israelites had with their animals than almost any alternative account of sacrifice. I have chosen to begin with Derrida's reflection on the "tamed, raised, sacrificed" animals of Abel, however, because I want to suggest that the context in which Derrida recalls Abel's dead animals points toward useful ways to think about biblical sacrifice, as well as the human, divine, and other animals who participate in it.

Derrida, Sacrifice, and the Chimera

In his reading of the story of Cain and Abel, Derrida refers back to observations made earlier in his lecture about another story from Genesis, that in which Adam names the animals. There God calls each animal to Adam "to see what he would call it" (2:19). The story of Adam catches Derrida's attention in part because of this emphasis on appellation, since he wishes to underscore the ways in which our words about animals and animality function not simply to describe animals but also to define humanity by way of contrast. Naming also creates a link between the animals and women, since Adam names the woman as well (Gen. 2:23; 3:20). But God's looking upon human and animal also plays a role in both stories. If, in 2:19, God wishes "to see" what Adam will call the animals, in 4:4–5 God "gazes" with favor on Abel's animal offering but not on the produce offered by Cain. The storytellers seem to assume that our relations with animals, the distinctions we draw between types of animals, and the distinctions we make between animals and plants are all being watched by God.

Derrida also links the tale of Cain and Abel in Genesis 4, and the two creation accounts in Genesis 1 and Genesis 2–3 (accounts that he simultaneously differentiates and hybridizes across the course of his reading), to the domestication of animals. Whereas the conflict between Cain and Abel concerns what he calls "tamed, raised" animals, earlier he has suggested that God "created man in his likeness *so that* man will *subject, tame, dominate, train,* or *domesticate* the animals."[8] Derrida's reading of the first four chapters of Genesis thus places some emphasis on the subjection of animals, especially domesticated animals, for human ends, and on the representation of God as a cause for this subjection.

In spite of making such links between the Genesis stories, however, Derrida does not turn to Cain and Abel immediately after his discussion of Adam. He has referred to Cain and Abel earlier, in passing, just after asking "what happens to the fraternity of brothers when an animal appears on the scene" (12). But his primary reflection on their story comes later in his lecture as a kind of interlude in his discussion of the killing of the Chimera, the Greek mythological monster whose body consisted of the combined parts of several different animal species. As part of that

The Chimera of Biblical Sacrifice 69

discussion, Derrida recalls another pair of brothers. Before killing the Chimera, Derrida reminds us, the Greek hero Bellerophon tamed the winged horse Pegasus. According to some traditions, Bellerophon and Pegasus were both fathered by Poseidon, though born to different mothers. Thus Bellerophon, a half-divine, half-human hero, and Pegasus, a half-divine, half-animal winged horse, are actually half-brothers.[9] As a pair, they confound and redraw what we normally think of as lines between humans and animals, lines between humans and gods, lines between animals and gods, lines between different species of animal (Pegasus is a horse but has wings), and lines of kinship. Bellerophon "ends up . . . taming a sort of brother, an other self," as Derrida puts it. It is only after noting this fraternal, cross-species relation between Bellerophon and Pegasus that Derrida shifts from one pair of mythical brothers to another when he raises this "matter of a dead animal between Cain and Abel" (42). After reflecting on Cain's story for a few pages, moreover, Derrida returns to Bellerophon, Pegasus, and the Chimera (45). In the development of Derrida's lecture, then, the Bible's first animal sacrifice is rhetorically associated with the Chimera and her mixed-species killers.

But how does Derrida come to be talking about Chimera in the first place? Just prior to his discussion of Chimera, Derrida has been considering problems with the use of the category "animal" in Western philosophical traditions. In a move that Derrida suggests may be foundational for philosophy, these traditions posit what he calls a "limit presumed to separate man in general from the animal in general." Although individual philosophers may disagree with one another about how, exactly, to define that "limit," nevertheless philosophers as a group, in the words of Derrida,

have judged that limit to be single and indivisible, considering that on the other side of that limit there is an immense group, a single and fundamentally homogeneous set that one has the right, the theoretical or philosophical right, to distinguish and mark as opposite, the set of the Animal in general, the Animal spoken in the general singular. It applies to the whole animal kingdom with the exception of the human. Philosophical right thus presents itself as that of "common sense." (40–41)

It will be important to ask whether such "common sense" is also found in biblical literature and its interpretations. The more salient point for the moment, however, is that Derrida repeatedly attempts to unsettle such "common sense" across his animal writings. Instead of denying differences between humans and animals, he calls attention to multiple types of difference, including differences among diverse animal species (some of which are closer to, and others more distinct from, humans, depending on the criteria used to differentiate); differences within species, including the human species (e.g., sexual difference is a recurring point of reference in Derrida's animal writings); and even differences among animals, plants, and minerals. Consistent with this differentiating project, Derrida, just before turning to the Chimera, famously coins a new term, *animot*, which sounds like the French plural *animaux* but carries within it the visible element *mot*, French for "word." By deploying this invented term, *animot*, Derrida reminds us graphically that the use of a singular term, "animal," to refer to the "heterogeneous multiplicity" of creatures (31), many of whom share little more with one another than their difference from humanity, is anything but a reflection of nature. It is, in fact, little more than the trick of a word (*mot*), "only a word, the word animal" (41). His neologism *animot*, incorporating multiple animals and multiple words, is, he tells us, "a chimerical word . . . a sort of monstrous hybrid, a chimera waiting to be put to death by its Bellerophon" (41). And it is immediately after this observation about chimerical words that Derrida turns to the discussion of Bellerophon that frames his reading of Cain and of Abel.

Derrida therefore arrives at the scene of Abel's animal sacrifice through a complex rhetorical itinerary. He has moved from his strategic introduction of a "chimerical" term to a mixed-species reflection on Chimera, Bellerophon, and Bellerophon's brother Pegasus; and only from there to his embedded reflection on "the matter of a dead animal between Cain and Abel," "a tamed, raised, and sacrificed animal." And after continuing his discussion of Bellerophon, Derrida returns to his discussion of animal terminologies. It is almost as if he is inviting us to explore further the relationship between "tamed, raised, and sacrificed animals" in the biblical texts and our problematic habit of drawing a line between "the human" and "the animal," a habit that his word *animot* is meant to expose and displace.

Derrida's discussion of Cain and Abel can also be read alongside other observations he makes about sacrifice, observations that raise additional questions about the ways in which lines are drawn and redrawn between, and among, humans and animals. In his interview "Eating Well," Derrida reflects upon the assumptions that structure a particular understanding of the subject (of thought, action, desire, law, ethics, and so forth) in Western traditions. Derrida argues that the writings of such influential thinkers as Heidegger and Levinas, who in many ways move beyond restrictive versions of the modern humanist subject, nonetheless "remain profound humanisms *to the extent that they do not sacrifice sacrifice.*"[10] "Sacrifice," here, refers not only to literal animal sacrifices such as we find in the Bible, but also to what Derrida calls the "sacrificial structure" of Western philosophical, religious, and political discourses, in which one finds "a place left open . . . for a noncriminal putting to death." These are places where the command "Thou shalt not kill" seems not to apply. The most obvious examples of "noncriminal putting to death" involve animals, which we allow ourselves to kill without penalty for food, clothing, experimentation, and other reasons. Our endless sacrifice of animals, understood in this sense, is facilitated by the fact that we seldom grant them the status of subject, which is one reason why some writers argue for making animals subjects of "rights."[11] Yet we do not actually restrict the "noncriminal putting to death" to nonhuman animals. We frequently sacrifice other humans as well, not only through literal and legal killing (one thinks of warfare, drones, the death penalty, police actions, and stand-your-ground laws in the United States) but also, Derrida notes, through symbolic forms of violence and appropriation that Dawne McCance, playing on Derrida's references to a "non-criminal putting to death," calls a "non-literal putting to death."[12] And it may be "very difficult, truly impossible," Derrida warns in "Eating Well," to erect a fence between literal and symbolic sacrifice (278).

Derrida's "sacrificial structure" thus informs what he calls a "dominant schema" for the Western subject, which is formed through a number of constitutive exclusions. While this subject is, in the first place, a human subject, and so defined by the exclusion of animals, that exclusion is only one of the assumptions that undergird notions of the subject. "There have been, there are still," Derrida reminds us in "Force of Law," also human beings "who are not recognized as subjects and who receive this animal treatment."[13] As many feminist thinkers also emphasize, the subject has been not simply human but "preferably and paradigmatically the adult male, rather than the woman, child or animal" (247).[14] And not just any male: "there was a time, not long ago and not yet over, in which 'we, men' meant 'we adult white male Europeans, carnivorous and capable of sacrifice'" (246). Here we see the dominant male subject characterized not only by additional specifications of race and nation ("we adult white male Europeans") but also by a particular relation to animality. The normative male subject dominates, kills, and eats animals, and so is characterized by what Derrida calls "carnivorous virility"; the "authority and autonomy" associated with the subject are "attributed to the man (*homo* and *vir*) rather than to the woman, and to the woman rather than to the animal."[15] In several places, Derrida refers to this structure of philosophical and political assumptions by what he indicates in *The Beast and the Sovereign* is a sort of "nickname": "carnophallogocentrism."[16] His addition of the prefix "carno-" to the more famous "phallogocentrism" encourages us to consider more explicitly the relationships between, on the one hand, our eating of meat, domination of animals, and ingestion of the other, whether physical or symbolic; and, on the other hand, our privileging of the masculine (phallus) and the word (logos) in constructions of meaning, subjectivity, and society. The exclusion of animals from ethical consideration cannot be separated from the exclusion of other humans as subjects of politics and meaning.

Now I may seem to be wandering at this point from *biblical* sacrifice. Even appreciative readers of Derrida can acknowledge that his discussions of sacrifice run some risk of obscuring particular characteristics of animal sacrifice in the various historical societies in which it was practiced, including ancient Israel.[17] Yet there is also little doubt that Derrida is attempting to associate biblical sacrifice with dynamics that appear in radically different contexts when he links such thinkers as Descartes, Kant, and Levinas to "a Greco-Judeo-Christiano-Islamic tradition" or, more graphically, "the Judeo-Christiano-Islamic tradition of a war against the animal, of a sacrificial war that is as old as Genesis."[18] As Aaron Gross notes, Derrida uses "the language of war" and sacrifice to "emphasize a continuity" between the suffering of living creatures on a massive scale today and "what is most ancient," such as the right to kill animals with impunity.[19] Sacrificial structures have been in some fundamental way constitutive for

"Abrahamic" religions, Gross suggests, although these religions, and particularly Judaism, include traditions attentive to animal welfare. Significant features of "Abrahamic religiosity" have "been soaked in the blood of sacrifice" (144). Moreover, the sacrificial dynamics of Abrahamic religions did not end with the cessation of actual animal sacrifice, in Gross's view. From the writing of biblical literature through to the modern world, religious texts and practices have conceptualized humans, animals, and God in ways that make it more permissible to kill animals. Such conceptualizations assume a clear distinction between humans and other animals, but paradoxically today entail a "common sense" assumption that religion "has little to do with animals" (60). As Gross demonstrates, the academic study of religion incorporates this "common sense" through its own "disavowal" of the importance of animals, and its uncritical adoption of the human–animal binary. Religious studies, like the philosophical tradition discussed by Derrida, has consequently failed to "sacrifice sacrifice." Thus it contributes to the fact that, as Derrida puts it in "Force of Law," "carnivorous sacrifice" is "fundamental" to "*our* culture."[20]

The suggestion that religious studies in general, or biblical studies in particular, has failed to "sacrifice sacrifice" may seem counterintuitive if one also considers the possibility that modern scholars, repelled by animal sacrifice, have made insufficient efforts to understand its importance for human practitioners.[21] But even scholars who study sacrifice seldom question certain "common sense" assumptions undergirding it, including the assumption that humans have a right, even a God-given obligation, to subject and kill animals for human purposes. Many discussions of sacrifice appear to be "sacrificial" in Derrida's sense, moreover, when they pay little attention to the animals involved. The focus lies most often on human actors and their views about God. And discussions of sacrifice are often grounded in the belief that a clear line, constitutive for both meaning and ethics, divides humans on one side from all animals on the other.

Derrida's rhetorical invitation to reconsider biblical traditions on sacrifice by focusing on the Bible's "tamed, raised, sacrificed animals," and to do so light of his "chimerical word" *animot*, may lead us to ask instead whether "biblical sacrifice" is not itself "chimerical" in nature. Like the Chimera and her killers, biblical sacrifice combines categories and redraws lines in ways that threaten to undermine those very lines and categories.

As Yvonne Sherwood shrewdly puts it, "sacrifice is all about clarifying the divisions between god, human, animal, and inorganic matter—and . . . it is also about dissolving those distinctions. It is about 'cutting up life,' in the sense of establishing the conceptual divisions that help us make sense of life—then putting those cuts in life under the knife."[22]

Reading Biblical Sacrifice

Animal sacrifice may seem strange to most people today, but it was widely practiced in the ancient world both before and after the Hebrew Bible was written.[23] It is hardly surprising, then, that the importance of sacrifice is assumed throughout the Bible. Certain texts, especially in the prophetic tradition, do express negative views on the practice of sacrifice and other rituals (e.g., Isa. 1:11; 66:3; Jer. 6:20; 7:21–2; Hos. 6:6; Amos 5:22; Mic. 6:6–8; Ps. 40:6 [Hebrew 40:7]); but such texts probably result from divergent views about the efficacy of ritual more generally and the relationship between ritual and ethics, divergent views that may correlate with social and institutional locations in ancient Israel.[24] As far as we can tell, they have little to do with concerns about animal welfare, or any squeamishness about blood.

Perhaps because sacrifice was familiar to ancient audiences, biblical and other texts that refer to it seldom give detailed explanations of the presuppositions of those who practiced it. While individual rituals may be described in great detail, only a few texts interpret their meaning with more than a gloss. As a result, modern scholars understand less, and agree less, about the meaning of animal sacrifice than many readers of the Bible realize. A few scholars outside of biblical studies have attempted to construct comprehensive theories of sacrifice, which might account for biblical sacrifice in the context of sacrifice more generally;[25] but little agreement exists about the relative plausibility of such theories or their relevance for biblical interpretation. Biblical scholars are generally more inclined to agree with Gary Anderson's conclusion that sacrifice in the Hebrew Bible is a "multivalent phenomenon" and that any single theoretical framework is unlikely to account for all of its instances.[26]

One indication of the multivalence of biblical sacrifice is the diverse Hebrew vocabulary, and the diverse translations, used to refer to different types of offerings.[27] Biblical literature uses a number of words to refer to sacrifices and other offerings, and it sometimes uses them inconsistently. A well-known example appears in the story of Cain and Abel, which refers to the offerings of each brother as a *minchah*, a "gift" or "offering" (Gen. 4:3–5). The use of this single term for both offerings of animals and offerings of grains, here and in some other texts, indicates that *minchah* could serve as a general term for various types of gifts, alongside other general terms such as *qorban* (an offering that is "brought near" the altar). Indeed, scholars have often emphasized the role of sacrifice as a kind of gift to God, even while acknowledging other functions; and when they have done so, they have long called attention to the story of Cain and Abel.[28] Yet such a conclusion can also lead one's explication of sacrifice in a direction in which its meaning in the story of Cain and Abel depends very little on the division between animals and plants. This is true, for example, of the opening pages of Moshe Halbertal's *On Sacrifice*. Halbertal uses the story of Cain and Abel, and the fact that they both bring a *minchah* to God, to underscore the possibility that, within a hierarchical relationship such as that between humans and gods, any gift from a subordinate may be rejected along with the cycle of gift exchange that follows from it.[29] Although this leads to an interesting interpretation of sacrifice, it also means that little attention is given to the specific difference between Abel's animal sacrifice and Cain's gift of produce. Animals tend to disappear in the explication.

On the other hand, certain portions of biblical literature, primarily those associated by scholars with "priestly" origins, use *minchah* in a more narrow sense than Genesis 4 to refer only to cereal offerings. Such usage probably resulted from the specialization of vocabulary required for priests and other religious functionaries, which we also find in other ancient societies. In distinction from the story of Cain and Abel, however, this use of *minchah* underscores the fact that grain offerings were certainly considered legitimate and may have been the most common type of gift given to the temple.[30]

Even if we restrict our attention to animal sacrifices, we find that generic English terms like "sacrifice" or "offering" are actually being applied to a number of types of biblical offering, which in some cases are distinguished by Hebrew vocabulary and in other cases by contextual considerations. One common term for sacrifice that may point toward its animal connections, *zebach*, comes from a verbal root for "slaughter" that is also the root for the Hebrew word for "altar." But other designations for types of sacrifices are discussed variously in English as "burnt offerings," "peace offerings" or celebratory "offerings of well-being," "sin" or "purification" offerings, "reparation" offerings, offerings for specific festivals (such as Passover), and so forth.[31] While some of these sacrifices require the complete destruction of an animal on the altar (as in the *olah,* or "burnt offering"), others entail the consumption of some portion of the animal by participants in the ritual. But the diversity of terms as well as the diversity of contexts in which the terms are used indicates that we are not talking about a single phenomenon of animal sacrifice, but rather a complex field of practice and meaning, which scholars attempt to order in various ways.

Anderson notes with some approval that Thomas Aquinas proposed a "distinction between offering and sacrifice as one of 'genus' and 'species.' Offering constitutes the more general category of gift or oblation, while sacrifice is a specialization of this category which entails a more specific means of delivery to the deity." Anderson himself considers this a "useful typology for biblical sacrifice," though he rightly notes that multiple terms are used in the Hebrew Bible at both levels.[32] But for my purposes here, this appeal to such terms as "genus" and "species," which today serve as levels in the nomenclature used to refer to animals, sets up an interesting parallel between our attempts to understand the larger system of biblical sacrifices and our attempts to understand different types of animals. In both cases, we are trying to make sense of a heterogeneous field of differences and similarities that may be obscured by the use of general categories like "animal" and "sacrifice."

The species of animals associated with different types of sacrifice in the Hebrew Bible are in fact far fewer in number than the species known to the Israelites. Only domesticated animals are considered appropriate for sacrifice. The animals that are sacrificed all come from Israel's closest companion species. It is not the case, moreover, that all domesticated animals are eligible for sacrifice. Rather, biblical guidelines for sacrifice cut across the category of domesticated animals. The Israelites sacrificed sheep, goats, cattle, and a small number of tamed or domesticated birds, such as pigeons and doves. They apparently did not, however, sacrifice donkeys, camels, horses, or dogs, all of which also lived among the Israelites.

One reason for this distinction is clear: animals eligible for sacrifice had to be considered edible. Both Leviticus 11:3 and Deuteronomy 14:6 attempt to define the category of "clean," edible mammals for the Israelites: such mammals must have hooves, the hooves must be cloven (divided into two toes), and the animals must chew the cud or ruminate. As noted in the Introduction, Mary Douglas devoted an influential chapter to these stipulations in her groundbreaking work *Purity and Danger*; and, since that time, numerous studies have attempted to find coherence in the biblical food laws.[33] For my purposes here, it is sufficient to note that the category of edible animals includes sheep, goats, and cattle; but does not include such domesticated animals as donkeys, camels, horses, or dogs, each of which is excluded by one or more of the criteria listed in Leviticus and Deuteronomy. Being "unclean" (Lev. 11:4–8) and even "abhorrent" (Deut. 14:3), they are inedible and so ineligible for sacrifice.

Edibility alone, however, does not make an animal eligible for sacrifice. Fish, though edible, are never sacrificed; and only a few edible birds are sacrificed. Deuteronomy 14:4–5 lists ten mammals that the Israelites may eat, all of which conform to the criteria for edibility in 14:6. Seven of these mammals, however, are never associated with sacrifice. Although the identification of some of these animals is uncertain, they all appear to be non-domesticated ungulates, including deer and gazelles, and possibly ibexes, antelope, and others.[34] If they are eaten, presumably they are hunted, since the Israelites are forbidden to eat carrion in Exodus 22:31 (Hebrew 22:30) and Deuteronomy 14:21 (which, however, allows carrion to be eaten by immigrants and foreigners). Leviticus takes a somewhat less restricted approach to carrion, apparently considering it unclean but edible for those who are not priests (cf. Lev. 11:39–40; 17:15–16; 22:8).

The practice of sacrifice thus presupposes at least two types of distinctions among animals: that between domesticated and wild, and that between edible and inedible. The latter distinction, moreover, is discussed in Leviticus 11 in relation to other ways of categorizing animals: "all the animals that are on the land" (11:2), water creatures, birds, flying insects, and swarming things of various types. Sacrifice, then, does not simply mark out animals as such, or domesticated animals as such, for ritual killing. It rather assumes the selection of particular species (domesticated sheep and goats, larger cattle, and a few tamed birds) against a background of several complex and overlapping biblical taxonomies. The category "animal" is not made simple by biblical sacrifice, or assumed to be what Derrida calls "an immense group, a single and fundamentally homogeneous set."[35] Rather biblical sacrifice articulates animal life in complex ways.

Animals that are available for sacrifice, moreover, cannot simply be substituted for one another randomly on any occasion of sacrifice. Various stipulations about sacrifice are more or less restrictive about which animals should be offered on which occasions, based on the species, sex, and age of the animals, as well as, in some cases, the economic or social status of the humans who bring the animal for sacrifice.

Indeed, rather than trying to understand biblical sacrifices, as many scholars have, by focusing on the names and types of offerings, we might imagine a kind of field of sacrificial situations involving greater or lesser specificity about the animals that are offered. In one part of the field, representing greater specificity, we find such practices as the Israelite daily offering (Exod. 29:38–46), which required that two yearling lambs be sacrificed on the altar every day, one in the morning, and one in the evening. Each offering is a "burnt offering" (*olah*), in which the entire animal is consumed in fire, in this case together with offerings of produce and drink. These offerings give off a pleasing odor to God (29:41), providing perhaps a kind of bait to ensure God's presence at the sanctuary (29:43) and among the Israelites (29:45). While the daily offering is one of several sacrifices that require a lamb, other occasions call specifically for a bull, a goat, or a ram. Sometimes these animals are sacrificed alone, as with the bull offered daily for atonement in Exodus 29:36, or the bull offered when a priest or the congregation sins unintentionally in Leviticus 4:1–21, or the male goat offered by a leader who sins unintentionally in Leviticus 4:22–26. A related example, which isn't always classified as sacrifice but which identifies a particular animal to be slaughtered for religious purposes, is the killing and burning in Numbers 19 of a red cow, whose ashes are used for purification rituals. In still other texts, particular species of animals are killed in rituals that combine more than one species, as with the young bull and two rams used in the consecration of priests in Exodus 29:1–35 (cf. Lev. 8:1–36) or the bull and goat who are sacrificed on the day of atonement in Leviticus 16, when a second goat is allowed to live and sent into the wilderness. All of these situations require very particular types of animals to be sacrificed, alone or in combination.

Elsewhere, however, we find occasions on which the animals eligible for sacrifice can be chosen from among several species. Some situations that seem narrow may actually fall into this category. At Passover, for example, which is often associated with a lamb, the young animal that is slaughtered and eaten is a yearling male without blemish, but either a sheep or a goat. A sacrifice of well-being, or "peace offering," might be either cattle, from the "herd" (Lev. 3:12–16), or sheep or goats, from the "flock" (Lev. 3:6–11, 12–16). Burnt offerings could involve bulls from the herd (Lev. 1:3–9), sheep or goats from the flock (Lev. 1:10–13), or a pair of either doves or pigeons (Lev. 1:14–17). Sin offerings might involve a female sheep or a female goat (Lev. 5:6), but a person who could not afford a sheep or goat could bring two doves or two pigeons (Lev. 5:7–10). If even these birds were too expensive, a grain offering could be substituted (Lev. 5:11–13). Thus, in contrast to sacrifices that require a very specific species of offering, there were also sacrificial occasions that allowed for the possibility of choosing among options, though the number of such options was always limited. And, as the option for a grain offering in place of an acceptable animal in Leviticus 5:11–13 indicates, the line between animals and produce is itself not altogether stable in such situations, notwithstanding God's preference for Abel's animal sacrifice.

The examples from Leviticus 5 also indicate, however, that the practice of sacrifice does not only involve differentiation among animals. It also involves differentiation among humans. The distinctions among a person who can afford to give a sheep or goat, a person who can only afford to give two doves or pigeons, and a person who can only afford to give grain mark differences of economic means. We have already seen in chapter 2 how the establishment of Passover—which involves the slaughter, preparation, and shared eating of a lamb or kid, and, like many sacrifices, some manipulation of blood[36]—occurs in a context where Israelites are differentiated from Egyptians. Exodus also prohibits foreigners from eating the Passover meal, though slaves or resident aliens could do so, as long as males were circumcised (12:43–49). The possibility of substituting birds or grain for a sheep or goat in Leviticus 5, however, shows that the practice of sacrifice can also involve lines of difference *internal to* Israel. The identification of specific people as those eligible to perform particular sacrifices (the high priest, Aaronid priests, Zadokite priests, Levites, various kings, prophets, or judges in certain contexts, and so forth) underscores other differences of status and holiness, many of which presuppose differences of gender as well. Indeed, specifications of gender are frequently applied to both humans and animals in the laws of sacrifice, often in ways that contribute to inequalities of power.[37] The exclusion of men with disabilities from offering "the food for his God" (Lev. 21:17) even if they belong to the line of Aaron inscribes and penalizes another type of difference among humans. It also corresponds to prohibitions on offering for sacrifice animals that are maimed or otherwise considered blemished. Specification of those who may, and those who may not, eat Israel's sacred gifts (Lev. 22:10–16) results in the drawing of still more lines of difference. These and other passages on sacrifice support the argument of Saul Olyan that biblical representations of ritual and cult produce and reproduce a "hierarchical social order" by making distinctions, often binary in nature (e.g., holy vs. common, clean vs. unclean, Israelite vs. alien, whole vs. blemished, male vs. female, etc.), and then privileging one side of such distinctions over the other.[38] Rather than assuming a single line between all humans and all animals, sacrifice articulates multiple lines of difference on both sides of that traditional divide.

Even the divide between human and animal is displaced by biblical sacrifice. A number of biblical passages condemn human sacrifice or make provisions for offering an animal in place of a child in the gift of the firstborn. As noted in chapter 2, however, a tension exists in the Bible between such passages and others that take a more ambiguous or positive view of child sacrifice; and even passages that condemn it sometimes reveal that it was being practiced.[39] Exodus 22:29–30 (Hebrew 22:28–29) requires the gift of a firstborn child without making provision for an animal substitute, while the rhetoric of Ezekiel 20:25–26 appears to confirm the existence of statutes requiring child sacrifice that, while "not good" (20:25), are nevertheless understood as having been given by God. The command to sacrifice Isaac as a "burnt offering" does, of course, come directly from God (Gen. 22:2). And although God never commands Jephthah to offer his daughter as a "burnt offering," Jephthah does so only after God's spirit comes upon him and after making a vow in exchange for a victory that God does deliver (Judg. 11:29–30, 35–36, 39). As Jon Levenson points out, the story lacks "any indication that child sacrifice, painful to father and offspring alike, was inappropriate from *God's* standpoint. Quite the opposite: Jephthah's actions are intelligible only on the assumption that his daughter—he had no son—could legitimately be sacrificed as a burnt offering to YHWH."[40] Susan Niditch argues that the biblical concept of *cherem*, which requires the Israelites to put to death all human and in some cases animal inhabitants of an enemy city, also has sacrificial connotations.[41] As a consequence of its own internal contradictions, then, the biblical discourse on sacrifice cuts across the barrier between humans and animals, making certain humans and certain animals eligible for ritual killing while eliminating other humans and other animals from such eligibility. Biblical sacrifice thus appears to confirm Derrida's observation that the "non-criminal putting to death" of animals and the "non-criminal putting to death" of humans are interrelated.

Moreover, the boundary separating humans and other animals from God may in some cases be destabilized by biblical sacrifice. A recurring interpretation of ancient animal sacrifice understands it as food for God. Numerous texts from the ancient Near East indicate that sacrifices were understood in just this way outside of Israel, a fact that scholars tend to agree upon when non-biblical texts are discussed. As JoAnn Scurlock puts it, "Ancient Mesopotamian deities expected to be fed twice a day without fail by their human worshipers."[42] Scurlock herself suggests that Israelite sacrifices can also be understood as food for a god. As noted above, Exodus 29:38–42 commands the Israelites to make an offering to God twice daily, replicating the model noted by Scurlock for feeding the Mesopotamian gods. More significantly, several biblical texts refer to offerings as God's "food" (e.g., Lev. 3:11, 16; 21:6, 8, 17, 21, 22; 22:25; Num. 28:2, 24; Ezek. 44:7; Mal. 1:7); and the altar is sometimes called a "table" (e.g., Ezek. 41:22; 44:16; Mal. 1:7, 12). Other texts use the vocabulary of "eating" to refer to God as a "devouring fire," whether in the context of sacrifice (e.g., Lev. 9:24; Judg. 6:21; 1 Kgs 18:38; cf. Lev. 10:2; Num. 16:35), covenant (Deut. 4:24; 32:22; Lam. 2:3; cf. Exod. 24:17) or warfare (Deut. 9:3; Isa. 30:27; cf. 2 Sam. 22:9; 2 Kgs 1:10–14; Ps. 18:8 [Hebrew 18:9]). Still other texts state that burnt offerings give a "pleasing odor" to God (e.g., Lev.

1:9, 13, 17; cf. Lev. 26:31; Exod. 29:18, 25, 41). When Noah offers burnt offerings after leaving the ark, this "pleasing odor" leads God to decide that he will never again destroy the earth and its creatures (Gen. 8:21). This image corresponds to scenes in the ancient stories of both Atrahasis and Gilgamesh, which represent Mesopotamian gods reacting to the good smells of sacrifice following the Flood.[43] It seems to have been understood in the ancient world that, in the words of Ingvild Gilhus, "both gods and humans were nourished with the meat of sacrificial animals, but the gods did not consume the animal flesh in the same way as humans, they did not chew and swallow the roasted meat but were fed by the aroma from those parts of the meat that had been burned at the altar."[44]

Although most scholars acknowledge that biblical literature contains this type of imagery, many attempt nonetheless to play down any frightening implications. Like modern-day Bellerophons riding Pegasus into battle against Chimera, they cry out that such references are, in Jacob Milgrom's words, "only fossilized vestiges from a dim past, which show no signs of life in the Bible."[45] What is the nature of the beast that needs to be slain here? In many discussions, rejection of the notion that sacrifice was food for God appears to involve anxieties around anthropomorphism. But perhaps another type of monster, in addition to anthropomorphism, lurks here. For among all the senses, the olfactory is arguably that which most distinguishes humans from other mammals. Images of God smelling savory sacrifices may frighten readers of the Bible not simply because they threaten to make God too human, but also because they threaten to turn God into an animal, a carnivore able to smell meat at a distance before "devouring" it with fire, a Chimera, appropriate perhaps for other ancient mythologies but surely not for the Bible.

The Divine Shepherd and the Chimera of Sacrifice

Biblical hints that God might have monstrous features are not limited to representations of God on the scent of a sacrificial carcass, or the threat that God might become a "devouring fire" against the Israelites as well as their enemies (Deut. 4:24). Chapter 5 considers other biblical images that associate God with wild animals and other frightening creatures.

But the Israelites clearly did not sacrifice only to appease a frightening God. Indeed, the passage on the daily offerings in Exodus 29, among many others, expresses a strong desire on the part of biblical writers that God would come to and remain with them. This desire for God's presence includes a desire for protection against enemies, but it cannot be reduced to that. A desire for divine care, flourishing, and fertility, not only for the human Israelites but also for their animals and crops, is apparent throughout the Bible. How does this desire relate to the Chimera of biblical sacrifice?

Jonathan Klawans has articulated an intriguing theory of sacrifice that highlights the Israelites' relations with their animals. What most interests me about his theory in this context is the light it may shed on the chimeric reading of biblical sacrifice toward which Derrida points.

This may seem surprising, since Derrida and Klawans write about sacrifice under the influence of different intellectual traditions and for very different purposes. Whereas Derrida opens his discussion of Cain and Abel by referring to "the matter of a dead animal," Klawans is concerned that too much attention has been given to dead animals in our attempts to understand sacrifice. Associating sacrifice primarily with killing, we modernists avert our eyes from it, and so find it difficult to understand what made it important for the Israelites. Klawans counters this in several ways.

Noting the importance of symbolic approaches to the Bible's purity and dietary guidelines (such as that offered by Douglas), Klawans proposes that a symbolic approach to sacrifice is preferable to interpretations that focus on historical origins. Building on a famous study by Henri Hubert and Marcel Mauss, he argues that we can only understand sacrifice if we reconceive it as a total ritual process, which begins long before the act of killing.[46] By extending this process back in time, Klawans is able to take seriously the fact that people who brought animals for sacrifice were in most cases intimately involved with those animals while they were alive. Indeed, Klawans picks up on Jonathan Z. Smith's suggestion that sacrifice might serve as a "meditation on domestication."[47] From this suggestion Klawans argues that "to trace Israel's sacrificial process—and to grasp fully its symbolic meanings—we also need to appreciate better Israel's relationship with its animal subjects."[48] Although he does not use this language, Klawans is in effect arguing that we cannot understand sacrifice without paying closer attention to the ways in which the domestication and raising of Israel's companion species shaped the lives and religious practices of the Israelites themselves.

Klawans reminds us that interactions between shepherds and flocks supply the Bible's writers with both political and religious symbols. Such imagery is not at all unique to the Bible. Long before the emergence of Israel, shepherding symbolism was used in Mesopotamia and Egypt for both kings and gods.[49] When the Bible utilizes these images, it picks up on a rich tradition of herding symbolism that developed out of the agro-pastoral "naturecultures" (to recall Haraway's hybridized term) of the ancient Near East. But as Howard Eilberg-Schwartz noted more than twenty years ago, the role of these "natural metaphors" in Israel's religious, political, and social self-understanding is often overlooked.[50] One of Klawans's contributions is to argue for the significance of such metaphors for our understanding of sacrifice as a religious "meditation on domestication."

The Hebrew Bible applies shepherd imagery to both human leaders and God.[51] While such imagery sometimes makes use of the figure of the bad shepherd, primarily for humans, more often the representation of God as a shepherd emphasizes the care with which God tends to and leads God's flock. This happens most famously in Psalm 23, where God is praised for knowing how to tend to, provide for, and protect his animals. But in Ezekiel too, God is a shepherd who will seek out the flock just as a shepherd searches for scattered sheep (34:11–12, 16). God will treat them as a shepherd should, leading them by streams, feeding them in good pastures in the mountains, and allowing them to lie down in good pastures (34:13–14). God will also distinguish among the animals, between rams and goats (17), between fat sheep and lean sheep (20), between one sheep and another (22); and then set up a Davidic shepherd over them (23). After this God will set up a "covenant of peace," banishing wild animals, who represent a threat to domestic animals, from the land (25), and providing the flock with plenty of food. When God is represented caring for the flock of Israel in such a fashion, God's actions correspond to actions that the Israelites would value in actual shepherds.

Yet as Klawans points out, the care and direction of domestic animals are also necessary for any successful animal sacrifice, prior to ritual purification and slaughter. When God is shown tending to the flock of Israel, God's actions correspond to those that human shepherds take to ensure that their animals are healthy, whole, and suitable for sacrifice by virtue of age, species, bodily condition, and even kinship relations (Leviticus 22:28, for example, specifies that an animal and its young should not be slaughtered on the same day). And when, as in Ezekiel 34, God separates lean sheep from fat sheep, or rams from goats, God is making choices that are necessary for a proper sacrifice. This correspondence between the actions of God as Israel's shepherd and the actions of the Israelites who bred, raised, ate, and sacrificed domestic animals therefore points to what Klawans calls one of the "organizing principles" of the symbolic meaning of Israelite animal sacrifice, the principle of *imitatio Dei*:

> Israel's sacrificial system presumes that Israelites themselves will be doing some good tending of their herds or flocks: if they did not, there would be nothing left to offer. Israel's theologizing frequently depicts God performing precisely that role vis-à-vis Israel, tending the flock. Thus it stands to reason that on some level, ancient Israelites understood tending their own flocks in light of this analogy: as Israel is to Israel's herds and flocks, so too is God to Israel, the flock of the Lord. The prophetic and hymnic metaphors based on this analogy . . . provide further confirmation of the case I am making: the process of sacrifice can be understood as an act of *imitatio Dei*.[52]

Klawans goes on to argue that we can better understand numerous elements of the biblical system of sacrifice, including the consumption of sacrificial meat, if we interpret them in light of this principle of *imitatio Dei*. Although it is not necessary here to discuss those elements in detail, sacrifice becomes an occasion to reflect upon the ways in which God provides for, protects, controls, allows to reproduce, but also sometimes kills humans, just as humans provide for, control, allow to reproduce, but also sometimes kill their domesticated animals. As Klawans puts it, there is "an analogy at the heart of sacrifice." According to the terms of this analogy, the humans who sacrifice

> play the part of God, and the domesticated animals—from the herd and the flock—play the part of the people. . . . This analogy can be fully appreciated only when both halves receive equal consideration: As God is to the people, so too—during the process of sacrifice—is the people of Israel to the domesticated animals offered for sacrifice. Indeed, one value of understanding sacrifice

metaphorically is that we are encouraged to think of the roles played by both the people and the animals . . . [T]he meaning of sacrifice was informed not only by what took place at the altar, but also by what transpired in their relationships with animals before getting to the altar. The sacrificial animals must be birthed, protected, fed, and guided—all things that Israel wished for themselves from their God. The meaning of sacrifice, therefore, derives not primarily from what the animals offered Israel, but rather from what Israel provided to its domesticated animals, which parallels the care that they wished their God to provide for them.[53]

Sacrifice is thus, for Klawans, a kind of imitation of the divine, an imitation that also seeks to draw the divine closer to the humans who belong to God's flock.

Now for my purposes there are several things to note about this theory. First, it places more emphasis on actual relationships between humans and animals than most accounts of sacrifice, and not simply on relations among humans, or between humans and God. Klawans's arguments therefore warrant particular attention from readers whose interest in sacrifice is grounded in an interest in animal studies. For Klawans helps us recall that the Israelites actually lived with animals, and raised them carefully over time (sometimes in their own houses, as archaeologists have noted,[54] and even as members of the household, as the prophet Nathan suggests in 2 Samuel 12). We are encouraged to take seriously that the Israelites even saw themselves in those animals, and saw the animals looking to their human shepherds for care (a fact that may remind us of Derrida seeing himself being seen by his cat).

Klawans makes no attempt to reconstruct a biblical view of animals in general, or, as Derrida might put it, "the Animal in the general singular." He focuses on domesticated animals because the Bible designates these animals as appropriate for sacrifice. We are dealing with what Derrida calls "tamed, raised, and sacrificed animal[s]." And even domesticated animals are not treated as a unified entity, but rather as "herds and flocks" of animals deemed suitable for sacrifice. Whether he would put the matter this way or not, Klawans's attention to animals differentiates among them, rather than falling into the homogenizing trap that worries Derrida; and it does so because, as we have seen, biblical texts on sacrifice differentiate among them as well.

Even as Klawans's account of sacrifice distinguishes and divides, however, it also destabilizes lines elsewhere. For the boundary between humans and animals, and the boundary between humans and God, are both blurred by the sacrificial system as Klawans interprets it. Humans are associated with domesticated animals inasmuch as they are the flock of God, who are bred, raised, cared for and protected, but also killed, on occasion, by God, just as Israel's flocks and herds are bred, raised, cared for and protected, but also killed, on occasion, by the Israelites. Yet humans are also associated with God, when they interact with their animals as God interacts with God's symbolic flocks and herds. Rather than saying, then, as we sometimes do, that sacrificial animals mediate the relationship between humans and God, perhaps we should ask whether it is not actually humans who, through sacrifice, bring animals and God together by playing now one role, and now another, or even both at the same time. Imitating God as they sacrifice animals, humans also imitate animals when, through the obedience of sacrifice, they serve God, their shepherd and domesticator, who in turn can be lured to the scene of sacrifice by the smell of animal flesh, much like an animal.

By conceptualizing sacrifice as a symbolic form of imitation of the divine, Klawans attempts to construct a more sympathetic account of it. Thus he tends to downplay some of the more troubling aspects of biblical sacrifice, including the problem of human sacrifice. Nevertheless, his own arguments for analogy and symbolism could be extended in such a way as to make more intelligible the practice of human sacrifice. If human care for flocks correlates symbolically with divine care for humans, then human *killing* of flocks may correlate symbolically with *divine* killing of humans. And if humans take on the role of God when they not only raise but also kill their domestic animals, it is only a short step to imagining that other living beings who are birthed, tamed, and raised inside domestic spaces—sons and daughters, for example—are also potential objects of sacrifice.

This symbolic logic may shed light on both Abraham's willingness to sacrifice his son at God's command, and Jephthah's actual sacrifice of his daughter in Judges 11. Of course, the fact that the latter sacrifice is carried out while the former is not requires a gender analysis.[55] The fate of Jephthah's daughter as a burnt offering reminds us of the tendency to associate women with animals noted in chapter 1. Her death is sometimes compared to those of two other women in Judges:[56] the wife of Samson who is burned alive in 15:6, and the young woman whose body is dismembered in 19:29 and used to send a message in ways that parallel Saul's use of butchered cattle parts in 1 Samuel 11. Carol Adams, the author of several influential pieces on the animalization of women, cites the story from Judges 19 as an example of what she calls the "sexual butchering" of women, which, in her view, continues in contemporary media.[57] But it is significant that all three of these women are also characterized explicitly as daughters. Human offspring, female *and* male, are understood in biblical literature in ways comparable to Israel's flocks and herds (e.g., Exod. 13:1–2; 22:29–30; 34:19–20; Num. 3:13; 8:17; 18:15). Human offspring fall under the authority of the head of a household (as do wives and slaves) and, like the young animals born into the flocks and herds, are evidence of God's provision of fertility. They dwell in domesticated space. Here it is useful to recall that our word "domesticated" is derived from the Latin *domus*, "house," and that the most common way of referring to the immediate family in the Hebrew Bible is *beyt ab*, "father's house." Domesticated inhabitants of the father's house are subject to both the care and the control of the paternal shepherd, whether human or divine. They benefit from the shepherd's protection, but they are available as objects of his slaughter.

The theoretical ruminations on sacrifice that we find in Derrida and Klawans initially appear to have little in common with one another. They are distinct species of intellectual engagement, with many differences between them that could be laid out in a more exhaustive comparison. By suggesting that we understand sacrifice better when we read them together, I may well be suspected of nurturing a new Chimera, a monster composed of incompatible theories, which must quickly be put to death.

It is striking, however, that both Derrida and Klawans call our attention to domestication. The idea that care, control, and killing of one's closest subordinates can go together is disturbing when we encounter it in extreme representations such as the story of the daughter of Jephthah. Yet studies indicate that our relations with domesticated animals are often structured by a combination of "dominance and affection," to quote the title of a book by Yi-Fu Tuan, who juxtaposes a discussion of "dominance and affection" toward one's animals with discussions of "dominance and affection" toward women and children, and toward slaves, all of whom may be judged "immature and naïve, animal-like, and sexual" by their superordinates.[58] Like Klawans, Tuan notes the care implied by biblical passages such as Psalm 23 and documents feelings of affection and love that herders may have for their livestock. Yet in the end, herders do often kill the animals they care for, even while constructing rationalizations for doing so. As Tuan puts it, "pastoralists do not exist for the sake of their livestock. It is the other way around, although this exploitative relationship is fudged by the care that cattle herders *must* give to their charges, a care that in specific instances can lead to genuine affection" (92; his emphasis). Thus we can't discount the possibility that domesticated animals could generate the affect attributed, for example, to the poor man in 2 Samuel 12:3, whose hand-raised lamb living in the house is said to be "like a daughter" to him. Jephthah, however, is characterized in terms of affect as well. Judges 11:35 depicts him as far more distraught than, for example, Abraham is about the prospect of killing his child. Yet in the end, he does so. Reading these stories together with Derrida and Klawans allows us to suggest that the cultural tolerance for a "non-criminal putting to death" of the subordinates one cares for, when applied routinely to animals, may have made such exceptional stories as the sacrifice of Jephthah's daughter easier to imagine for the Israelites than they are for us.

Klawans is rather more circumspect than Derrida about the matter of dead animals. But if Derrida reminds us of "the *unprecedented* proportions" of our "subjection of the animal" today, which "go well beyond the animal sacrifices of the Bible,"[59] so also Klawans notes that the end of the biblical system of sacrifice has not made things better for animals.[60] It has simply created a gap between the act of killing and the act of consumption, and reduced the direct experience most of us have of care for those species of animals that are routinely eaten. And he is surely right about this. As Timothy Pachirat argues in his excellent ethnographic study of the slaughterhouse, the distance we have put between ourselves and the animals we kill facilitates our ability to ignore the staggering numbers and horrific conditions associated with modern industrial meat production. It also allows us to ignore the dehumanizing effects of the meat industry on the human workers who slaughter the animals we eat, workers who are mostly people of color, immigrants, and members of lower socioeconomic classes. In distinction from Klawans, Derrida proposes continuity between our contemporary practices of killing animals and "the Judeo-Christiano-Islamic tradition of a war against the animal, of a sacrificial war that is as old as Genesis."[61] Both accounts of sacrifice encourage us, however, to refrain from using biblical sacrifice simply as an occasion to recoil in horror from the supposed barbarism of a primitive past. They encourage us instead to look at our animal "brothers" today as they look back at us, and to ask how our own world is constructed through new chimeric monsters of our own making, and the matter of dead animals.

4

From Animal Hermeneutics to Animal Ethics

Moshe ben Maimon, the twelfth-century Jewish scholar also known as Maimonides, attempts in book 3 of his *Guide of the Perplexed* to clarify the nature of divine providence in relation to the distinction between humans and animals. For humans, Maimonides suggests, divine providence extends "over all the human individuals . . . watching over human individuals and exercising a surveillance over their actions." For animals, on the other hand, divine providence extends "over the species and not to individual providence." God "prepares for every species the food necessary for it and the matter for its subsistence," as such texts as Psalm 104:21 and 147:9 indicate. But God does not watch over them one by one as God does over individual humans.[1]

Maimonides does not conclude from this postulated difference that humans can treat individual animals any way we wish, however. For as he notes, his own tradition puts constraints on the treatment of animals. Jewish sources that urge the avoidance of "suffering to animals" appeal to the Torah for support, citing among other texts, according to Maimonides, the biblical "dictum 'Wherefore has thou smitten thine she-ass?'" Maimonides goes on to suggest that the purpose of avoiding animal suffering is to foster human virtue, rather than the flourishing of individual animals. As Elijah Judah Schochet puts it, Maimonides' interpretation emphasizes "the acquisition of habits of kindness that will enhance relations between human beings, and the avoidance of the cultivation of noxious habits that will vex and pain other humans."[2] If we treat animals well, Maimonides seems to believe, we may be more disposed to treat one another well likewise. He acknowledges nonetheless that humans "should not inflict pain gratuitously without any utility, but . . . we should intend to be kind and merciful even with a chance animal individual, except in case of need . . . for we must not kill out of cruelty or for sport."[3] Maimonides makes distinctions between humans and animals, then; but he does so in dialogue with his tradition's emphasis on avoiding the mistreatment of animals, an emphasis he believes is grounded in Torah.

The specific biblical text that Maimonides cites here for avoiding animal suffering is Numbers 22:32, where God's messenger asks the prophet Balaam, "Why did you strike your she-ass these three times?" The donkey herself asks Balaam a similar question (22:28). The story of Balaam and his talking donkey thus comes to be included among the biblical passages that Jewish tradition associates with the duty to avoid *tsaar baalei chayyim*, "the suffering of living creatures."[4] Although no single biblical verse articulates this principle exactly, a number of passages are identified in Jewish texts as sources for it, in addition to Numbers 22:32.[5] Some of these passages offer more straightforward guidance for the treatment of animals than Balaam's story. Modern biblical scholars, moreover, seldom identify the treatment of animals as an issue in the interpretation of the story of Balaam's ass, though scholars advocating for religious compassion for animals sometimes do.[6] Yet biblical scholars also disagree about the meaning of the story, and about the best approach to take when reading it.

The story of Balaam's donkey and its history of interpretation thus highlight certain challenges readers face when attempting to discern the significance of the Bible's animal references. How do interpreters decide upon such significance? Is it the role of biblical scholarship to tame the unruly meanings that circulate around the Bible's animal texts? Do decisions about the meanings of those texts take into account the fact that other readers, taking other approaches to the Bible, reach different conclusions about the animals who appear there? And what possibilities exist for reading the story of Balaam and his she-ass in relation to matters of animal ethics, not simply in the context of Maimonides and the traditions he refers to, but also today?

These sorts of questions animate the current chapter. They call our attention to possibilities and challenges for developing a "multifaceted, critical 'animal hermeneutics,'" to return to Gross's phrase. And they do so specifically in relation to biblical interpretation. What I would like to suggest here is that an animal hermeneutics does well to learn from multiple interpretive approaches, rather than narrowing its focus in a quest for a single meaning. To remain open to differences in interpretation may be as important for an ethics of reading as openness to differences among humans is for conventional ethics, and as openness to differences among species is for animal ethics. I will also consider briefly the role that affect may play in moving us from animal hermeneutics to animal ethics, in dialogue with Kathy Rudy's contributions to animal studies. But it will be useful to begin with some additional attention to the story of Balaam and his ass.

The Prophet and the Donkey

The biblical traditions about the prophet Balaam present several challenges in addition to the obvious problem of the talking donkey. For example, the Bible thwarts attempts to state unambiguously whether the character Balaam is represented positively or negatively. Although not an Israelite, Balaam in Numbers 22–24 clearly communicates with Israel's god (whom he refers to as "my god" [Num. 22:18]), attempts to follow God's commands (though contradictory messages given to Balaam by God make that difficult), and pronounces blessings upon the Israelites rather than the curses requested by the Moabite king Balak. Yet Deuteronomy 23:5 (Hebrew 23:6) indicates, in contradiction to Numbers 22–24, that Balaam did try to curse Israel. Numbers 31:8 and Joshua 13:22 report that the Israelites kill Balaam in a battle commanded by God. Numbers 31:16 blames a "word of Balaam" for encouraging Midianite women to cause the Israelites to do wrong in a mysterious "matter of Peor," though Numbers 25 does not bear this out. Biblical scholars generally explain these difficulties by positing multiple sources.[7] But however one accounts for them, such divergent traditions lead readers to evaluate the character Balaam in contradictory ways. Partly as a result, the study of Balaam's story often focuses on his reputation.[8]

For my purposes, however, the more important questions about Balaam's story involve the role in it of his female donkey, who tends to receive less attention than the prophet she carries. The donkey first appears in the narrative after Balak has twice sent messengers to Balaam asking him to come to Balak and curse the Israelites. On the first occasion, God tells Balaam not to go (Num. 22:12). On the second occasion, God tells Balaam to "get up and go with them, but only do the thing that I tell you to do" (22:20). Obediently, Balaam "got up in the morning and saddled his donkey and went with the officials of Moab" (22:21). Inexplicably, however, God then "flared up in anger that he was going, and a messenger of YHWH put himself in the road as an adversary" (22:22). God's contradictory responses to Balaam's journey thus present more difficulties for interpreters. As Michael Moore observes, "the deity demonstrates a perplexing propensity for reversal—a disturbing divine characteristic which surfaces repeatedly in the Balaam cycle."[9] Not only Balaam, but also God, is difficult to categorize here in unambiguously positive or negative terms.

At this point, however, the donkey becomes an active character in the story. Three times, she "sees" (22:23, 25, 27) God's messenger standing in the road with a sword, though Balaam does not. Thus the story's reader shares information with the donkey that the prophet does not have. Three times, she moves her body in an attempt to avoid the armed messenger: once by leaving the road and moving into a field, once by scraping against a wall, and once by sitting down under Balaam. Yet each time she takes action to avoid the danger in front of her, Balaam responds by striking her. Indeed, after the donkey's third attempt to avoid the messenger, the narrator states that Balaam "flared up in anger" at her (22:27), using the same terminology for becoming angry that is applied to God's anger at Balaam in 22:22. After Balaam hits her a third time, God "opened the mouth of the she-ass and she spoke to Balaam" (22:28). Rather than pointing out the danger in front of them, she asks Balaam, "What did I do to you that you struck me these three times?" Her voice calls attention to her treatment by Balaam. Oddly, Balaam expresses no surprise at being addressed by a donkey. Instead he retorts that he would kill her if he had a sword in his hand; for she has, in his view, made a fool out of him (22:29). But the donkey responds with more questions: "Am I not your donkey, on whom you have ridden continually until today? Has it been my habit to treat you thus?"

To the second question, Balaam replies, "No" (22:30). He seems to agree that the donkey has previously interacted with him consistently—more consistently, we might suspect, than God. At this point, God "opened the eyes of Balaam," who now sees the messenger standing in the road with a sword. Balaam "bowed down, and fell on his face" (22:31). And God's messenger chastises Balaam with words that include the question quoted by Maimonides:

Why did you strike your donkey these three times? Look, I came out as an adversary, for your journey is contrary to me. The donkey saw me, and she turned away from me these three times. If she had not turned from me, surely now I would have killed you; but her I would have let live. (22:32–33)

The messenger neglects to mention that Balaam is on this journey because God told him to take it. But like the donkey, God's messenger emphasizes Balaam's treatment of his animal. Balaam is contrite, and expresses a willingness to go back home if that is what God wants. In another inexplicable change of mind, however, God's messenger tells Balaam to proceed with Balak's men.

Although Balaam's story continues, his donkey is not mentioned again. She appears and disappears without much explanation, as do numerous other donkeys who populate the Bible's pages. If it weren't for the striking fact that this donkey speaks, it is unlikely that she would receive any more attention than, say, the donkey in Genesis 22:3 who accompanies Abraham, his son Isaac, and his servants as they travel to offer Isaac as a burnt offering; or the donkey in Exodus 4:20 who carries the wife and sons of Moses when Moses returns to Egypt; or the donkey in Judges 1:14 who carries the young woman Achsah to her father; or the donkeys in Judges 19 who carry the Levite and his servant to retrieve a woman whose body is later carried home on one of those same donkeys; or the donkeys in 1 Samuel 9–10 whose straying from Saul's father plays a role in Saul's anointing as king; or the donkey in 1 Samuel 16:20 who carries the bread, wine, and young goat that David takes to his brothers; or the donkey in 2 Kings 4:22, 24 who carries the Shunammite woman to Elisha after her son dies; or the young donkey in Zechariah 9:9 who will carry the hoped-for messianic king, and who is later taken up by Christian tradition and associated with a donkey ridden by Jesus; or the many other donkeys, too numerous to list here, who are referred to in biblical literature. Donkeys appear throughout the Bible, in numbers that testify to their role as another "companion species" for Israel. Yet readers hardly notice that most of them are there.

Among these biblical donkeys, however, only the she-ass in Numbers 22 talks. It is easy to understand, then, why philosopher Élisabeth de Fontenay asserts, in one of her animal writings, that "the donkey of Numbers will go down in history as a one-off, or what is otherwise known as a hapax."[10] She thus applies to Balaam's donkey the same term, "hapax," that Derrida uses to refer to Levinas's essay on Bobby. And many readers do treat this donkey as a strange kind of hapax, a unique animal who is difficult to understand, with no connection to the Bible's other creatures. Scholars even read her story as an intrusion in the longer Balaam complex. Thus Baruch Levine calls "the Tale of the Jenny" a "fable . . . deriving from a separate source." The story was probably added, Levine suggests, to mock Balaam, who, "for all of his reported clairvoyance . . . could not see the angel of God standing in his path, even though his jenny could."[11] Levine's conclusion is plausible as far as it goes, though it is striking how quickly the presence of remarkable animals leads scholars to label a text a "fable" or otherwise categorize it according to genre. But if we approach this donkey's story out of an interest in interpreting the Bible's animals, must we treat her as a hapax? Might Balaam's ass have more to say if we pay attention to her as one among other ancient animals?

Fontenay does note that the donkey is not entirely unique when she compares Balaam's ass to Achilles' horse Xanthus, who is granted the ability to speak by the goddess Hera in Homer's *Iliad*. Others also make such comparisons, including the scholar of ancient literature Cyrus Gordon, who considered the speaking of Xanthus to be "of a piece with the talking of Balaam's ass."[12] And a few biblical scholars recognize other ways in which Balaam's donkey may be interpreted as something other than a hapax. Placing more emphasis on the story's animal elements, they invite us to read her story in relation to stories about other animals who appear in the Bible.

To interpret Balaam's ass by reading her story alongside references to other biblical animals seems consistent with an animal hermeneutics, but it may not be as simple as one imagines. Which, among the Bible's diverse creatures, will serve as our point of comparison? Here I explore that question by calling attention to three ways in which biblical scholars have contextualized her tale: by placing Balaam's donkey among other ancient donkeys, by placing Balaam's donkey among other fantastic animals, and by placing Balaam's donkey among other subjugated equines. The last interpretive move, which calls for an ethics of reading, will return us to the possibility raised by Maimonides and others that her story can also be read as an occasion to move from hermeneutics to animal ethics.

Balaam's Donkey among Ancient Donkeys

The story of Balaam's ass is one of many narratives, fictional and otherwise, told about what Jill Bough calls one of "the most used, and abused, animals in history": the domesticated donkey.[13] Since their earliest domestication in Africa, donkeys have lived among, and worked for, humans for thousands of years.[14] Among many contributions as a companion species, the extraordinary ability of donkeys to carry heavy loads, over long distances or in dry or rocky terrain, has been especially prized and helps to explain their frequent appearances in the Bible and other ancient Near Eastern texts and images, where they often carry humans or other cargo.

Readers who wish to interpret Balaam's ass by contextualizing her story in terms of information we have about other donkeys in the Bible and the ancient Near East will find their task made easier by Kenneth Way's comprehensive study *Donkeys in the Biblical World: Ceremony and Symbol*.[15] Way's volume is one of several recent works that explore biblical references to animals by applying to them one or more of the literary, historical, and comparative methods conventionally accepted among biblical scholars. An impressive example of such a study is the volume on lions by Brent Strawn, which examines a range of lion images and metaphors in the Bible and beyond.[16] Such studies encourage readers to interpret the significance of the Bible's animals by asking about the range of connotations animals might have carried for authors and audiences in the ancient Near East. While this historicist-contextualist approach is only one way to read the Bible, it helpfully reminds us that the Bible was written in a world full of rich animal imagery and sheds considerable light on biblical examples of such imagery.[17]

Before turning to biblical donkeys, then, Way devotes considerable attention to references to donkeys in a wide range of ancient Near Eastern sources. One of the better known examples is a fragmentary inscription found at Deir 'Allā, in modern Jordan, that refers to "a seer of the gods" named Balaam.[18] Although the inscription does not refer to talking donkeys, it does include what Way calls "role reversals" among animals, communication by birds, and, depending upon one's translation of a contested verse, the presence of at least one donkey.[19] In addition, Way identifies numerous references to donkeys in various genres of ancient literature. Rather than reducing such references to two or three summary conclusions, he lists no fewer than twenty-one conclusions about the donkey's diverse symbolic roles in the ancient Near East. Thus the overall impression one is likely to draw from Way's discussion is that the donkey, quite common in the ancient Near East as a "beast of burden par excellence" (97), was also capable of carrying a large number of meanings and associations. This impression is confirmed by Way's summary of archaeological evidence, including evidence for numerous donkey and other equine burials. Many of these burials are associated with human graves, or have other characteristics indicating that they resulted from ceremonial functions; but some do not. After offering several frameworks for understanding such burials, Way concludes that donkey burials, like the donkey's textual associations, "are obviously diverse and complex" (158). It appears to be difficult to restrain donkey meanings.

By the time one gets to Way's discussion of donkeys in the Hebrew Bible, then, one is prepared for his suggestion that biblical donkeys, too, fill "diverse and complex" roles. Way argues, in fact, that no fewer than ten of his twenty-one observations about the symbolic significance of donkeys in the ancient Near East are also relevant for the Hebrew Bible. Some of these observations shed little light on Balaam's ass, but do illuminate other biblical donkeys. Ancient characterizations of donkeys and other equines, such as wild asses and horses, as lustful have biblical counterparts in such passages as Ezekiel 23:20, Jeremiah 2:24 and 5:8, and possibly Song of Songs 1:9, though they tell us nothing about Balaam's ass. Way also considers the possibility that non-Israelite uses of donkeys for sacrifice, or in covenant ceremonies, shed some light on the odd fact, noted in chapter 2, that donkeys are the only animals other than humans whose firstborn are redeemed with a sheep in Exodus 13:12–13 and 34:19–20. But he is cautious in his conclusion about this: the donkey's special status in Exodus may result simply from its economic value or its close partnership with humans.

Other ancient ways of understanding donkeys clearly resonate with Balaam's story, however, such as the role of the donkey for "personal transportation" (98); the use of donkeys "as a mount for people of high standing," including prophets (172); recurring characterizations of donkeys as "stubborn," which can lead to beatings; and a widespread association of donkeys with divination and omens. Way argues that such connotations are skillfully deployed in the Numbers story, where the traditional roles of prophet and donkey are reversed. Balaam becomes a figure who, like the horse and mule in Psalm 32:9, lacks understanding; while the donkey becomes "YHWH's mouthpiece" (185). Balaam, who is a seer at Deir 'Allā, here cannot see God's messenger, whom the ass sees and tries to avoid. Balaam is stubborn as well, repeatedly trying to beat his donkey into moving forward, though it is clear to the reader why she refuses to do so. Way also proposes an explanation for the striking fact that Balaam seems unsurprised when his donkey talks: given the associations made in some texts between donkeys, divination, and omens (99), Balaam may take the donkey's speech as an omen. His task as seer is to discern what the omen means, though initially he is unable to do so. The meaning is found, according to Way, in the words of the messenger to Balaam in 22:35: "Go with the men, but only the word that I speak to you, that you will speak." This message, Way concludes, "is the whole reason for the story of Balaam's encounter with the angel. The jenny merely serves as the vehicle (both literally and figuratively) that reinforces this message to Balaam" (187). Indeed, the donkey and the adversary "are both employees of YHWH" (191). For Way, then, the story of the donkey is an integral part of Balaam's story rather than an intrusion. Underscoring Balaam's inability to see God's messenger, it highlights by contrast the importance of delivering a message that comes specifically from God.

But Way also notes that the story contrasts Balaam's "brutish" behavior in striking his donkey (185) with the donkey's own "loyalty" (189–90). Here Way sees a distinction between the biblical story and ancient non-biblical sources, which do not often represent donkeys in terms of faithfulness. Balaam's jenny herself highlights this aspect of their relationship when she asks in 22:30, "Am I not your donkey, on whom you have ridden continually until today? Has it been my habit to treat you thus?" Way notes possible parallels in 1 Kings 13:24, where a donkey stays near its dead rider in spite of the presence of a lion, and Isaiah 1:3, which states, "An ox knows its owner, and a donkey its master's manger." Balaam's donkey, like these others, is a faithful companion. At the same time, Way emphasizes the messenger's statement that he would have killed Balaam but let the she-ass live if she had not stopped. Why, Way wonders, would such "immunity to death" be extended to a mere donkey? The answer apparently lies in the donkey's unusual status as God's "agent":

> YHWH not only employs her natural behavior for his purposes (vv. 22–27), he also endows her with supernatural ability for his purposes (vv. 28–30). The jenny is the vehicle that YHWH uses in this story to remind Balaam that he may only speak the words of YHWH. The jenny is therefore quite exceptional and shares a status akin to that of the angel of YHWH. The reason why the angel feels differently about this jenny is that they are both employees of YHWH. (190–91)

We can understand Balaam's donkey, then, when we read her alongside other ancient Near Eastern donkeys. But it would appear that we still have to allow for her status as an "exceptional" animal, used as a messenger by God.

Balaam's Donkey among the Bible's Extraordinary Animals

How, then, to think further of Balaam's ass as an "exceptional" animal? While Fontenay and Gordon associate Balaam's donkey with Achilles' horse Xanthus, these equines are not the only examples of talking animals in ancient literature. Texts from several ancient societies represent animals speaking, though not always to humans.[20] Indeed, one of the more striking examples of ancient animal speech comes from the Bible itself. Balaam's donkey is not nearly as well known as the snake who talks in Genesis 3. At first glance, they appear to have little in common other than speech. The snake, though hardly the evil figure he is made out to be in later traditions, is punished for his role in the disobedience of Adam and Eve (Gen. 3:14–15). The donkey's behavior, by contrast, is approved by God's messenger. Whereas the donkey's mouth has to be opened by God in order for her to talk, the snake's ability to talk is simply assumed in the text.

Nevertheless, the two stories do share features in addition to animal speech. George Savran notes that both tales involve cursing, blessing, a sword-bearing divine emissary, and animals interrogating and persuading a human.[21] The snake is only able to persuade Eve to eat fruit from the forbidden tree because he already has information that God has withheld from humans: specifically, that they will not die on the day they eat the fruit, that their eyes will be opened, and that God is worried about the humans becoming like God (Gen. 3:4–5, 7, 22–23). Thus the snake, like Balaam's ass, is able to perceive things that humans cannot perceive. Both animals are characterized, not only by speech, but also by an exceptional knowledge of the divine that humans do not share.

If we wish to understand Balaam's donkey among the Bible's extraordinary animals, however, we need not limit ourselves to other talking animals. We can also place her among other animals whose characterization involves unexpected or extraordinary acts. David Marcus attempts something like this in a monograph on "anti-prophetic satire," though for reasons quite different from mine.[22] After describing literary features that he considers characteristic of satire, and identifying various biblical texts that, in his view, contain one or more such characteristics, Marcus explores in more detail four texts as primary examples of satire aimed at prophets. These examples, it turns out, all involve animals in unusual situations. In addition to the story of Balaam, Marcus considers the story of Elisha and the she-bears who maul the boys who make fun of him in 2 Kings 2:23–25, the story of the "man of God" who is killed by a lion while riding home on his donkey in 1 Kings 13, and the story of Jonah. Though his reasons for classifying these stories as anti-prophetic satire go beyond their uses of animals, in every case the actions of animals contribute to his argument that the stories contain literary features that he associates with satire, especially "fantastic situations."

What do we find in these other animal tales? In 2 Kings 2:23, Elisha is on his way to Bethel when "small boys came out of the city and mocked him, and said, 'Go away baldhead, go away baldhead.'" After Elisha curses the boys "in the name of YHWH," two female bears come out of the forest and maul forty-two of the boys. The specification of the bears' sex is consistent with other passages that recognize the ferocity of mother bears in particular (2 Sam. 17:8; Hos. 13:8; Prov. 17:12), though bears generally are considered dangerous, like lions (1 Sam. 17:34; Amos 5:19; Prov. 28:15; Lam. 3:10). But this bear attack is not a natural event. The structure of the tale implies rather that the bears exact retribution on the boys for making fun of God's prophet.

The story of "the man of God" in 1 Kings 13 is significantly longer, and more complex; and much of it concerns matters that take place without animals. After delivering an oracle against King Jeroboam, the man of God begins traveling home to Judah. God has told him, "Do not eat food, or drink water, or return on the way you came" (13:9). Yet an old prophet, claiming to receive a different message from God, sets off on his donkey and persuades the man of God to come home with him for food. While they are eating, the very prophet who deceptively persuaded the man of God to return home with him delivers an oracle against the man of God, announcing that he will die for his disobedience. After they have eaten, the man of God sets off on the old prophet's donkey. On his way home, "a lion found him on the road and killed him. His body was flung in the road, and the donkey was standing beside it, and the lion was standing beside the body" (13:24). People passing by see "the lion standing beside the body" (13:25). When the old prophet hears about this, he rides another donkey to the scene "and he found the body flung in the road, and the donkey and the lion standing beside the body. The lion did not eat the body or attack the donkey" (13:28). The old prophet carries away the man's body on the donkey and buries it, asking his sons to bury him in the same grave.

These two stories from Kings about prophets and animals are indeed quite strange, and unknown to many readers of the Bible. The story of the bears is one of several episodic tales that represent Elisha or Elijah in unusual situations. Some of these other tales also include animals, such as the ravens who bring Elijah bread and meat when he is hiding in the desert (1 Kgs 17:4, 6); the dogs who drink the blood of Ahab (1 Kgs 22:38) and eat Jezebel (2 Kgs 9:35–6), as Elijah predicted (1 Kgs 21:23; 2 Kgs 9:10); and the horses of fire who carry Elijah away in a chariot (2 Kgs 2:11). In those stories, animals accomplish God's purposes. Thus it seems plausible to conclude that the bears in 2 Kings 2 are also working with God and God's prophet. Such a conclusion raises unsettling questions about the character of Elisha and the character of God; but God is represented in unsettling ways in many stories that feature animals, including the story of Balaam. The role of God is unsettling as well in the story in 1 Samuel 6 where the non-maternal behavior of two nursing cows who carry the ark of the covenant away from their calves reveals to the Philistines that God is behind strange events taking place in their cities in the presence of the ark. We might even wonder whether animals appear in stories where God's actions are unsettling precisely because animals, like God, were experienced by Israelite storytellers as being simultaneously predictable and unpredictable. Animals become something like an index for the unpredictability of God.

As for the unusual pairing of donkey and lion in 1 Kings 13, such pairing does have parallels in the ancient Near East.[23] An illuminating example is found in the Egyptian *Instruction of Any*, where a "savage lion abandons his wrath, and comes to resemble the timid donkey" (31). The significance of such descriptions emerges from both the contrast between lion and donkey, and the contrast with more common representations of lions in the Bible and the ancient Near East. As Strawn's study of lion symbolism demonstrates, "the fearsome aspects of the lion—its roar, killing, rending, devouring, and so forth," tend to dominate such symbolism.[24] Elsewhere in the book of Kings, God explicitly sends lions to kill non-Israelites who are moved into Israel by the Assyrians (2 Kgs 17:23–26). Thus, when we come upon a text such as 1 Kings 13, where the lion refrains from eating either the prophet he has killed or the donkey who stands beside him, we are understandably led to ask about the significance of such an odd picture. And here it is helpful to recall that lions also refrain from eating in a more famous story found in the book that Jennifer Koosed and Robert Seesengood call "Daniel's zoo."[25] When Daniel is thrown into a pit of lions in Daniel 6, it is clear that the lions' unusual behavior is divinely inspired. As Daniel tells the king, "My god sent his messenger, and he shut the mouths of the lions" (6:22 [Aramaic 6:23]). When Daniel's enemies and their wives and children are thrown into the lions' pit, however, "the lions overpowered them and crushed all their bones" (6:24 [Aramaic 6:25]), behaving as we expect lions to behave. The parallels from 2 Kings 17 and Daniel may lead us to conclude that God is behind the lion's behavior in 1 Kings 13 as well. Because the lion does not act as lions are expected to act, one suspects that the death of the man of God results from divine punishment for disobedience, and not simply from routine predatory behavior. The donkey's behavior reinforces the conclusion that something unusual is taking place, since it stands beside the lion rather than running from it. As Way observes, "the text here seems to portray the lion and the donkey as collaborative partners who carry out YHWH's mission."[26]

Like the story of Elisha and the bears, the story in 1 Kings 13 provokes questions not only about the role in it of animals, but also about the roles of both prophets and God. The actions of the old prophet are particularly strange: he uses a deceitful oracle to cause the man of God to disobey God, delivers an actual oracle from God announcing punishment for that disobedience, and then asks to be buried with the man of God because of the latter's oracle against Jeroboam's altar. Yet God's actions, too, are perplexing, relying as they do on a deceitful prophet while causing the death of the prophet who sincerely tries to follow God's wishes. They lead Mordechai Cogan to recall God's use of a "lying spirit" in 1 Kings 22:20–23 and to remark on the storyteller's "seeming acknowledgment of the devious ways of divine justice."[27] Such stories highlight the obstacles faced by those who attempt to communicate with or understand God and one another, a feature that, I argue elsewhere, is also underscored by the larger story of Balaam.[28]

These stories from Kings are seldom understood as satire by scholars other than Marcus, however. The book of Jonah, on the other hand, is frequently read as satire or parody. Among several arguments for such a reading, one sometimes finds comments about the book's representation of animals. Steven McKenzie, for example, notes that the idea of a man literally living for three days inside a great fish as Jonah does is "ridiculous," a claim most scholars are likely to agree with. Whether one agrees in addition that such a detail was "intended to be preposterous" when the book was written is more open to question.[29] Modern decisions about what ancient writers would have considered "preposterous," in the absence of biblical or other ancient statements to that effect, are inevitably made under the influence of cultural assumptions about biblical literature, animals, and divine activity that may well be different from those held in ancient Israel. This is not to deny that the story of Jonah may have satirical elements, a suggestion I return to briefly in chapter 6. But scholars who make such a suggestion generally agree that the object of satire in the book is Jonah, "the butt of the story,"[30] who has to be taught lessons by God with the assistance of animals. Whatever the story's genre, the fish and, later in the story, the worm that God sends to teach these lessons to Jonah can be included among the Bible's numerous extraordinary animals who act under God's command.

Like the story of Jonah, the story of Balaam and his donkey can certainly be read as containing satirical elements, including ironic contrasts between donkey and prophet noted earlier. Satirical readings of the stories in 1 Kings 13 and 2 Kings 2:23–25 are perhaps less compelling, though Marcus is right to suggest that our tendency to read the Bible overseriously, perhaps under the influence of Protestantism, causes us to miss humorous elements in biblical literature.[31] For my purposes, however, Marcus makes a more important contribution by calling our attention to the presence in all these stories of "fantastic" animals.

Indeed, rather than trying to force all four stories into a shared genre of satire, we might understand them as examples of a recurring biblical tendency to represent animals acting in extraordinary ways to accomplish God's purposes. For the Bible's extraordinary animals are not limited to texts that Marcus and others read as satire. In addition to animals noted above such as Daniel's lions and Elijah's ravens, we may recall the snakes that are formed from the staffs of Aaron and the Pharaoh's wise men and magicians in Exodus 7:8–12; the frogs, gnats, flies, and locusts sent by God to torment the Egyptians and their animals in Exodus 8 and 10; the quails sent by God as food for the Israelites in Exodus 16:13 and Numbers 11:31–33; the poisonous snakes sent by God to punish the Israelites in Numbers 21:6; the bees who produce honey in the body of the lion killed in Judges 14:8 by Samson, who also uses foxes with torches tied to their tails to burn Philistine fields (15:4–5); and the locusts who come upon Israel in conjunction with a drought in the book of Joel, causing havoc, hunger, and thirst for humans and animals, cattle and sheep (1:4–20). Joel's locusts, though presumably actual insects, stimulate additional animal symbolism, as when their destructive nature is compared to "the teeth of a lion and the fangs of a lioness" (1:6). This animal imagery reminds us of the still more fantastic creatures who roam through the Bible's images of the future, from Isaiah's vision of predators who refrain from eating prey in Isaiah 11:6–8 to apocalyptic visions of horses and donkeys in Zechariah (1:8; 6:1–7; 9:9) and of chimerical beasts in Daniel 7.[32] If we articulate such images with other representations of wild animals that I discuss in the next chapter, we may even begin to see vast sections of the Hebrew Bible as a savannah full of extraordinary animals, rather than simply a "book of God and man," to borrow a phrase one scholar used to refer to the book of Job.[33]

Recognition that so many animals roam through the Bible, often acting at the bidding of God, is a significant gain for an animal hermeneutics. In the raucous cacophony that results, however, even a talking donkey may go missing. And the specific question that she and God's messenger raise about her treatment by Balaam receives even less attention: Why did you strike me these three times?

Balaam's Donkey among Subjugated Equines

In her essay "Through the Eyes of Horses," Heather McKay suggests alternative directions for an animal hermeneutics in the course of reflecting critically on the Bible's representation of horses and other equines, including donkeys and mules. Unusually for a biblical scholar, McKay takes into account, not only issues of power and representation that have been raised by feminist and postcolonial studies, which she brings to bear on the Bible's animals, but also several early contributions to non-biblical animal studies. As McKay notes, the equines who appear in biblical literature do so not of their own accord, but as objects of human power and language. Donkeys, mules, and horses worked for the Israelites, carrying out more strenuous tasks than most other domesticated animals, with the possible exception of oxen; and they are frequently represented doing such work in biblical texts, though most often in the background. This has the effect of naturalizing their labor for us. We rarely read about them struggling under heavy loads, or being beaten or otherwise subdued, as they go about their literary tasks. Our picture of them and their docile labor is a product of their subordination, not simply to ancient masters, but also to literary representation.

McKay points out, moreover, that equines also do another sort of work when they are used metaphorically with respect to human characters, as when Ishmael is described as "a wild ass of a man, with his hand against everyone and everyone's hand against him" (Gen. 16:12); when the legendary ancestor of a non-Israelite clan is given the name Hamor, "Donkey" (Gen. 34); and when Egyptians and their gods are associated with the genitals of donkeys and the emissions of stallions (Ezek. 23:20). It also happens when Israel is compared to a wild ass "sniffing the wind in her heat" and to a lusty female camel (Jer. 2:23–24); when the men of Jerusalem are described as "well-fed, lusting stallions, each neighing for the wife of his neighbor" (Jer. 5:8; cf. 50:11); and when Issachar, legendary ancestor of an Israelite tribe, is described as a "strong donkey, lying between sheepfolds," apparently a way of accounting for some association with "hard labor" (Gen. 49:14–15). Of course, equine associations can also be positive. Horses, for example, sometimes serve as what McKay calls "a means of attribution of wealth, power and military might" to human characters (133).[34] So too, the woman in Song of Songs is compared by her lover to "a mare among the chariots of Pharaoh" (Sg 1:9).[35] Whether represented negatively or positively, however, animals are subordinated to their usefulness for humans and appear through that prism. One of McKay's provocative moves is to suggest that we should approach this textual subordination of animals with the same suspicion that we bring to the textual subordination of women, recognizing that such representation reflects in part the actual social subordination of the subjects in question and, concurrently, that such representation also distorts the interests and perspectives of those subjects by filtering them through the perspectives of a dominant class—male, Israelite/Judahite, and human—that gave us biblical literature.

Against this background, Balaam's ass both fits a larger pattern and threatens to disrupt it. On one hand, she appears in a text written by humans and plays a role that is thoroughly conventional, carrying a human character to his destination. Commentators often suggest, moreover, that she functions primarily as a foil to Balaam. The fact that she sees a divine messenger and speaks the truth, while the prophet cannot see the messenger and speaks without knowledge, certainly casts the prophet in a bad light; but the story remains his rather than hers.

On the other hand, we do hear her voice. We also know as readers that she sees and attempts to avoid God's messenger. The text thus provides something that is rare in biblical literature: an animal's perspective. Of course, her perspective is mediated by the narrator. But rather than simply reducing the donkey's perspective to that of the storyteller, McKay attempts to take into account what we actually know about "the sensory powers of equines." Can our knowledge of equine eyesight shed light on the donkey's ability to see what the human prophet cannot see? Does the reputation of horses for "truth telling" shed light on this story about an "ass as the truth teller" (139–40)? Although these are unusual questions for biblical scholarship, McKay's attempts to bring knowledge about actual animals into the humanities and allow such knowledge to play a role in our engagement with literary and other texts are consistent with work done in animal studies by Haraway and others, such as the philosopher Vinciane Despret or the late poet, philosopher, and animal trainer Vicki Hearne.[36] By raising such questions in relation to Balaam's donkey, however, McKay effectively recasts our tendency to treat her as a hapax. We begin to wonder whether this biblical donkey would appear less unusual if we took the time to pay attention to real donkeys, who are still around and still being mistreated; to wonder what it is that they see when they act the way they do; and even, on occasion, to speak with them.

Given her attention to the mistreatment of donkeys, and her assertion that Balaam's donkey "upbraids him as an equal partner in their joint enterprise" (140), it is somewhat surprising that McKay does not discuss explicitly the questions asked by the donkey about her mistreatment and her faithful service. McKay does, however, expand the range of questions that we can imagine asking as readers of the Bible about its animals. By encouraging us to analyze the ways in which equines are treated at multiple levels—in the text, behind the text, and even by the text, as well as by its readers—McKay moves the interpretation of Balaam's donkey in the direction of an ethics of representation and an ethics of reading. To borrow from a different discussion of the Bible and the ethics of reading, McKay invites us to ask what it would mean to read the Bible "as if lives depended on it."[37] But whereas that type of question is more often asked where human characters and readers are concerned, McKay raises a very different possibility: the lives of nonhuman animals, including donkeys, may depend on the ways in which we read biblical texts in which they appear.

Balaam's Donkey among Animals Who Deserve Compassion

Questions about ethics and reading bring us back to Maimonides, and to his observation that his Jewish tradition appeals to the story of Balaam's donkey as a way of encouraging kindness to animals. At first glance, that way of reading her story seems quite different from the others we have discussed. It does not emerge from modern biblical studies, even of the less conventional sort. There is no appeal to ancient Near Eastern sources as in Way's discussion of ancient donkeys, no appeal to literary genre as in Marcus's discussion of satirical animals, and no appeal to the politics of representation as in McKay's discussion of subjugated equines. Yet one might argue that Maimonides and the authorities he cites do encourage us to interpret Balaam's she-ass by placing her among other animals, rather than considering her a hapax. Specifically, we can read her story in relation to other biblical animals whose welfare is either identified explicitly as a matter of concern, or can be interpreted as a matter of concern; and who therefore deserve our compassion.

We have already encountered some of these animals, including donkeys, while tracking the dogs of Exodus. Exodus 23:4–5, for example, contains two stipulations that refer to donkeys. In 23:4, the Israelites are commanded to return either a donkey or an ox to its owner even if that owner is an enemy. In 23:5, they are commanded to relieve a donkey who has fallen under its load even if that donkey belongs to "one who hates you." The latter stipulation recognizes the donkey's role as beast of burden, a role that humans often exploit. (It is striking, for example, that archaeologists sometimes distinguish the skeletons of donkeys from those of wild asses by looking for "extreme pathologies on the vertebra," caused by carrying "heavy loads.")[38] But both commandments assume that relief for overburdened donkeys and help for lost donkeys and oxen would normally be required. Obligations to animals are presupposed, and they must be met even under circumstances where one might wish to avoid them, such as when they belong to enemies. Indeed, more general obligations to help such animals are made explicit in other passages. Deuteronomy 22:1–3 specifies that a neighbor's ox, sheep, or donkey should be returned if it wanders away. Deuteronomy 22:4 then extends the obligation to help an animal fallen on the road, so that it refers not only to donkeys but also to oxen. A concern about the working conditions of laboring animals also shapes Deuteronomy 25:4, which forbids muzzling an ox while it is threshing. If the ox chooses to eat some of the grain, it should be allowed to do so.

Exodus 23:12 stipulates that donkeys and oxen should be allowed to rest on the Sabbath, as do both versions of the Ten Commandments. Exodus 20:10 specifies that "your animals" should rest, along with humans; while Deuteronomy 5:14 is even more explicit, referring to "your ox and your donkey and all your animals." Animals are also included in passages on the Sabbath year, not only in Exodus 23 but also in Leviticus 25. Every seventh year, the latter passage states, the Israelites should refrain from sowing and reaping and let the land rest. Whatever the land produces may be eaten, not only by humans but also by "your animals" and "the living creatures in your land," apparently a reference here to wild animals (25:7). In Exodus 23:11, food left in the field goes first to the poor but then to "the living creatures of the field."

These types of explicit references to the welfare of animals in legal texts can be read alongside texts elsewhere in the Bible that also encourage compassionate treatment, such as the passage in Proverbs 12:10 which observes that "a righteous man knows the life [*nephesh*] of his animals." Here *nephesh* is sometimes translated as "needs," as in "the needs of his animals" (NRSV). The verse draws a contrast between the righteous who care for animals and the "wicked" whose "mercy" is "cruel." Care for animals is also presupposed in Proverbs 27:23, which encourages readers to tend to their flocks and herds. Though the passage goes on to point out that healthy animals will supply wool, milk, and food to humans, the importance of caring for animals is clear (and, as Patricia Tull notes, contrasts with the treatment of animals on modern industrial farms).[39]

Texts that explicitly point toward concern for animals can also provide an interpretive frame for texts that might be read as encouraging compassion for animals but are not always so read. A good example comes, again, from Exodus 23. Exodus 23:19 is one of several passages that forbid boiling a young goat in its mother's milk. Although no explicit rationale is given for this prohibition, an interpretive tradition extending from such ancient sources as Philo and Clement of Alexandria down to such modern biblical scholars as Menahem Haran suggests that it is grounded in principles of "humane behaviour."[40] To eat a mother and young together this way would be "morally revolting." Such an interpretation of 23:19 and other versions of the prohibition (e.g., Exod. 34:26; Deut. 14:21) place it among such stipulations as the command to let a mother bird go free if you take her eggs or fledglings (Deut. 22:6–7) or the prohibition against slaughtering an ox or a sheep on the same days as its young (Lev. 22:28). Haran suggests that "humane considerations" informing these texts may also explain why a newborn animal is supposed to remain with its mother for at least a week before being sacrificed (Exod. 22:30 [Hebrew 22:29]; cf. Lev. 22:27).[41] Even laws that seem further removed from such considerations are sometimes read in light of the admonitions for compassion. The prohibition against plowing with an ox and a donkey yoked together in Deuteronomy 22:10, for example, is sometimes read as preventing "harm" to the "weak animal,"[42] though we may also read it in light of concerns about impure admixtures that occur in the same chapter and elsewhere.[43]

All of these biblical passages, when read together with other passages that discuss God's creation of the animals in Genesis 1 and 2 and Job 38–41, God's preservation of animals at the time of the Flood, God's covenant with animals immediately after the Flood (Gen. 9:9–17), God's provision of food and homes to animals in such texts as Psalm 104, Psalm 146:9, and Job, and so forth, contribute to a foundation on which Jewish tradition built its commitment to ameliorate *tsaar baalei chayyim*, "the suffering of living creatures." Aaron Gross notes that this tradition often combines an "assertion of a human ascendancy over animals that articulates a special ontological and ethical status for the human within creation," with an "assertion of limits on this ascendancy that recognizes certain commonalities between humans and other animals and that highlights human responsibilities to animals."[44] Both of these dynamics are found already in the Hebrew Bible. The question remains, however, of whether readers give "relative priority" (166) to human ascendancy or to commonalities and responsibilities. Greater attention to the commonalities with, and responsibilities to, animals that are noted in religious texts, biblical and otherwise, can result in the development of more compassion overall.

In his discussion of forbidden foods in *The Guide of the Perplexed*, Maimonides considers the prohibition against slaughtering an animal on the same day as its offspring (Lev. 22:28). Although Maimonides elsewhere draws clear distinctions between humans and animals, here he appeals to similarities between human suffering and the suffering of animals. The commandment, he tells us, is

a precautionary measure in order to avoid slaughtering the young animal in front of its mother. For in these cases animals feel very great pain, there being no difference regarding this pain between man and the other animals. For the love and tenderness of a mother for her child is not consequent upon reason, but upon the activity of the imaginative faculty, which is found in most animals just as it is found in man.[45]

Because animals can have feelings similar to our own, Maimonides suggests, including feelings of pain and suffering, we should adjust our behavior in a more compassionate direction.

There are two points to underscore about this quote. First, although the reference to "reason" hints at Maimonides' assumptions about differences between humans and animals, the appeal to shared maternal affect and "the imaginative faculty" simultaneously undermines such assumptions. Calarco has highlighted the important role that the "breakdown of the human/animal distinction" plays in animal ethics.[46] Although the "grid" of contemporary approaches to this distinction that Calarco constructs does not map easily onto premodern sources, it is striking that Maimonides, attempting to give an ethical interpretation to a biblical commandment, does so by acknowledging important *similarities* between humans and animals, specifically in the areas of love, tenderness, and pain. A "breakdown of the human/animal distinction" takes place on some level in his interpretation of Leviticus 22:28, even if he attempts to shore it up elsewhere.

Second, this breakdown occurs in the context of recognition of animal emotion. Maimonides, who famously synthesizes Jewish and Aristotelian thought, is careful to note that the quality shared by humans and animals is not reason. Aristotle, after all, is well known for arguing that, because animals in his view lack rationality, they cannot participate in politics and justice, and are naturally subjugated to humans;[47] and this position has been mediated to Western culture and religion not only by Maimonides but by influential Christian thinkers such as Aquinas. Such a view seems much less compelling today, as our understanding of animal minds continues to change. Maimonides' acknowledgment here of similarities between humans and animals is not based on an argument about reason, however, but rather on recognition of shared affect. We look at animals, and we recognize "the love and tenderness" that they share with us, as well as the "pain." And this becomes a rationale for treating them with more compassion.

What is the significance of such a rationale? In her book *Loving Animals*, Kathy Rudy suggests that many theories associated with animal advocacy (utilitarianism, the extension of "rights" to animals, etc.) are insufficient for sustaining or expanding it.[48] Writing partly in dialogue with animal studies and partly in dialogue with theories of affect, Rudy argues that animal activists need to give more attention to affect and narrative rather than relying solely on rational argumentation. Like most affect theorists, Rudy understands affect to involve more than simply emotion, though emotions play an important role (as the title of her book indicates). Affect also involves our bodies, and our embodied relationships to others, including other animals. When we are moved to act on behalf of animals, it is often because of affective relationships with them as well as stories about such relationships. Affect and narrative do not simply provide a sentimental background for animal activism. Rather, they are the reasons why many activists get involved in the first place. Giving more attention to affect and narrative can play a role, then, in expanding animal activism and politics. Stories about animals, and human relationships with animals, may lead to "affective shifts" (xvi) that generate compassion and action for animals.

Rudy is not the only scholar to call for more attention to affect in animal ethics.[49] Her emphasis on affect and narrative, however, may help us reframe both Maimonides' rationale for Leviticus's prohibition of killing an animal on the same day as its offspring, and the usefulness of the story of Balaam's donkey for Jewish authorities who cited it to encourage compassion for animals. Although the prohibition in Leviticus 22:28 does not appear in narrative literature, Maimonides' interpretation of it positions us in a narrative scenario in which a mother animal sees its offspring killed in front of her. Noting that such animals feel the same pain that we would feel in a comparable situation, Maimonides invites us to suffer with the animal. By doing so, he seems to assume that his readers will understand the wisdom of the biblical injunction and act accordingly. The recognition of animal emotion affects us, and moves us to compassion. Rather than appealing here to reason, as he does in other texts, Maimonides makes an argument that almost seems closer to a famous assertion of Jeremy Bentham that is often quoted in animal studies, including by Derrida. Against tendencies to use reason or speaking abilities as the foundation for determining our ethical obligation, Bentham insisted that "the question is not, Can they *reason*? Nor Can they *talk*? But, Can they *suffer*?"[50]

Balaam's donkey, in distinction from the animal mother in Leviticus, appears in a narrative context already. As McKay and Way note, she plays a familiar role that many biblical donkeys play, with which a pre-industrial audience would have been familiar: carrying a human rider. No doubt such an audience would also have seen real donkeys carrying heavy loads, and sometimes being mistreated. In distinction from other biblical donkeys, however, this donkey is a developed narrative character, with perspective and voice. She sees a dangerous obstacle on the path, and attempts several times to avoid the danger. Her rider, a seer who can't see the obstacle, beats her each time. And when God allows her to speak, the first thing she speaks about is her physical mistreatment at the hand of Balaam: "What did I do to you, that you struck me these three times?" When Balaam responds angrily, she reminds him that they have a relationship. It is in fact an embodied relationship: He has ridden her for a long time, and she has not been in the habit of acting this way (Num. 22:30). And when God's messenger finally speaks, he also focuses on Balaam's mistreatment of the donkey: "Why did you strike your donkey these three times?" The structure of the narrative encourages readers to adopt the donkey's perspective and so to feel outraged at the donkey's unfair abuse. It triggers an affective response. It implies that God's messenger is concerned about the donkey's beating, which opens the possibility that God, too, is concerned about animal welfare. Thus her beating comes to be understood, not simply as an example of *tsaar baalei chayyim*, "the suffering of living creatures," but also as a divine mandate for lessening such suffering.

It is certainly possible to read the story of Balaam and his donkey, as many scholars do, without worrying about the donkey's treatment. As we have seen, even scholars who focus on the donkey interpret her story in different ways. It is not my intention here to suggest that one or more of these ways of reading is "right," and the others, "wrong." On the contrary, various approaches shed different types of light on Balaam's donkey and on the other animals who share biblical literature with her. The interpretations that an animal hermeneutics finds worth exploring need not be limited, however, to those originating in modern biblical scholarship. Traditional readings that found encouragement to reduce "the suffering of living creatures" in the donkey's story should also be included among the multiple forms that an animal hermeneutics can take.

They help to carry the Bible's readers along a road from animal hermeneutics to animal ethics.

5

Israel's Wild Neighbors in the Zoological Gaze

Hosea 13 reminds Israel of God's care in the past. After noting that God was with Israel "in the wilderness, in the land of drought" (13:5), the poet, speaking in God's voice, observes, "in their pasturage they were satisfied" (13:6a). As in other texts, Israel is represented as a grazing flock; and God, by implication, is a good shepherd. Once they were satisfied, however, the Israelites "forgot" the one who fed them (13:6c). Thus God declares that punishment is coming for Israel. And, strikingly, God's declaration contains images of wild animals:

> I will be like a lion to them,
>   like a leopard I will lurk on the road.
> I will meet them like a bereaved she-bear,
>   and tear open the covering of their heart.
> I will eat them like a lion,
>   as a living creature of the field would tear them apart. (13:7–8)

This passage is one of several texts from the Bible and the ancient Near East in which the familiar "pastoral metaphor is turned upside down . . . denied or reversed."[1] In this case, the reversal involves a different type of divine metaphor. While God is a good shepherd to the flock of Israel in many other texts, here God is a fierce predator devouring it.

The use of this metaphor shows that familiarity with animals supplied the Bible's writers, not only with positive symbols of care and sustenance, but also frightening symbols of danger. It comes from a world in which the risk of losing domesticated animals to wild ones was real. Thus David, pressed by Saul about his ability to kill Goliath, recounts his experiences with lions and bears who snatched members of his father's flock. According to David, he rescued his father's animals from the mouths of predators and, when necessary, killed the wild animals to do so. If he was able to kill lions and bears, he was surely able to kill "this uncircumcised Philistine" (1 Sam. 17:33–37). David's tale, though frequently recounted in children's Bible stories, is fraught with political symbolism. Against the background of ancient Near Eastern shepherd imagery, the representation of David as a shepherd who is able to kill predators to protect his flock hints that he is a leader able to protect Israel from its enemies. At the same time, the association of "this uncircumcised Philistine" with lions and bears underscores the beastly nature of a foreign enemy, who needs to be slain. Such connotations also raise questions, however, about the use of predator imagery by Hosea and other texts. Does Israel understand God, at least on some occasions, to be beastly as well?

As these examples indicate, the Bible's wild animals deserve careful consideration. The Israelites lived most intimately with sheep, goats, cattle, donkeys, and other domesticated animals, but they were also familiar with wild animals, and interacted with them in various ways. The Bible's writers may not have seen wild animals as often as they saw domesticated animals, but they saw them frequently enough to mention them many times, sometimes even describing their habits. Those animals were also companion species. Or, since their relations with the Israelites were not quite as close as those of goats, sheep, cattle, and dogs, perhaps it would be better to consider them "neighbor species," to borrow a phrase from the ecological philosopher Timothy Morton.[2] In either case, their presence shaped biblical literature and the religions that make use of it. And although numerous texts, including Hosea 13 and 1 Samuel 17, represent wild animals as frightening, some passages do adopt alternative perspectives.

The study of the Bible's wild animals presents several challenges, however. A number of Hebrew words used for particular animal species are very rare, and so the specific animals referred to are not always certain.[3] Moreover, the Hebrew Bible does not have a term or phrase that corresponds exactly to our English phrase, "wild animals." Two terms that are sometimes used by translators to distinguish wild from domesticated animals are *chayot* (singular *chayah*), "living creatures," which can also appear in such phrases as "living creatures of the earth" and "living creatures of the field," and *behemoth* (singular *behemah*), "animals" or "beasts." When these two terms appear in the same passage, the former is sometimes understood as referring to wild animals and the latter to domesticated animals or "cattle."[4] Although such an understanding makes sense of particular passages (e.g., Gen. 1:24–26; 2:20; 3:14; 7:14, 21; 9:10; Ps. 50:10; 148:10; Isa. 46:1), the terms are not used this way consistently. In some texts they are used interchangeably, as in the discussion of clean and unclean animals in Leviticus 11. Certain passages where one or the other term occurs alone indicate that each term can also refer inclusively to all animals, or perhaps more narrowly to all land mammals.

Moreover, ecological and animal studies scholars point out that contemporary notions about wild animals, and wildness or wilderness more generally, are themselves historically and culturally determined.[5] In addition to changing over time, competing ideas of wildness and wilderness exist concurrently, sometimes in hybridized forms. Our contemporary understanding of wildness and wilderness is also changing rapidly as human degradation of the environment continues to accelerate. And as Kerry Harris and Yannis Hamilakis note, "the term 'wild' as a blanket description for 'non-domestic' animals homogenizes the widely varying characteristics of different species and prevents the detailed exploration of species-to-species interactions."[6]

In order to approach the Bible's wild animals while keeping these challenges in mind, I borrow here from a certain strand of animal studies the notion of a "zoological gaze." The zoological gaze does not result in a single way of understanding all wild animals, however. Thus, after discussing the zoological gaze below, I turn to three, rather different, examples of the ways in which Israel's zoological gaze, or zoological gazes, brought into focus the wild animals that the Bible's writers knew, as well as the God they worshipped and sometimes represented as a wild animal. All three of these examples acknowledge the dangers associated with wild animals and the God who creates them. The third example, however, also underscores the ways in which the biblical zoological gaze, in some texts as least (such as Psalm 104 and Job 38–41), catches sight of a world of animals more akin to what Derrida calls "a heterogeneous multiplicity of the living."[7]

The Zoological Gaze

The environmental historian Roderick Nash has noted that "civilization created wilderness."[8] For hunter-gatherers, relations with the rest of the environment, including the animal world, are often conceptualized differently.[9] Notions of wilderness are less meaningful without the contrast of organized, sedentary habitation. But "lines began to be drawn—on the land and in human minds—with the advent of herding, agriculture, and settlement." Now distinctions between domesticated and undomesticated spaces, and animals, became meaningful. In the process, "wilderness became dangerous."[10]

If "civilization created wilderness," then we should keep in mind that the wild spaces and wild animals who appear in biblical texts are always represented from the perspectives of ancient civilization. Thus I want to suggest that the Bible's wild animals can usefully be interpreted as products of what the sociologist Adrian Franklin calls "the zoological gaze."[11] Although the study in which Franklin discusses this gaze is focused largely on relations between humans and animals in Western modernity, Franklin notes that "looking at animals" is "neither confined to the West nor to the present."[12] Humans across time and space observe animals, but "people from different cultures and times look at animals in different ways." In order to understand this "changing zoological gaze" (64), one must take into account the wide range of cultural assumptions and social concerns that shape perceptions of animals in different societies. For as Franklin argues, "Animals convey meanings and values that are culturally specific; in viewing animals, we cannot escape the cultural context in which that observation takes place. There can be no deep, primordial relationship underlying the zoological gaze since it must always be mediated by culture" (62). Franklin also observes that since "animals are like us and different, they can be incorporated into discourses of similarity (of me, us, we, etc.) and difference (of they, other, etc.) within the social."

This means, first, that even animals who are quite distinct from us are understood in terms of human norms and values. In order to illustrate this point, Franklin calls attention to the contemporary passion for watching whales and dolphins. Here Franklin is referring not to scientific or ethological studies of whales and dolphins (which in themselves can be fascinating),[13] but rather to the popular pastime of watching whales and dolphins from boats. While such marine mammals are clearly very different from humans in terms of morphology, habitat, and modes of locomotion and communication, interactions among them are nevertheless often read in terms of perceived similarities to the interactions humans have with one another. Thus modern humans look at whales and dolphins and see such qualities as "family togetherness, nurturing, and even leisure," all of which are valorized in the modern West. Franklin therefore suggests, "We will go to some lengths to see large marine mammals in the wild but when we see them we are just as likely to say they are just like us.... We have always to interpret, to provide the meaning for what we see, and for that we can only draw upon human values, emotions, and interpretations. When we gaze at animals we hold up a mirror to ourselves" (62) Our interpretations of animals are not only structured in terms of perceived similarities and differences between humans and other animals, however. The perception of relations between distinct groups of humans also plays a role in the zoological gaze. During the era of European colonial expansion, for example, "non-Europeans" were often represented by Europeans as "animal-like" (69). Europeans who gazed at exotic animals in menageries therefore found a dangerous otherness originating from distant lands, which "positively confirmed the civilizing influence and European ordering" of those lands (66). Similar dynamics are apparent today when members of other races and religions are denounced as beasts.

But changing sociopolitical circumstances also sometimes correlate with changes in the ways in which humans look at animals. Franklin notes, for example, that as urbanization increased in nineteenth century England, efforts were made "to change working-class comportment and behavior" by replacing forms of sport and leisure that urban immigrants brought with them from the countryside with forms of recreation that were supposedly more rational (67). Such developments shaped the rise of the modern zoo, which came to be associated with "instruction or improvement" of the new urban masses (68).[14] Today, of course, efforts at conservation and anxieties about ecological change or the global economy are more likely to shape the ways in which we look at animals. Across multiple contexts, however, "the zoological gaze is not merely social and cultural, it is also historically specific" (69).

Here, then, I want to consider biblical representations of wild animals as products of the Bible's zoological gaze. As Gene Tucker notes, "the eyes that see the world" in many biblical texts "are those of the farmer and the shepherd. This view has depth, but it also has limitations."[15] Although we should probably add the eyes of scribes and priests to farmers and shepherds, from all these perspectives domesticated animals tend to be viewed positively. Wild animals, on the other hand, are often seen as threats that roam beyond the bounds of human habitation but also sometimes encroach upon it. God may have told Noah after the Flood that animals would henceforth fear humans (Gen. 9:2), but it appears that some of the Bible's writers feared wild animals in turn. There is, however, no single zoological gaze in the Bible. Diverse texts represent animals from multiple points of view, as we shall see. And in at least a few texts, fear of the Bible's wild animals turns into awe and admiration, not only of and for the animals, but also of and for the God who created and feeds them.

Destructive Predators, Animal and Divine

As we have seen, Hosea 13:7–8 represents God as predator—a lion, a leopard, a bear—who will tear apart Israel in judgment. Although all three of these animals appear elsewhere in the Bible, the lion is by far the most common. As Brent Strawn notes, the lion may be referred to more often in the Bible than any other wild animal.[16] Given the sheer number of biblical references to lions, as well as textual and iconographic representations from the ancient Near East (which Strawn also examines), it is difficult to draw exhaustive conclusions about them. Lion images are "polyvalent—open to multiple uses." Yet most of these uses draw their force from recognition of "the power and threat" of the lion (284). This power and threat can be applied to a number of different mighty entities, particularly human leaders (such as kings) and gods. But whether the mighty are perceived as threatening or not depends upon the writer's location and context. When an Israelite poem lauds Saul and Jonathan as "swifter than eagles" and "stronger than lions" (2 Sam. 1:23), animal power is understood positively. But when biblical writers represent Assyrian and Babylonian kings as lions hunting the flock of Israel and chewing on their bones (Jer. 50:17), the lions are clearly menacing. Similarly, the Psalms frequently depict the speaker as menaced by lions (who represent the speaker's human enemies), while God is appealed to as a savior from such lions as well as dogs, wild oxen, and other threatening animals.[17]

Strawn makes the intriguing point, however, that the Hebrew Bible applies lion symbolism infrequently to Israelite kings compared with other ancient Near Eastern texts.[18] This divergence results in Strawn's view from "the ideology and theology of kingship in ancient Israel" (282). Perhaps the writers of the Bible, like the characters Samuel (1 Sam. 8:6–22) and Gideon (Judg. 8:22–23), preferred a divine king and lion to a human king and lion. Of course, since much biblical literature was written under the threat of annihilation by foreign powers, or during or after exile, the Bible's "ideology and theology of kingship" also developed in the wake of the failure of Israelite and Judahite kings, minor potentates in minor western Asian provinces, to resist the domination of the more powerful empires of the ancient Near East. Lion imagery was thus more appropriate for foreign kings and powers who, according to much biblical theology, were used by God to punish Israel. It is foreign kings rather than Israelite ones who thus show themselves to be lions, and sometimes other carnivores as well (Jer. 2:15; 5:6; 50:17; cf. 51:34–35; Isa. 5:29–30).

In contrast to the relative paucity of instances in which the lion metaphor is applied to Israelite kings, the Hebrew Bible frequently applies the lion metaphor to the Israelite god. As Strawn notes, this type of association with lions is, among some of Israel's neighbors, actually more common for goddesses than male deities. Strikingly, however, most biblical references to God as lion are, from the perspective of Israel, frightening rather than reassuring. Occasionally a text may represent God as a lion who roars on Israel's behalf, thus protecting them (Isa. 31:4; Hos. 11:10; Joel 3:16 [Hebrew 4:16]). But more often, God as lion threatens the assumed Israelite audience, whether the lion's ferocity is directed toward individuals (e.g., Isa. 38:13; Job 10:16; cf. 16:9) or a nation (e.g., Jer. 25:30, 38; 49:19; 50:44; Amos 1:2; 3:4, 8; Hos. 5:14; Lam. 3:10). Hugh Pyper, noting this change from protection to threat, recalls that in the ancient Near East lion statues guard entrances, "for the very good reason that there is a world of difference in being face-to-face with a lion and standing behind it. Once allowed past the threat of the lion, one moves into its protection. The lion does not move, the spectator moves; but its symbolic force changes. What is strong and fierce enough to protect me can also threaten me."[19] Biblical images of God as a lion or some other predator may be illuminated, not only by such ancient representations, but also Pyper suggests, by Derrida's reflections in *The Beast and the Sovereign* on the ways in which modern political thought sometimes creates a "symmetry of the two living beings that are not man, i.e. the beast and the sovereign God."[20]

The writers of the Bible were, of course, clearly familiar with the ferocity of actual lions, bears, leopards, and wolves. Such predators play roles that Strawn calls "naturalized" when they appear as ferocious actors in a biblical scene, as when Samson tangles with a roaring lion in Judges 14:4–5 or she-bears attack the boys who make fun of Elisha in 2 Kings 2:24. But the presence of these animals in ancient Israel, and the threats they represented, also made them available for biblical symbolism to an extent that is no longer true for those of us who rarely encounter dangerous animals outside of zoos or nature documentaries. If God is experienced not only as a good shepherd but also as "a bear waiting for me, a lion in hiding" (Lam. 3:10), this does not simply reinforce the fear of predators but turns God into one. The roar of God (Jer. 25:30), like the roar of a lion, can generate fear and dread.

Of course, as metaphors, fearsome creatures can have differing connotations. When Jeremiah 13:23 asks rhetorically whether "Ethiopians can change their skins, or leopards their spots," the comparison of the stiff-necked Israelites to leopards alludes to the animals' appearance, not to the danger they represent. Even the lion's roar can have ambiguous meanings. In Jeremiah 12:8, for example, lion imagery is apparently a metaphor not for God or Israel's enemies but for the land of Israel itself. God's "heritage" has become "like a lion in the forest who lifted up her voice again me." Now it is God who "hates" the lion. Immediately after this, however, we read that hyenas, birds of prey, and "living creatures of the field" are assembling against her (12:9), apparently a reference to enemies aroused by God.

The Bible assumes, moreover, that God can send real lions and other dangerous animals against humans, whether Israelites who break their covenant with God (Lev. 26:6, 22; Deut. 32:24; Jer. 15:3) or non-Israelites in the land of Israel who worship other gods (2 Kgs 17:25). According to some texts, non-Israelites were allowed by God to remain in the land after the Israelites entered it so that wild animals would not proliferate and overrun Israel (Exod. 23:29; Deut. 7:22). At the same time, a few texts look forward to a day when God will remove the threat of wild animals. This need not involve removal of the animals themselves, however. In Hosea 2:18 (Hebrew 2:20), God announces,

> I will make for them a covenant on that day with the living
>   creatures of the field and with the birds of the skies and
>   creeping things on the ground.
> And the bow and sword and warfare, I will abolish from the
>   land.
> And I will cause you to lie down in safety.

This new "covenant" (the same term, *berit*, that is used throughout the Bible for covenants between God and humans) appears to be a reversal of God's punishments of Israel in 2:12 (Hebrew 2:14), which include being eaten by "the living creatures of the field." The new relationship with animals is articulated with desires for peace. The reference to a covenant with animals may also recall God's covenant, not only with humans, but also with all animals and birds after the flood in Genesis 9:9–17.

But a more elaborate, and better-known, transformation of human relations with wild animals is anticipated in Isaiah 11. Here the hope for a future Davidic leader who embodies the ancient Near Eastern ideal of restoring justice and righteousness (11:1–5) is linked to a vision of peace that extends to animals in 11:6–8:

> The wolf will dwell with the lamb,
>   and the leopard will lie down with the kid,
> The calf and the young lion and fatling together,
>   and a little child will lead them.
> The cow and the bear will graze,
>   and their young will lie down together,
> and the lion will eat straw like an ox.

> The nursing child will play over the hole of the serpent,
>   and over the viper's den the weaned child will put its hand.

So too, Isaiah 65 contains a description of the "new heavens and new earth" that God is going to create, when "the former things will not be remembered or come to mind." After recounting changes that will take place in an ideal Jerusalem, the writer's gaze turns from humans to animals in 65:25:

> The wolf and the lamb will feed together,
>   the lion will eat straw like an ox,
>   but the serpent will have dust for its food.
> They will not hurt or destroy on all my holy mountain,
>   says YHWH.

Scholars who take an ecological approach to biblical interpretation sometimes point out that, as attractive as these passages may be for their vision of peace, they also assume a negative view of "the food chain and the ecosystem as we know it."[21] Such passages hope for a world in which the essential nature of wild predators will be changed. It is important to remember, however, that the people who wrote these passages actually lived alongside predators. Some of these predators, such as lions and bears, have long been exterminated from Israel; while other predators found in the Bible, such as leopards and wolves, are nearly extinct in Israel as well. Yet the potential threat of such predators was real to the Bible's ancient audience. And that threat shapes the way in which many of them appear under the Bible's zoological gaze.

The Desolate Places Where Wild Things Are

The animals who inspire fear in the Bible are not limited to predators. A number of animals who live in wild places are associated with what Joseph Blenkinsopp calls a "back to nature" theme in the Bible.[22] In these cases, "back to nature" does not mean a week spent watching wildlife in Yellowstone or on safari. It refers rather to the destruction of cities and to the wild creatures from desert and forest who return to live where humans lived previously. It is, in Gene Tucker's words, "a return to the 'chaotic' state of the uncultivated and uncultured land."[23] Texts associated with this theme fit into a strand of biblical thought that understands wilderness negatively, and that influences later readers of the Bible who understand wilderness negatively as well.[24]

The most developed examples of this theme occur in connection with oracles against non-Israelite cities. Isaiah 13, for example, looks forward to a time when Babylon will be destroyed "like the overthrowing by God of Sodom and Gomorrah" (13:19). Human inhabitants will no longer be found in the ruins of Babylon. The prophet does see in those ruins several other sorts of creatures, however:

> But wild cats[25] will lie down there,
>   and its houses will be full of owls.
> There ostriches will live,
>   and there goat creatures[26] will dance.
> Hyenas will cry in its bereaved dwelling places,
>   and jackals in the pleasant palaces. (13:21–22a)

The picture of a destroyed city inhabited by multiple wild creatures occurs again in chapter 34. There we find an oracle against Edom, which is given an ominous new name, "No Kingdom There" (34:12). Edom is represented as being destroyed under circumstances that sound similar to the fiery destruction of Sodom and Gomorrah (34:9–10), which was mentioned explicitly in chapter 13. In this scene of devastation, described in 34:11 with words (*tohu* and *bohu*) that recall the chaos that precedes God's creative activity in Genesis 1:2, human inhabitants are missing. Other creatures do live in Edom, however, which has become "a dwelling place for jackals, an abode for ostriches" (34:13) and a home for numerous other beasts. Although some of the creatures mentioned in chapter 34 are difficult to identify, they include not only the ubiquitous jackals and ostriches but also the wild cats, hyenas, and goat creatures mentioned in chapter 13 as well as other wild animals (which Blenkinsopp translates as hawks, hedgehogs, owls, ravens, and buzzards)[27] and the mysterious entity Lilith. These particular creatures seem to represent the antithesis of civilization and order. The inclusion of Lilith, known in Jewish tradition as Adam's first wife but here apparently a kind of demonic figure, indicates (as may the goat creatures) that the line between real animals and mythical creatures is blurred in these types of passages, as in other ancient texts that imagine wilderness as a place where demons and other strange creatures live.[28]

Blenkinsopp proposes that here Lilith is "queen of this spooky realm of death in place of the king and princes who are no more."[29] But these creatures have been called to the ruins of Edom by the "command," indeed, the "spirit," of God (34:16b). God's "hand" has given them Edom as a place to possess "forever, from generation to generation" (34:17). They may be instruments of God's judgment and the antithesis of civilization, but they do not stand in opposition to God. God is rather aligned with the creatures of chaos.

The assumed ancient audience for Isaiah 13 and 34 was no doubt pleased by descriptions of the destruction of Babylon and Edom, or by Zephaniah's description of Nineveh as a "wilderness" full of wild creatures (Zeph. 2:13–15). The presence of some of these same animals in other passages, however, indicate that Israel or Judah was also at risk of falling prey to such devastation. Micah, for example, while describing the destruction of Samaria and Jerusalem, declares that he "will make a wailing like the jackals, and mourning like the ostriches" (1:8). An association of jackals and ostriches with lamentation and mourning is also implied in Job 30:29, where Job refers to himself as "a brother of jackals and a companion of ostriches." The jackal is found in desolate circumstances in Judah in Jeremiah 9:11 (Hebrew 9:10) and 10:22, as well as Psalm 44:19 (Hebrew 44:20). In Jeremiah 49, a prediction of the destruction of Judah by the Babylonians refers to the city of Hazor as a "lair of jackals" (49:33) in addition to describing the capture of Israelite camels and cattle (49:29, 32). Ironically, Babylon itself becomes a "lair of jackals" in 51:37; and 50:39 refers to ostriches, hyenas, and other wild animals living in a destroyed Babylon.

Since the appearance of jackals and ostriches, among other creatures, is associated with lamentation and mourning over the destruction of cities, it is hardly surprising that they show up together in the book of Lamentations, written in the wake of the destruction of Jerusalem. But Lamentations indicates that, as a conventional pair, the combination of jackals and ostriches also provided opportunities for literary innovation. The book notes twice (2:20; 4:10) that circumstances grew so bad in Jerusalem that women were reduced to eating their own children (cf. Lev. 26:29; Deut. 28:53–57; Jer. 19:9; Ezek. 5:10). In order to express the horror of such a situation, the writer in 4:3 bewails the fact that "even the jackals offer the breast and nurse their young, but the daughter of my people has become cruel, like the ostriches in the wilderness." This notion that ostriches were bad parents, which is presupposed as well in Job 39:13–18 (albeit with different vocabulary), may have been derived from the fact that female ostriches lay eggs on the ground and allow a single mating pair to care for the eggs and offspring of several females; but it clearly sheds more light on the ancient zoological gaze than on the natural history of ostriches. The contrast between the parenting behavior of the jackal and that of the ostrich underscores the chaotic conditions in Jerusalem.

Jackals and ostriches play yet a different role in Isaiah 43. Here a well-known oracle focuses on the "new thing" (43:19) that God is about to do for Israel at the end of the Babylonian exile. In spite of God's admonition not to "remember the former things, or give heed to the things of old" (43:18), the oracle opens with language that recalls the Exodus from Egypt and God's victory at the Sea. God is described as creating "a way in the sea, and a path in the mighty waters" (43:16); and references are made to "chariot and horse, army and power" (43:17). God's ability to master the forces of chaos is thus reaffirmed.[30] By emphasizing the "new thing" that "springs forth," the prophet indicates that a new journey to Israel rather than the one associated with Moses is in view. This journey, like the former one, will entail passage through wilderness. And in connection with this passage, the prophetic gaze, which claims to mediate a divine gaze, falls upon animals:

> I am making a way in the wilderness,
>   and rivers in the desert.
> The living creatures of the field will honor me,
>   jackals and ostriches.
> For I give water in the wilderness,
>   rivers in the desert,
> To give drink to my chosen people,
>   the people whom I formed for myself
>   so that they might declare my praise. (43:19b–21)

This passage is clearly informed by the ominous connotations that jackals and ostriches carry elsewhere. Far from lamenting or mourning, however, these jackals and ostriches stand in for animals who will "honor" God for providing "water in the wilderness, rivers in the desert." Their "honoring" of God parallels the "praise" that comes from the people God creates in 43:21. Given the frequency with which jackals and ostriches are associated with desolation and lament, this image of jackals and ostriches in Isaiah 43 may well have been startling. Humans looking at jackals and ostriches in the desert expect them to lament or mourn, as humans do under similar circumstances. Yet the prophet's gaze reveals a zoological scene that provokes surprise, a scene of jackals and ostriches honoring God.

Perhaps such a scene is grounded in actual experiences: the ancient writers must surely have noticed that even animals who live in desolate places need water and rejoice when they get it. They also understood God as the source of water for wild animals, as we will see in a moment. But this unconventional vision of jackals and ostriches here contributes to the writer's project of describing developments that neither conventional wisdom nor the recent circumstances of the exiles in Babylon would lead one to anticipate. The "new thing" is proclaimed to an audience whose feelings are represented in 49:14: "YHWH has abandoned me, my Lord has forgotten me." The hopelessness and desolation of this statement coheres with the connotations carried by jackals and ostriches in most passages. No doubt those who experienced Babylonian destruction and exile believe they have good reason to lament and wail, just as jackals and ostriches are expected to do. Jackals wail and ostriches mourn because the zoological gaze finds them in the uncivilized chaos of wilderness, desert, and ruin. Yet the "new thing" in Isaiah 43 emphasizes water, rivers, and drink, necessary prerequisites for both human civilization and animal flourishing. The zoological gaze continues to shape the way in which jackals and ostriches are represented in chapter 43, even though a reversal in Israel's circumstances (return from exile) leads to a change in the habitat in which animals are viewed (water instead of drought) and a reversal in characterization. The exiles may feel that they have little reason to praise God, as the prophet says they soon will (43:21); but the image of jackals and ostriches honoring God for "rivers in the desert" reiterates the writer's contention that God is about to do amazing and praiseworthy things for Israel. Jackals and ostriches, more often associated with devastation and despair, become symbols of hope. But they are also represented in relationship to God.

Beautiful and Ferocious Creatures of God

Most of the texts referred to so far in this chapter see wild animals in a negative light. Even the startling image of jackals and ostriches honoring God, intended as a source of hope in Isaiah 43, gets its force from the way in which it reverses a more common association of both animals with desolation and wilderness. It is therefore easy to see why Tucker concludes that, while domesticated animals are viewed positively in biblical literature, the Bible's wild animals "are beyond the fringe of culture, for the most part symbolizing danger and destruction."[31]

In an intriguing footnote to this statement, however, Tucker adds, "In only two texts, Job 38–39 and Ps. 104, are the wild creatures viewed with unambiguous admiration." Phrased like that, Tucker's observation might imply that these passages are relatively insignificant. We may be led to wonder about the ways in which biblical scholars and other readers decide which texts are most important for our conclusions about the Bible's views on animals, and which texts are herded into footnotes. But what do we find if we turn to these passages and highlight, rather than downplay, their particular zoological gaze?

Psalm 104 does have some unusual characteristics in comparison with other biblical texts, such as long-noted similarities to an Egyptian Hymn to the Aten, or sun-disc.[32] It also plays an important role in our understanding of the importance of creation themes across the Hebrew Bible.[33] But Psalm 104 does not actually recount the process of creation. What we see here, rather, is what Jon Levenson calls "a panorama of the natural world," described in such a way as to celebrate God's role in maintaining "such an astonishing place."[34] And whereas Genesis 1:26–28 and Psalm 8:5–8 (Hebrew 8:6–9) can be read as granting humans a special role as rulers over other animals, Psalm 104 simply includes humans among the many creatures sustained by God's activity, playing a relatively minor part.

Thus we read that God causes springs to flow in the valleys in order that "all the living creatures of the field" can quench their thirst, including specifically wild asses and the birds who sing in trees watered by God (104:10–12, 16–17). If God causes plants to grow for people to use, giving them bread, wine, and oil (the famous "Mediterranean triad" known from biblical and non-biblical sources),[35] God also causes grass to grow for grazing animals (104:14–15). God provides animals with specific places to live, including cedar trees for birds; fir trees for storks; mountains for the mountain goats, possibly the ibexes that still live at Ein-Gedi (cf. 1 Sam. 24:1–2 [Hebrew 24:2–3]); and rocks for the hyraxes, which still live at Ein-Gedi as well (104:17–18). When it is night, "all the living creatures of the forest" come out (104:20); and "the young lions roar for their prey, seeking from God their food" (104:21). But when the sun comes up, these animals return to their dwelling places, and humans go out to do their work (104:22–23). "Creeping things" live in the sea, "living creatures small and great" (104:25). Ships sail upon it, as they do in the Hymn to Aten; and as in that hymn, there are water creatures as well as ships in Psalm 104. But here one finds the great sea monster Leviathan, "which you formed to play in it" (104:26). Ultimately, all of these creatures, including humans, depend upon God:

> All these look to you to provide their food in its season.
> When you give to them, they gather it.
>   When you open your hand, they are filled with good things.
> When you hide your face, they are dismayed.
>   When you take away their spirit [or "breath," *ruach*], they die
>   and to their dust they return.
> When you send forth your spirit [or "breath," *ruach*], they are renewed,[36]
>   and you replenish the face of the ground. (104:27–30)

It is therefore easy to agree with Tucker's suggestion that this Psalm views "wild creatures . . . with unambiguous admiration," though the admiration for God as the one who sustains these creatures and the rest of creation is just as striking. It is doubtful, however, that this passage needs to be understood entirely in opposition to better-known texts such as those in Genesis. There is, to be sure, no hint here of human "rule" over animals, such as we find in Genesis 1:28, or of the animals' "fear" of humans, such as we find in Genesis 9:2. And as already noted, the process of creation, for example, of animals, is not described in Psalm 104. Yet the order in which various elements of creation are referred to in the Psalm is similar to the order of elements in Genesis 1, which also shares vocabulary with Psalm 104.[37] If the two texts are read together, rather than separately as more often happens, they might be seen to balance one another in ways that later traditions have forgotten. In Genesis 1, God creates many creatures, commands them to multiply in their various habitats, and declares them to be good. This important feature of the opening creation accounts tends to be downplayed when readers focus on the role of humans at the end of the story. But the diversity of such creatures, and God's ongoing care for them in multiple habitats, is affirmed here in Psalm 104. If animals and humans are created in Genesis 1, here the focus is on "*sustenance, support, provision*" for those same creatures; "it is the *continuance* of life that is emphasized," in the words of James Barr.[38] Barr, who suggests that the Psalm contains something rather close to a "natural theology" (in which the activity and attributes of God are discerned in various features of the natural world), acknowledges that it might be understood instead as expressing a kind of "theology of nature," with some relevance for "our modern awareness of ecology and ecological crisis" (83). But we might go further and suggest that in Psalm 104 we have an ancient theology of wild animals, which finds a place for them as well as humans. Indeed, the Roman Catholic feminist theologian Elizabeth Johnson, in the course of developing an ecological theology of the natural world, emphasizes Psalm 104 for its attention to "the diversity of species," its lack of "a mandate for human dominion," and its assertion that animals have their "own relation to the Creator," independent of humans.[39]

Johnson places even more emphasis, however, on the other text that Tucker associates with "unambiguous admiration" for animals: the speeches of God in the book of Job. The radicality of the book of Job, in comparison to other parts of the Bible, is not always appreciated.[40] It is not an orderly treatise, but rather a cacophonous argument, incorporating multiple points of view and conflicting positions as it probes such issues as radical suffering, the motivations for piety, the nature of God, justice and retribution, chaos and creation, and the tension between our individual experiences and the categories given to us by tradition and society.[41] It is also a book full of images from nature, including animals.[42] For much of the book, Job and his friends disagree about whether Job deserves his fate and whether he is right to complain about his treatment by God. Thus a reader may anticipate that, when God finally joins the conversation, issues raised in the debate between Job and his friends will be resolved. Surprisingly, however, God appears to ignore that debate almost entirely.

The fact that God speaks to Job out of a storm hints from the beginning of chapter 38 at something that remains clear over the course of God's speech: the image of God evoked by these chapters is spectacular but unsettling. For some readers, God seems to be doing little more than putting Job in his place. "Who is this," God demands in 38:2, "who darkens counsel with words without knowledge?" The implied answer is "Job"; and, after warning Job to "gird up your loins like a man" (38:3), God interrogates Job with a series of questions that emphasize distance and distinction between Job and God ("Where were you . . . ?" "Have you entered . . . ?" "Can you . . . ?" "Do you know . . . ?").

In terms of content, however, God's discourse focuses largely on matters of creation. As one might expect from an ancient Near Eastern creation text, and similarly to Psalm 104:3–9, the early parts of God's speech evoke a cosmos in which the created order and its foundations are established by restraining such mythological forces of chaos as "Sea" (38:8, 16), "Deep" (38:16), and "Death" (38:17). The process by which such restraints are put in place is represented, in the ancient world, as a kind of struggle or battle between the forces of chaos and a deity, often a male deity; and biblical literature frequently appeals to a fund of mythological images that were associated with this "chaos battle."[43] Here, though, in a gender-related twist on those images, language about a "womb" (38:8) and a "swaddling cloth" (38:9) invites one to imagine God as "the midwife who births the sea and wraps it in the swaddling bands of cloud and darkness."[44] This picture of God as something like a mother of the forces of chaos indicates that God's speeches, while making use of traditional creation imagery, take that imagery in directions for which conventional piety does not prepare us.

Such a possibility seems to be confirmed in Job 38:39 when, at the beginning of a lengthy reflection on the world of animals, God asks Job whether he is able to "hunt prey for the lion, or satisfy the appetite of young lions." The point here is clearly that God rather than Job finds prey for the lions, a belief that we have already seen in Psalm 104:21. As Edward Greenstein points out, whereas Psalm 104 understands God's concern for the animals within a wider framework that also includes concern for human beings (but without granting humans any special role), God's speech to Job affirms that God is busy hunting with the lions while giving no indication that God is much concerned about the fate of individual human beings.[45] Indeed, since the lion is sometimes understood in the Bible as a hunter of sheep and hence an opponent of shepherds, God's supply of prey for the lion may hint that God is aligned more closely with the foes of human beings than with humans themselves.[46] So, too, God provides food for ravens, whose young "cry out to God" (38:41). Ravens of course serve important roles in other texts, surveying the waters after the Flood (Gen. 8:7) and feeding Elijah at God's command (1 Kgs 17:4, 6); but God's explicit reference to supplying their food may remind us that they are also predators and scavengers. In Job 39, moreover, after observing that God but not Job knows where mountain goats and deer give birth to their young, the divine speech associates God with other animals whose characteristics oppose them to human civilization and order. The wild ass, for example, is understood elsewhere in the Bible to wander about alone (e.g., Hos. 8:9) and to be at odds with others (Gen. 16:12). Job himself has earlier used the wild ass in the desert to symbolize the chaos brought about by the wicked (24:5). In Job 39:7, the wild ass both scorns the city and ignores humans who attempt to master it. Yet God takes credit for setting the wild ass in opposition to human domestication and giving it the barren steppes and salt wastes as a home (39:5–6). The wild ox, too, perhaps the aurochs, a now extinct species of wild cattle known for its size and ferocity (cf. Deut. 33:17) and hunted by kings,[47] is described in terms of its unwillingness to accommodate human constraints and commands (39:9–12).

Also standing outside the realm of human comprehension and control is the ostrich described in Job 39:13–18.[48] As we have seen, other passages indicate that ostriches were understood to inhabit ruins and deserts, along with jackals, hyenas, and other strange creatures. In biblical imagery, ostriches represent the antithesis of human civilization and order. Job, in fact, has earlier described himself as "a brother of jackals and a companion of ostriches" (30:29) in order to indicate, in a moving passage, the chaotic state to which suffering has reduced him. God's speech to Job accepts the notion, also found in Lamentations 4:3, that ostriches are poor parents, and even elaborates upon it in more detail (39:14–16). Yet God also asserts that God made it the way it is, without the wisdom one expects to see (39:17). Thus God is associated here not with human values but rather with values that stand in opposition to those which humans consider good and proper. This strange creature of God's, far from being subject to human beings or fitting neatly into functional human categorizations, flaps her flightless wings wildly (39:13) and "laughs at the horse and its rider" (39:18).

And the horse, too, is one of God's creatures, as God goes on to remind Job. It is God who creates this mighty animal; and, in fact, the horse is described with language that in the ancient Near East is associated with deities themselves, so that the horse appears here as "a magnificent godlike figure . . . a warrior god poised for battle," in Norman Habel's words.[49] Such an association between God and the horse may be unsettling, however, when one recognizes that the qualities of the horse underscored in Job 39:19–25 have to do with the horse's excitement for battle. The possibility that God, too, may be characterized by such blood lust seems to be hinted at further in the subsequent sketch of the eagle (39:26–30), which soars at God's command (39:27); for its young "suck up blood, and where the slain are, there it is" (39:30). The implication here seems to be that God provides food—meat, carrion—for the bloodthirsty eagle chicks just as God supplies food for the lions and ravens.

The picture of nature drawn in God's first speech is therefore hardly a peaceful, harmonious realm. The animal world appears rather as a wild and raucous space, in which some creatures prey upon others, with God's assistance; and human values seldom prevail. The fact that this realm is associated so closely with God hints at the notion that God, too, may act according to principles that humans cannot fathom, and sometimes in frightening ways.

This possibility becomes even more likely in God's second speech, beginning in Job 40:7. Here God speaks of two mighty beasts, Behemoth and Leviathan. In some commentaries, Behemoth and Leviathan are understood respectively as the hippopotamus and the crocodile. On the basis of our increased knowledge of ancient Near Eastern symbol and myth, however, most commentators now conclude that Behemoth and Leviathan, though perhaps modeled in part on such real animals, are in fact mythological beasts, "liminal creatures" that "represent the frightening and alien 'other,' bearing the terror of the chaotic in their very being."[50]

These frightening creatures are, however, closely associated with God. The association is perhaps more obvious in the case of Behemoth, since God states that Behemoth is just as much a creation of God as Job himself. Literally, in fact, God calls Job's attention to "Behemoth, which I made with you" (40:15). Such an assertion is potentially disquieting, for it raises the possibility that God is as concerned about Behemoth as with humankind and treats it in a similar fashion. As William Brown observes in a startling comparison, Behemoth is "with" Job here much as the woman is "with" the man in Genesis 3:6, 12.[51] Moreover, Behemoth is not just any creature but, according to 40:19, "first of the ways of God." This enigmatic statement is often understood to mean simply that Behemoth is the greatest of all creatures, or the first to be created; and both interpretations are possible. Yet it may also point toward some priority of interest, as if Behemoth (whose name is literally formed from the plural of the Hebrew word *behemah*, "animal" or "beast") actually has a greater claim on God's time and attention than Job. Behemoth's explicit association with "the ways of God" reminds us that this speech sheds light on God as well as on Behemoth. Since the poem emphasizes Behemoth's spectacular strength, fearlessness, and potency (note how a euphemism, "He makes his tail stiff like a cedar," seems to refer to Behemoth's erect penis in 40:17),[52] it is God's awesome nature rather than God's intimate involvement with individual human beings that is here underscored. Creation imagery is thus used once again in an unexpected fashion. As Timothy Beal notes, the encounter with Behemoth produces not a sense of "order and harmony" but rather awareness of "a kind of dangerous otherness in creation," a "dangerous otherness" partly associated with God.[53]

The climax of God's speeches, however, occurs in the lengthy poem about the sea monster Leviathan in Job 41. Job has invoked Leviathan earlier in the book (3:8); but God's description of Leviathan seems designed rhetorically to call into question the wisdom of any such invocation on the part of mere humans:

> Can you draw out Leviathan with a fishhook,
> or with a rope press down his tongue?
> Can you put a cord through his nose,
> or with a hook pierce his jaw?
> . . . .

> Will you play with him like a bird,
> or tie him down for your young women?
> . . . .
> Can you fill his skin with harpoons,
> or his head with fish spears?
> Put your hands on him, think of the battle!
> You will not do it again! (41:1–2, 5, 7–8 [Hebrew 40:25–26, 29, 31–32])

In light of Job's earlier reference to Leviathan, such rhetoric implies that Job has been treading onto territory that it might be wise to avoid. But another implication of God's questions is that while Job cannot engage Leviathan, God can. Scholars note that Leviathan traditions are used in the Hebrew Bible with two, rather different, emphases: an emphasis on Leviathan as the creature or even "plaything"[54] of God, as we saw in Psalm 104:26; and an emphasis on Leviathan as the opponent of God or the gods in divine battles against forces of chaos (e.g., Ps. 74:14). God's speech in Job 41 presupposes familiarity with the latter tradition of battle, for 41:25 (Hebrew 41:17) refers explicitly to the fears of the gods when they are confronted with Leviathan; and in some ancient manuscripts 41:9 (Hebrew 41:1) does so as well. Clearly, then, the awesome power of God is underscored in the passage, since God's ability to do things with this fearsome creature that Job cannot—drawing out Leviathan with a fishhook, pressing down his tongue with a rope, putting a cord through his nose and so forth—is presupposed by God's rhetorical questions. God appears to be asking how Job, who cannot engage mighty Leviathan, dares to do battle with a god who can.[55]

But is Leviathan represented here only as God's enemy? Does God stand only over against creatures such as Leviathan who are associated with chaos? The implication of Job 41:5 that God is able, not only to battle Leviathan, but also to play with him "like a bird," indicates that the relationship between God and the forces of chaos may be more complex than simple opposition. We cannot help being reminded of the assertion in Psalm 104:26 that God "formed" Leviathan "to play." Indeed, in Hebrew, God in Job 41:3 (English 41:11) asserts that Leviathan is "for me" or is "mine." Most English translations obscure an oscillation between third-person and first-person personal pronouns in the Hebrew text of 41:1–3 (English 41:9–11) that actually make it difficult to differentiate Leviathan from God. Thus, as Beal shrewdly observes, in the divine speech about Leviathan "the identity of the monstrous blurs with that of God, and vice versa. God identifies with the monster over against all challengers."[56] Given this identification, it is perhaps less surprising that the speeches of God end, not with a description of God's successful battle against Leviathan (a description that would reassure readers of God's intention to overpower forces of chaos that threaten to overwhelm us), but rather with an admiring description of Leviathan that culminates in the unexpected image of Leviathan as a king (41:34 [Hebrew 41:26]). Whether God is able, or even necessarily desires, to subdue this magnificent creature of chaos altogether remains unspecified.

Thus we find in these speeches a representation of a God who is centered elsewhere than on human beings. To the extent that God's speeches allow us to locate a sphere for divine activity, they point us in the direction of creation. It is almost as if God is saying to Job and his friends: if you truly want to understand me, look to the world of nature, and especially to the world of animals. Here we find a world that is complex, beautiful, and even playful. It is, like the world found in Psalm 104, a world characterized by what Derrida called the "heterogeneous multiplicity of the living."[57] It is a world that a powerful God sustains, a God tender enough to notice young birds crying out for food (39:26–30), but mighty enough to engage Behemoth and Leviathan. Yet the world evoked here also seems, much like the ostrich, to be at odds with human wisdom and order. Here we find instead a world of carnivores and monsters, a world of bloodthirsty young eagles and snorting warhorses, a world of creatures that cannot be tamed and secrets that cannot be found out, a world in which beauty and brutality are difficult to disentangle.

Tova Forti has made the important observation that God's speeches in Job qualify human knowledge of, and power over, wild creatures. Although Genesis 1:26–28 may speak of "a certain control over animals," that "power is in fact quite limited." The animals here are "free to choose their habitat away from human society and live according to their own zoological systems and behavioral traits."[58] But hints of this qualification of human dominion may be found in other passages as well, such as the statement in Proverbs 30:18 that the speaker does not understand "the way of the eagle in the skies" or "the way of a snake on a rock." The focus of so many biblical interpreters on Genesis 1:26–28 to the exclusion of such texts as Job 38–41, Proverbs 30:18, and Psalm 104, an exclusion that is in need of explanation, as some writers on animals and religion have noted,[59] has produced a skewed impression of the ways in which the Bible's zoological gaze, taken in its entirety, actually sees the relationships between humans and wild animals.

It is not only our view of human dominion, however, but also our view of biblical representations of God that is skewed by the overemphasis on Genesis 1 in comparison with Job 38–41 and Psalm 104. What does it mean that God finds prey for lions? What does it mean that God supplies eagle chicks and ravens with meat? What does it mean that God creates creatures who stand outside human values and knowledge such as the wild ass, the wild ox, and the ostrich? What does it mean that God cares for Behemoth and Leviathan as much as Job? What does it mean that, when pressed by Job and his friends to give an account of human suffering, God calls their attention to the existence in God's creation of predators and prey? Although such questions do not have easy answers, they may point us toward issues that some writers in religious studies and environmental ethics have identified as especially challenging for our attempts to come to terms with Darwinism and natural selection: the necessary role of such phenomena as predation and animal suffering in the ongoing evolution of life.[60] They may remind us of recurring connections between animals and God, beyond the understanding or control of humanity, that led Derrida to observe, in *The Beast and the Sovereign*, that "there are gods and there are beasts, there is, there is only, the theo-zoological, and in the theo-anthropo-zoological, man is caught, evanescent, disappearing, at the very most a simple mediation, a hyphen between the sovereign and the beast, between God and cattle."[61] And so they may also remind us that our religious traditions and our ways of reading the Bible run some risk, not simply of ignoring the beauty and ferocity of its wild animals, and the wild animals who still live in our own time, but also of domesticating the Bible's wild and ferocious God.

6

The Psalmist, the Primatologist, and the Place of Animals in Biblical Religion

Chapter 5 noted several passages that point toward direct relationships between God and wild animals. God creates these animals, feeds and waters them, and gives them homes in diverse habitats. They serve to accomplish God's purposes. And as frightening as some of these animals were to the Israelites, both Psalm 104 and the speeches of God in Job 38–41 suggest that God might be as concerned about animal lives as about human ones.

God's concern for animal lives is also apparent in a very different type of psalm. Like many lament psalms, Psalm 36 opens with a complaint about "the wicked" that enumerates several of their characteristics. Beginning in 36:5 (Hebrew 36:6), the psalmist expresses confidence that God can intervene on behalf of the petitioner and against the wicked. As in other such expressions of confidence, Psalm 36:5–9 (Hebrew 36:6–10) affirms both God's interactions with the so-called natural world and God's interactions with humanity:

> YHWH, your steadfast love extends to the skies,
> and your faithfulness as far as the clouds.
> Your righteousness is like the mountains of God,
> your judgments like the great deep;
> You save human and animal, YHWH.
> How precious is your steadfast love, God;

Humans take refuge in the shadow of your wings.
They are saturated from the abundance of your house,
and from the river of your delights, you cause them drink.
For with you is a fountain of life,
with your light we see light.

For my purposes here, the important thing to note about Psalm 36 is its affirmation that the extent of God's activity includes but exceeds the human realm. Far from being focused solely on humans, God is represented in verses 5 and 6 (Hebrew 6 and 7) as working throughout creation. And, as if to punctuate this emphasis on the scope of God's concern, the Psalmist exclaims clearly in 36:6 (Hebrew 36:7), "You save human and animal."

The affirmation that God "saves human and animal," though rarely discussed by readers, ought to make us reconsider many assumptions that have been made about Israelite, and biblical, religion. As noted earlier, for much of the twentieth century, scholars argued that biblical religion was uniquely centered around human history, salvation, and covenant, while other ancient religions were supposed to have been concerned with nature and fertility. These stark oppositions between history and nature, or between salvation and fertility, have now been discredited by scholars who emphasize instead the Bible's significant attention to creation, cosmos, agriculture, and fertility alongside history and salvation.[1] Such attention clearly shapes Psalm 36, which uses terms and images that are associated elsewhere in the Hebrew Bible with creation and cosmos (such as "skies" [or in older translations, "heavens"], "mountains," and the "great deep") or with fertility and agriculture (such as "saturation" with "abundance," or the supply of drink). The psalmist represents God engaging directly with elements that are often associated with nature, including nonhuman animals. Indeed, even God is represented with animal features when the psalmist refers to God's protective "wings," an image that also appears in other psalms (e.g., 17:8; 57:1 [Hebrew 57:2]; 91:4).

But the psalmist's notion that God "saves" animals does not simply place animals in the context of creation. The verb translated as "save," *yasha*, is not a minor word in the Hebrew Bible. It is a common verbal root used in many different contexts for salvation, deliverance, and liberation. It is used for example in military contexts, sometimes accompanied by miraculous intervention, such as when it describes God's salvific activity in delivering the Israelites from the Egyptians at the Sea (e.g., Exod. 14:30), or from the Midianites and Amalekites under the judge Gideon (Judg. 7:7), or from the Assyrians at the time of Hezekiah and Isaiah (2 Kgs 19:34; cf. Isa. 37:35). It is used multiple times in the Psalms and in other poems to refer to God's salvation. Indeed, most references to God as a "savior" in the Hebrew Bible, and most references to "salvation," rely upon words derived from this root. By making animals as well as humans the objects of God's salvation, and using such vocabulary to do so, Psalm 36 allows us to think about animals and religion beyond the confines of questions about the use of animals in human religion, or even religious responsibilities toward animals. It places animals firmly within the redemptive activity of God that is often understood as central to biblical religion.

What might it mean to locate animals at the center of biblical religion? Are our notions about religion and theology adaptable enough to account for the animal salvation affirmed by the Psalmist? Do we need to revise our understanding of religion in order to propose more adequate interpretations of the presence of animals in such texts as Psalm 36? In order to reflect on these questions, I make another detour here through animal studies.

The Question of Animal Religion

In 2000, the *Harvard Theological Review* published an article by Kimberly Patton, a scholar of comparative religions, titled "'He Who Sits in the Heavens Laughs': Recovering Animal Theology in the Abrahamic Traditions." There Patton raises a series of startling questions: "Do animals have spiritual awareness? Can they pray? Do they know God? Does He know them? . . . [A]re animals theological *subjects* rather than animated *objects* in the consecrated landscape?"[2] These are not questions that one often finds in scholarly journals of religious studies. Indeed, they might sound at first like questions uncovered in the myths of some religion deemed exotic by Western observers, or practiced by so-called primitives. Yet the subtitle of Patton's article points toward a focus on monotheistic traditions. Her title, in fact, is borrowed from Psalm 2:4: "He who sits in the heavens laughs." And her article both opens and closes with reflection on a Talmudic opinion that divine laughter takes place because of the way in which God chooses to close each day. According to Avodah Zarah 3b, God spends the first three hours of every day studying Torah and the next three hours judging the world. The following three hours are devoted to "feeding the whole world, from the horned buffalo to the brood of vermin." But during the final three hours of every day, God plays with Leviathan, as indicated by the reference in Psalm 104:26 to "Leviathan whom you made to play in/with it."

The biblical image of God playing with Leviathan can seem charming and even humorous. Jon Levenson once referred to Leviathan in Psalm 104 as God's "rubber duckey."[3] But Levenson also makes clear that biblical references to God's interactions with Leviathan and other mythical creatures are crucial, rather than peripheral, to an understanding of biblical religion. Patton, for her part, notes that the relationship between God and other creatures in this and other texts is not "mediated by human beings." Thus, we can say about such texts that "animals are construed as theological *subjects* rather than as mediated *objects*."[4]

Patton clearly believes that scholars of religion have paid insufficient attention to "the nature of the relationship between the divine and animal realms" (403). When such attention is given, she notes, religious traditions tend to be placed in a kind of "developmentalist schema" (405), according to which "increasing theological sophistication" is correlated with "fewer sacred animals" (404). Monotheism is then understood to represent the most advanced point in religious development because it is supposed to place less religious emphasis on animals. One problem with this conceptualization, however, is that particular religious traditions are too complex to fit into it neatly. A focus on the tendency of Abrahamic religions to privilege relationships between God and humanity (whether this tendency is pointed out in affirmation or critique), for example, can cause us to miss the fact that these religions also acknowledge direct relationships between God and animals. Patton therefore highlights three "aspects" of divine-animal relationships in Judaism, Christianity, and Islam: "first, divine compassion or special regard for animals; second, communication and mutual awareness between God and animals; and third, animal veneration of God, particularly in its ritual dimensions" (409).

In addition to texts from Judaism, Christianity, and Islam, however, Patton engages contemporary literature on the study of actual animals. This engagement is motivated in part by Patton's attention to religious texts that represent "animal veneration of God," since such veneration leads to questions about the forms that animal praise takes. After asking whether animals "have spiritual awareness," "pray," or "know God," Patton turns to research on animal cognition and consciousness as a way of critiquing our tendency to "assume, along with so many modern and postmodern sociologies of religion, that religious thought is humanly constructed thought that only encodes social and cultural values" (424). Given some of the conclusions that have been made in contemporary studies of animals, Patton asks provocatively, "what is left to militate against the possibility that animals can think about God?" (424). Reminding her reader of several now-famous statements by Jane Goodall about the "awe" with which chimpanzees studied by Goodall observed a waterfall, Patton notes that Goodall's "decades of familiarity with the chimpanzees led her to place their response *on* the spectrum of religious consciousness rather than utterly apart from it" (425, her emphasis). Indeed, Patton links Goodall's observations about chimpanzee awe to Goodall's own awe at both the beauty of the Tanzanian forests where she studied chimpanzees (which Goodall calls "a most sacred place")[5] and the beauty of the Notre-Dame de Paris cathedral. One might, of course, conclude from this comparison that Goodall was simply being anthropomorphic when she attributed awe to chimpanzees. But Patton, observing that charges of "anthropomorphism" seem to become most heated when we talk about animals and when we talk about God, goes on to suggest that in some religious discourses humans and animals actually share a kind of "theomorphism," according to which all animals, including ourselves, reveal something about God that is distinctive to the particular forms and actions of each species. Thus she attempts to rethink our notions about humans, animals, and God in ways that allow animals to be recognized as "creatures . . . of deep, original, and abiding interest to God" (432). It may even be the case, she suggests in her conclusion, with another nod to the Psalmist and the Rabbis, that when we search for "the unique religious orientation to animals, in their idiosyncratic and joyous devotion to the One who brought them into being—and in [God's] reciprocally fierce and tender devotion to them—we can strain to hear the echoes of [God's] laughter" (434).

One of many remarkable features of Patton's article is its ability to weave together things that are more often kept apart. Thus the discourses of comparative religion in which she is trained are intertwined with a kind of "nature mysticism," to borrow a phrase she applies to Goodall (426); and the relationships between animals and deity that are often associated with "primitive" or "exotic" religions are entangled with, and embedded in, texts from Abrahamic traditions. Even more surprising is the conversation Patton stages between religious texts (including the Bible) and studies of animal cognition and behavior. Expressing some weariness with our now-routine recourse to social constructionist accounts of religion, Patton's engagement with traditional texts that refer to animals causes her to turn to writers like Goodall who study actual animals. The psalmist is introduced to the primatologist.

As unusual as her article may appear in the landscape of religious studies, Patton is not alone in raising the possibility of animal religion. Donovan Schaefer, for example, builds on Patton's suggestions in his article "Do Animals Have Religion?"[6] Casting a wider net among religions than Patton, Schaefer emphasizes the embodied nature of animal religiosity across traditions. Numerous texts indicate that "animals are consummately religious bodies" (177), whose "bodies express their religious being in singular ways, through bodily-specific channels" (177–78). Noting with Patton that Saint Francis is said to have recognized in the singing of birds praise for the creator, Schaefer weaves together texts from several traditions to reveal a widespread understanding of "animal bodies as designed to praise God each in their own ways" (179). Like Patton, Schaefer engages contemporary research on actual animals to rethink the nature of religious studies. Expanding on Patton's attention to animal cognition, however, Schaefer emphasizes animal emotion, "embodied affects," and "the heterogeneity of bodies" (185) in order to call for a view of religion that "affects animal bodies no less than human bodies, and . . . affects humans no less than the bodies of animals" (186). Indeed, in his more recent book *Religious Affects: Animality, Evolution, and Power*, Schaefer expands his argument for an affective approach to religion that can "rewrite the parameters . . . of what gets called religion" so that we "better understand not only other animals but the terms and conditions of our own human religions."[7] One of the problems with our approaches to religion, Schaefer suggests, is that we focus too much on its rational and linguistic dimensions. As a consequence, we fail to recognize crucial characteristics of human religions as well as the possibility that some of their building blocks are found already among animals. Rather than working with restrictive definitions of religion, we should approach religion with the same openness to "heterogeneous multiplicity" that Derrida suggests we bring to both human differences and the many differences that characterize animals.[8]

Aaron Gross, too, has challenged religious studies scholars to abandon prejudices that shape the field and consider "an ontology that does not restrict personhood exclusively to human beings and its important corollary: some animals too can be loci of religious action and meaning (can be religious 'subjects' in the sense of not being mere objects of unwitting participants, but agents within the phenomenon of religion)."[9] Gross comes at this issue from a different perspective than Patton or Schaefer, placing less emphasis on ethological studies of animal cognition or affect (though these are not ignored [see, e.g., 128–29]) and more emphasis on compassion for the suffering of the animals we eat, grounded in our "shared vulnerability" with animals (130). Rather than ranging widely over several religious traditions, he focuses on the treatment of animals in Jewish practices of raising and slaughtering animals deemed kosher, practices that necessarily involve the participation of animals. But as noted in chapter 3 in connection with Derrida and sacrifice, Gross also argues that many definitions of "religion" and "religious studies" make it difficult to take these animals seriously. Such definitions almost invariably rely upon distinctions between humans and animals that associate religion and the study of religion with humans, even at the cost of animalizing "primitives" whose statements and practices do not honor that distinction. Building in part on the work of anthropologist Tim Ingold,[10] Gross calls for "a way of thinking a religious actor that is no longer strictly a human (or divine) subject." Instead, "persons are agencies, and they come in human and nonhuman forms" (114). Such agencies emerge, exist, and respond to one another in webs of sociality and practice that include much that we would consider religious, as well as much that we normally exclude from religion. By making explicit "the coemergence of *homo sapiens* with the more-than-human world and thus religion's coemergence with both humans and animals" (201), Gross asks us to reimagine animals as participants in religion, like Patton and other advocates for rethinking "animals as religious subjects."[11]

One of the challenges faced by those who wish to carry out such reimagining—but also one of the opportunities—is that no single definition of "religion" lies ready at hand, allowing us to distinguish clearly between what is religion and what is not. As Schaefer puts it (appropriately enough using an animal metaphor), the attempt to provide such definitions too often "assumes that the word has a fixed point of origin, a moment where the pin of the term 'religion' first punctures the butterfly of religion as such and sticks it to a board."[12] The difficulty here is not that the term "religion" has no pragmatic use, but rather that it can be used in so many different ways. Efforts to provide a single definition that includes all religions, but only religion, inevitably exclude some phenomena that others might consider religion. All too often, these phenomena are dismissed with alternative labels ("primitive," "superstition," "mere ritual," and so forth), raising suspicions that boundaries are being drawn in ways that privilege some culturally bound practices and ideas over others. Scholars of religion are aware of the difficulty, of course. But the exclusion of animals from most definitions of "religion" may be no less culturally bound, and no less damaging in its effects, than other definitions that rely upon arbitrary exclusions. Indeed, humanistic definitions of religion, and the study of religion as a "human science," may simply provide one more example in a long list of attempts to identify characteristics supposed to mark a clear distinction between human and animal. Such definitions may contribute, Gross suggests, to what Agamben calls the "anthropological machine," which functions to produce a distinctive humanity by identifying features that are supposed to be proper to it and excluding from it all elements of animal life, even when they appear among other humans.[13]

Primatology, Religion, and Human/Animal Distinctions

As was noted in chapter 1, Matthew Calarco asserts that "one of the defining characteristics of our age is the radical breakdown of the human/animal distinction."[14] Some of the most compelling challenges to traditional ways of drawing this distinction have come from empirical studies of animal behavior, cognition, and emotion, which have increased significantly in both quantity and sophistication over the past few decades.[15] Although attempts have been made since the ancient world to identify characteristics or capabilities that separate humans from other animals, researchers continue to find examples of one or more animal species who share such characteristics and capabilities, even if only in a limited way. As the primatologist Frans de Waal puts it, "humanity never runs out of claims of what sets it apart, but it is a rare uniqueness that holds up for over a decade."[16]

It is no longer surprising that a primatologist would make such a remark. Some of the most famous discoveries of animal behavior and capabilities that have undermined previous conceptions of boundaries between humans and animals come from the study of nonhuman primates. This has been particularly true of research on the great apes—chimpanzees, bonobos, gorillas, and orangutans—who, among all living animals, are genetically our closest relatives. Thus, when Goodall first observed chimpanzees modifying and using sticks to extract termites from a mound in the 1960's, deeply held beliefs that tool-making was a distinctive characteristic of humans had to be put aside.[17] Goodall's discovery may seem unremarkable today, when tool-making has been documented in several other species in addition to great apes.[18] But it is worth recalling that, when Goodall's observations were first announced, some scientists refused to believe her, going so far as to accuse her of training the chimpanzees.[19] The study of apes has subsequently shown that groups of chimpanzees living in different areas share distinct tool-making traditions, indicating that some animals in addition to humans participate in and transmit "cultures."[20] More ominously, but consistent with other similarities to humans, groups of male chimpanzees also participate in something like warfare against enemy chimpanzee communities.[21]

The Psalmist, the Primatologist, and the Place of Animals 149

Even the identification of language as a unique characteristic of humans has been challenged. Although great apes are physically incapable of producing spoken words, experiments involving American Sign Language or the use of other symbols created by humans indicate that some great apes have a larger capacity for communicating using *elements that we associate with language* than had previously been imagined. These experiments generate both insight and controversy.[22] To the extent that we focus on modes of communication that seem most like our own, or on the abilities of great apes to communicate with us, we risk missing sophisticated forms of communication that apes use among themselves.[23] At the very least, however, research into, and debates over, the capacity of great apes or other animals to participate in what Vicki Hearne calls "some condition of language"[24] demonstrate that the conclusions we draw about language as a boundary marker between humans and animals depend in part on how we define such terms as "language." Although differences clearly exist between human language use and forms of communication among animals, when we break language down into its constitutive elements and look for those elements elsewhere, we may discover more points of overlap than we anticipated between our communication and the communication that takes place among animals of certain species.

Might something like this be true for religion? "Religion" is no more amenable to single definitions than "language," and it may even be less so. But even as religious studies scholars begin to speak of "animal religion" and "animal theology," some research on animal behavior can be read as implying that particular elements associated with various definitions of "religion" might also be found among animals. And as with language, so also with religion, the work of primatologists can lead to striking suggestions.

Consider, for example, the work of de Waal, whose observation about the supposed uniqueness of humans was noted above. De Waal made a name for himself by analyzing political maneuvering in a colony of chimpanzees. In *Chimpanzee Politics*, he called attention to social manipulation and struggles for power among these chimpanzees, which he associated at the time with Machiavelli.[25] Already in this early work, de Waal describes chimpanzee social life in ways that question assumptions about the boundary between humans and great apes. More significantly for my purposes, the political machinations of the chimpanzees involved not only phenomena that we view negatively, such as deception, but also such phenomena as solidarity and empathy. De Waal's subsequent work has highlighted these more positive features of the lives of primates, especially chimpanzees and bonobos. Across a series of both specialist and popular publications, de Waal argues against what he calls a "curious dualism, which pits morality against nature and humanity against other animals."[26] This dualism, which understands morality to be uniquely human, also represents morality as a phenomenon overlaid on top of, and in opposition to, evolutionary processes. According to this perspective, we are moral because we fight against, and overcome (more or less successfully), our inherited animal natures. De Waal detects this dualism in diverse thinkers from Sigmund Freud to Richard Dawkins, but he also proposes a connection to certain forms of religion: "The image of humanity's innate depravity and its struggle to transcend that depravity is quintessentially Calvinist, going back to the doctrine of original sin."[27]

Against such notions, de Waal, like Darwin himself, argues that many building blocks of morality are already present among nonhuman animals, and especially among great apes (though de Waal also cites examples from other species including elephants, certain species of monkeys, and even dogs). Referring to both scientific experiments and anecdotes, de Waal notes the occurrence among animals of such phenomena as empathy, sympathy, friendship, cooperation, consolation, helping responses, gratitude, reciprocity, impulse control, conflict avoidance, reconciliation, fairness, community concern, social codes, and even altruism. If the social interactions of humans also incorporate such phenomena, this is partly because of an evolutionary history that we share with other mammals, especially great apes. Consistent with Schaefer's emphasis on affect, de Waal notes that these phenomena are often grounded in emotion as much as cognition. Of course, de Waal does not deny that violence, selfishness, and deception also take place among animals, as they do among humans. But taking what he calls a "bottom up approach" to morality, de Waal argues that we do not need to suppress our "animal nature" in order to act in ways considered moral. Rather, we build upon pro-social impulses that we share with other social animals.

How does this argument relate to religion? De Waal accepts that morality and social organization are more developed among humans than among our closest animal relatives. And here he proposes one possible reason for the development of religion. Religion, among other functions, can encourage the further development of moral tendencies we have inherited by motivating moral behavior, fostering communal bonds and social support, and threatening consequences for failing to act according to community norms. De Waal, who is not himself religious, acknowledges that religion also has negative features. It can reinforce the in-group/out-group dynamics that we, like our primate relatives, tend to use when making decisions. It is clear that he dislikes superstition (though he notes that it is extremely widespread among humans, and not only where religion is concerned) and would prefer a humanistic support for religion's positive functions. Indeed, he actively promotes "expand[ing] morality's reach," and using our intellect to do so.[28] Yet he is also critical of anti-religious positions adopted by such "new atheists" as Dawkins and Sam Harris. "Religious community building comes naturally to us," in de Waal's words; and that may be because it is grounded in, and stimulates, our evolved pro-social tendencies, tendencies that he sees at work already among animals.[29]

Religion and sociality are also linked in the work of the anthropologist and primatologist Barbara King. King too notes the presence of empathy among great apes, and she suggests that "at some point it combined, I believe, with other foundational elements to push human ancestors toward the expression of a religious imagination."[30] As this statement indicates, King does consider religion a human phenomenon.[31] But which of its "other foundational elements" are also found among animals? Exploring this question, King builds upon her research into the ways in which African great apes use gestures and bodily movements to communicate with one another. Rather than focusing on individual gestures, King emphasizes larger "social interactions" between apes that involve "moment-by-moment mutual adjustments and fluidity." These "interactions can be termed *co-regulated* because they are highly unpredictable and contingent, reminiscent of a dance between two highly attuned partners." But they also produce "meaning" between participants. Such meaning does not inhere in the individual gestures, but emerges from the total social communication. Meaning "is constructed socially" among the apes as they interact.[32] But humans also create meaning through co-regulated social communication. We use human language in addition to other forms of communication, of course; but chimpanzees incorporate vocalization into their meaning-making as well. And this capacity for meaning-making, like empathy, forms part of the inherited platform, shared with great apes, upon which religion has evolved: "Fundamentally, the quest for the sacred is about a search for meaning in the deepest sense, going beyond making sense of shared communication between social partners to encompass a search for making things *matter*."[33] Our inherited desire to *make meaning* with others, whether other humans, gods, or spirits, leads us to participate in social rituals, including those we associate with religion.

Other characteristics that we share with great apes are, in King's view, also important for the development of religion. She calls attention, for example, to the presence among apes of social rules, a desire for "belongingness," a "capacity for imagination" (57), and self-aware consciousness. King goes so far as to argue "that there clearly exists some degree of continuity in symbolic ritual among nonhuman primates and among humans" (55–56). Among surviving primate species, humans are in King's view "the spiritual ape" (153). But the evolution of our spirituality depended upon attributes that we can observe, not only among humans, but among at least some animals. The ways in which we look at animals play a role here. King notes that there seems always to have been a "spiritual dimension" to our own creation of images of animals.[34] And while the burials and mummification of animals by humans that she discusses in *Being with Animals* testify to our continued attempts to draw animals into such quintessentially religious practices as those associated with death, burial, and afterlife, King has turned more recently, in *How Animals Grieve*, to the presence among animals themselves of both love and grief, two of the most significant emotions at play in religious contexts.[35]

But a much closer link between animals and religion is made by Goodall. Like de Waal and King, Goodall notes the presence among chimpanzees of such qualities as empathy and compassion, which "in both chimpanzees and humans . . . lead to altruistic behaviour and self-sacrifice."[36] As indicated above, Goodall also recounts, in several places, actions she saw chimpanzees taking when they arrived at a waterfall. The males would display in front of the waterfall—swaying rhythmically; swinging on vines, sometimes over the water; charging along the stream; or throwing rocks and branches. Goodall refers to these displays as "ritual"[37] and "dance."[38] On some occasions, the displaying chimpanzee would then "sit on a rock, his eyes following the falling water."[39] And these activities lead Goodall to questions that are nearly as surprising coming from a primatologist as are the questions coming from Patton and Schaefer about religion:

Is it not possible that the chimpanzees are responding to some feeling like awe? A feeling generated by the mystery of water; water that seems alive, always rushing past yet never going, always the same yet ever different. Was it perhaps similar feelings of awe that gave rise to the first animistic religions, the worship of the elements and the mysteries of nature over which there was no control? Only when our prehistoric ancestors developed language would it have been possible to discuss such internal feelings and create a shared religion.[40]

Goodall does appear here to leave some space between the "awe" of the chimpanzees and "shared religion" among humans. She nevertheless invites us elsewhere to consider "primate spirituality," raising the possibility, noted by Patton and Schaefer, that animals themselves participate in experiences that we reasonably associate with spirituality when we find them among humans. Goodall tells, for example, of seeing "chimpanzees 'dance' at the onset of a very heavy rain, reaching up to sway saplings or low branches rhythmically back and forth, back and forth, then moving forward in slow motion loudly slapping the grounds with their hands, stamping their feet, and hurling rock after rock." And she explicitly disagrees, she writes, with the "many theologians and philosophers [who] argue that only humans have 'souls.'"[41]

Neither de Waal nor King is willing to go as far as Goodall in attributing to chimpanzees or other apes anything like "spirituality." De Waal, who reports having also seen the "rain dance" among chimpanzees, acknowledges that when he first observed it, "I had trouble believing what I saw."[42] Noting Goodall's interpretation, de Waal proposes as an alternative that perhaps "the apes believe, for whatever reason, that they can influence the course of nature. Perhaps a fortuitous event, such as the ceasing of the rain in the middle of a charging display, created the superstitious belief that if they display hard enough, they can stop precipitation"

(200). King, for her part, grants that Goodall's interpretation is "possible" while wondering "if the awe response emerges as much in us as in the chimpanzees when we learn that our closest living relatives connect in an emotional way with their natural world."[43]

Yet religious studies scholars continue to find in Goodall's work and similar arguments a basis for redefining religion to take into account some animal activities. Stewart Guthrie, in a discussion of "animal animism," invokes Goodall among others to suggest that religion is grounded in part in a tendency among both animals and humans to find in the world animate agents who could be dangerous.[44] More recently Schaefer uses what he calls "the chimpanzees' religious reaction to the waterfall" and a notion of "religion as dance," associated with the waterfall dance, to articulate a powerful theory of religion as an affective, embodied economy suffused with relations of power.[45]

For my immediate purposes here, however, it is unimportant whether one is ultimately persuaded by Goodall's suggestion that chimpanzees experience a kind of spiritual awe. Each in his or her own way, with arguments that sometimes overlap and sometimes go in distinctive directions, de Waal, King, and Goodall arguably bring animals closer to what we call religion. They do so, not by speaking explicitly about "animal religion" as some religious studies scholars do, but by calling attention to the existence in some animals of emotions, capabilities, and capacities for meaning and ritual that we associate with morality and religion when we find them in ourselves. They are not alone, moreover. Other scholars of animal behavior also speak about animals in ways that seem to associate them with something quite close to ritual and morality, from Barbara Smuts's references to certain baboon behaviors as "an almost sacramental procession" and "a baboon sangha"[46] to discussions of animals' "social morality," "wild justice," and "moral lives" by Mark Bekoff and Jessica Pierce.[47]

Animal Religion and the Bible

Now even in comparison with earlier chapters, my circuitous route through a certain type of animal studies may seem to have led me quite far at this point from biblical interpretation. How can the writings of primatologists shed light on the writings of a psalmist such as the author of

The Psalmist, the Primatologist, and the Place of Animals   155

Psalm 36, whose reference to the salvation of animals I referred to at the beginning of this chapter? After all, it is not likely that writers of the Bible even had opportunities to see any of the great apes. The "apes" that are brought by ship to Solomon along with gold, silver, ivory, and peacocks in some English translations of 1 Kings 10:22 and 2 Chronicles 9:21 are more likely to have been monkeys (though still, like us, also primates). And there is no point in trying to correlate biblical literature with modern science in any literalizing sense, at least in my view.

On the other hand, biblical writers were in a position to observe animals, as I noted in connection with the zoological gaze. When they looked at various species of animals, they sometimes drew conclusions about God's activities in the world. The divine activities that most interest the writers of the Bible are clearly activities believed to have the biggest impact on humans. But a number of texts also indicate that the writers of the Bible imagined God in some relationship to animals themselves.

What I want to ask, then, is whether both the writings of primatologists who take seriously questions about morality, animal meaning, and in some cases spirituality, and the writings of religious studies scholars who take seriously questions about animals and animal religion, can play a useful role in *reshaping the hermeneutical imagination that readers of the Bible bring to biblical texts*. For they encourage us to pause over animal references, refusing to hurry along out of some misguided sense that biblical religion must, by definition, exclude animals from its agents. They encourage us to wonder, for example, about the full range of possible meanings for such biblical statements as the affirmation in Psalm 36 that God saves both humans and animals, or the affirmation we saw in Isaiah 43 that animals praise God. And they encourage us to think about how such texts relate intertextually to a series of other biblical references to animals that we may otherwise be tempted to neglect, including not only texts that refer to God's agency for animals but also texts that hint at animal agency in relation to God.

With respect to God's agency, of course, and specifically God's agency for salvation, we have already seen in chapter 2 the explicit biblical statements in Exodus 11:7 and 13:15 that God protects the animals of the Israelites along with humans when the Israelites are delivered from death on the night of the first Passover, even as God kills both human and animal Egyptians. For just this reason, the Israelites believed they owed to God the firstborn of both humans and animals (Exod. 13:11–16). But this shared religious fate of humans and animals in the Hebrew Bible's most famous salvation narrative follows a series of appearances of animals in the stories of the Egyptian plagues. It is not simply that God uses certain types of animals, such as frogs, gnats, flies, and locusts, to inflict these plagues. The fates of both humans and animals, their salvation and their judgment, are also at stake in the plagues. Thus, the gnats go out "on humans and on animals" in 8:17–18 (the vocabulary, *adam* and *behemah*, is shared with Psalm 36). Boils come upon "humans and animals" in 9:9–10 (again, vocabulary is shared with Psalm 36). So too, hail falls on "humans and animals" in 9:22, 25 (again, vocabulary is shared with Psalm 36), including explicitly slaves in the field (9:21); but no hail falls in Goshen, where the Israelites live. A plague falls on the Egyptian animals, including horses, donkey, camels, herds and flocks; but God "makes a distinction" between "the livestock of Israel and the livestock of Egypt" (9:4). As a consequence, "all the livestock of the Egyptians died; but from the livestock of the Israelites, not one died" (9:5). Pharaoh tells Moses and Aaron that the Israelites should take their flocks and herds with them when they leave Egypt (Exod. 12:32); and Exodus 12:38 confirms that the Israelites journey with "flocks and herds, very many livestock." Although animals are not identified explicitly at every turn throughout the Exodus story, these and other recurring references to them—such as the indication that Egyptian horses as well as soldiers are killed when God allows the sea to resume its normal depth in Exodus 14:23–15:1; the explicit inclusion of animals alongside humans who need water that God provides by ordering Moses to strike a rock in Exodus 17:2–6; or God's warning to the Israelites in Exodus 19:13 that anyone, animal or human, who touches the holy mountain will be put to death—continually remind attentive readers of Exodus that animals participate throughout this paradigmatic story of divine deliverance.

Looking at the Exodus story from another angle, and continuing to take the theme of animal salvation seriously, we should keep in mind the increasing recognition that creation and salvation are not separable or contradictory emphases in the Hebrew Bible. The Exodus story, with its dramatic representation of God's power over both the cosmic forces of

The Psalmist, the Primatologist, and the Place of Animals 157

chaos associated with the sea and the social forces of chaos associated with Egypt, reminds us of the affirmation in such texts as Genesis 1 that God's creative power involves mastery of the "deep" and the waters, and the ability to bring order from the formless void of chaos. Indeed, the great poem celebrating Israel's salvation in Exodus 15, though not always associated with creation and nature by readers, "employs the language, style, and literary structure of the creation myths of the ancient Near East," as Terence Fretheim puts it.[48] As a consequence, the exodus from Egypt is likened to a cosmic, creative enterprise. We should not be surprised, then, that animals as well as humans populate the Exodus story, since they also play prominent roles in the creation narratives. And it is worth recalling that Psalm 36:6 (Hebrew 36:7), with its affirmation of the salvation of humans and animals, also places that salvation in a cosmic, creation context when the Psalmist refers to the skies, the clouds, the mountains, and the great deep (36:5–6a), using words for skies and deep that also appear in Genesis 1. God's actions to save humans and animals in both Exodus and Psalm 36 are congruent with God's actions to create humans and animals in Genesis.

I hasten to note again that I am not trying to turn the Exodus story into a manifesto for animal liberation. The fates of many animals referred to in Exodus—attacked by swarms of gnats, afflicted with boils, struck down by hail in the fields as well as by illness, slaughtered by the angel of death, drowned in the sea with their Egyptian riders and chariots—are horrific. But this is true, too, for the Egyptians and their slaves who are afflicted and die alongside their animals. On the other side, Israelite animals are saved from such fates, delivered from Egypt, and given water in the wilderness. Their firstborn are owed to God, but so are the firstborn of Israelite humans. The problems raised by the Exodus texts for modern notions of liberation are not resolved by the distinction between human and animal, but *rather cut across that distinction*. The same religious promises, and the same religious threats, affect both humans and animals. The species line is disrupted in this story of deliverance and death.

Between the creation narratives and the story of Exodus, another famous story of salvation and judgment contains similar dynamics. The story of Noah and the Flood, which I return to in the next chapter, certainly relies upon assumptions about God's mastery of the forces of chaos, represented by the waters. But whereas, in Genesis 1 and Exodus 14 and 15, God separates waters to allow the safety of dry land to appear, the sequence is reversed in the Flood story. In Genesis 7:11 God sets loose "the fountains of the deep" and opens "the windows of the skies." Here too, the vocabulary of "skies" is shared with Genesis 1 and Psalm 36, while the "deep" can be found in Genesis 1, Psalm 36, and Exodus 15. But if God's judgment in the story falls upon both humans and animals (who are included together in the category "all flesh" at several points [e.g., Gen. 6:12–13; 9:11, 15–17]), so too humans and animals are saved together on the ark that Noah builds at God's command. The waters of chaos that God lets loose eventually recede, thanks in part to a "wind" that God is said in Genesis 8:1 to cause to blow upon the earth (using for "wind" the same word, *ruach*, that refers to God's "wind" in Genesis 1:2 and Exodus 15:10). As Ronald Simkins notes, "The result of the flood is a new creation."[49] Genesis 9:9–17 makes clear that, after the Flood, God establishes a "covenant" not only with humanity, but also "with every living thing that is with you, with the birds, with the animals, and with all the living creatures of the earth" (9:10). Consistent with Psalm 36:6, the stories of Creation, the Flood, and Exodus all include animals alongside humans in scenes of creation, judgment, and salvation that are associated with one another through shared imagery and vocabulary. Animals participate at every one of these exemplary points in the narrative explication of biblical religion.

Given the presence of animals in such key biblical texts, we should not be surprised that animals appear elsewhere as well, alongside humans, as objects of judgment and salvation. Jeremiah refers several times to the judgment of "humans and animals" (again *adam* and *behemah*) by God (e.g., 7:20; 21:6; 36:29; 50:3; 51:62). As Jeremiah notes, God created humans and animals and can give them to anyone, including the Babylonian king Nebuchadnezzar (27:5–6; 28:14). But judgment does not last forever, and God eventually will "sow the house of Israel and the house of Judah with the seed of humans and the seed of animals" (31:27; cf. 33:10, 12). Ezekiel, too, refers repeatedly to the judgment of "humans and animals" (e.g., 14:13, 17, 19, 21; 25:13; 29:8, 11). Eventually, however, God will again "multiply humans and animals" in Israel (36:11). When God's house lies in ruins in Haggai, the drought that follows as a consequence falls upon both "human and animal" (1:11).

In their respective articles on "animal theology" and "animal religion," Patton and Schaefer also call attention to the book of Jonah and its striking representations of animals. As noted in chapter 5, God uses both "a great fish" (Jon. 1:17) and a worm (4:7) to achieve divine ends in Jonah's tale. Less often noted, however, is the fact that, after Jonah delivers God's message in Nineveh, the king calls for a fast by proclaiming: "the humans and the animals, the herds and the flocks, will not taste anything. They will not feed, and they will not drink water. The humans and the animals will be covered in sackcloth, and they will cry out to God mightily" (3:7–8). The fast is carried out, which causes God to refrain from destroying Nineveh rather than following through on the judgment Jonah had announced. And at the very conclusion of the book, in response to Jonah's petulant complaints, God asks rhetorically, "Should I not have pity on Nineveh, the great city, in which there are more than a hundred and twenty thousand people, who do not know their right hand from their left, and many animals" (4:11).

Although Jonah's animal imagery is remarkable, I noted in chapter 4 that some scholars believe the book was written as satire or parody. Arguments for this conclusion sometimes include comments about the book's representation of animals. Steven McKenzie observes that the idea of a man living for three days inside a great fish is "ridiculous" and was "intended to be preposterous," but he goes on to say a few pages later:

> In spite of the curtness of Jonah's oracle, it is enormously successful—to a ridiculous extreme.... The king issues a decree requiring all the people *and the animals* in the city to fast, dress in sackcloth, pray; and repent of evil deeds and violence.... However, the royal decree highlights the ridiculousness of the extent of effectiveness of Jonah's oracle in the story. Imagine sheep, cattle, and other animals dressed in sackcloth refusing to eat or drink, preferring instead to lament their evil deeds and pray for mercy! The idea is ludicrous. No other scene in the book quite so clearly illustrates the satirical nature of the story with its ridiculous images and hyperbole.[50]

In order to make his case for the book's satirical genre, McKenzie assumes that readers will agree that the participation of animals in this religious ritual is "ludicrous."

Of course, not all scholars agree that the book of Jonah was written as parody. Dissenting scholars note that, in the ancient world, the book was usually read as a more straightforward account; and it has been interpreted in many different ways.[51] For my purposes, however, it is not necessary to deny its humorous or satirical elements. What matters more is the point that we as readers imagine the book to be making. When the book is read as parody, who or what is the target of its humor? Jonah is, in Athalya Brenner's words, "the butt of the story," who has to be taught lessons by God with the assistance of animals.[52] Although the repentance of humans and animals in Nineveh, a city long destroyed by the book's likely date of composition, may be represented in exaggerated fashion, one point made by such exaggeration is that even ostentatious repentance is unable to cause this misguided prophet to recognize God's merciful response. But if "God's word is the final word" in this humorous book (191), as Brenner suggests, then it is surely relevant that God rather than Jonah or the king expresses divine concern in the closing verse for Nineveh's animals as well as its humans. In spite of its humorous elements, the book of Jonah is consistent with the psalmist's observation that God saves human and animal. Indeed, vocabulary for human and animal—*adam* and *behemah*—is shared by Psalm 36:6 (Hebrew 36:7) and Jonah 4:11. What Jonah has to learn, as do other prophets who would limit the scope of God's activity, is exactly the message of Psalm 36:5–6 (Hebrew 6–7): that God's faithfulness extends to the skies, to the clouds, and to both human and animal.

And other texts reiterate God's concern for animals. In Psalm 50:10–11, we find this affirmation put into the mouth of God:

> For all the living things of the forest are mine,
>   all the animals on a thousand mountains.
> I know all the birds on the mountains,
>   everything that moves in the field is with me.

The context for this affirmation is intriguing, since Psalm 50 is one of several biblical texts that cast animal sacrifice in a negative light. This poem, like others, criticizes those who sacrifice while disobeying God in other ways. But whereas some biblical texts use the belief that animals belong to God as a rationale *for* sacrifice, this passage might be read as deploying that same relationship between animals and God as a mark *against* animal sacrifice.

Explicit references to animals in such texts as Psalms 36 and 50 should be kept in mind when one reads other texts that refer more generally to God's relationship with the nonhuman world. When Psalm 24:1 states that "the earth and those who dwell in it" belong to God, for example, we understand that animals are among those inhabitants. And when the speaker in 1 Chronicles 29:11 tells God that "everything in the skies and on the earth are yours," animals are again included.

Some readers may assume that this belonging to God implies no positive relationship, and simply affirms a belief in God's power over all creation. But such misunderstanding is corrected by Psalm 104, as we have seen. Its lengthy reflection on the natural world includes numerous references to God's active creation, not simply *of* animals, but also *on behalf of* animals. Thus God provides water to "every living creature of the field," including the wild asses (104:11) whose independence, wandering nature, and association with wilderness cause them to be represented elsewhere as unsettling animals (e.g., Isa. 32:14; Jer. 2:24; 14:6; Hos. 8:9; Job 24:5; 39:5–8 cf. Gen. 16:12). God provides trees and branches as habitation for birds (Ps. 104:12, 17), mountains for mountain goats or ibexes, rocks for hyraxes (104:18), and the sea for numerous living creatures (104:25) including Leviathan (104:26). God provides food for both humans and animals (104:14–15 [the vocabulary *behemah* and *adam* are again used here as in Psalm 36:6], 27–28), as well as the breath or spirit (*ruach*) that allows them to live (104:30).

Notably, however, Psalm 104 also offers a shift in perspective on the relationship between God and animals. While attributing significant agency to God in that relationship, the psalmist also attributes some agency to animals. For example, the "young lions" in 104:21 "seek from God their food." Here the lions are active subjects of seeking from God. This statement follows, in poetic parallelism, an observation that "the young lions roar for prey," which probably indicates that the writer understood such roaring as a kind of plea to God for food. A similar observation is made in Job 38:41, which also refers to young lions crying to God for help when they lack food. And in the summary statement of Psalm 104:27–30, the psalmist, as we have seen, notes that "all of these," referring to the animals who have been described throughout the psalm as well as the humans who appear briefly, "hope for you to give their food to them" (104:27). A similar idea appears in Psalm 145:15–16, where the psalmist exclaims:

> The eyes of all wait for you, and you give them their food in its season,
> opening your hand, and satisfying the desire of every living creature.

The verb used here for "waiting" appears elsewhere in the Psalms when a speaker hopes for God's salvation (119:166).

Animals are represented in the Psalms, then, as relying actively on God for their food and calling out to God for it. As Psalm 147:9 also observes, God "gives to the animals their food, to the young ravens when they call out." Note that here, as with the lions in Psalm 104, the sounds made by animals are understood as calls to God. And such calls may be lifted up when food is missing as well, as noted in Joel 1:20: "The animals of the field also cry to you, because rivers of water are dried up, and fire has consumed the pastures of the wilderness." So too the animals "groan" in 1:18 for lack of food; but they are told not to fear in 2:22, since God is restoring fertility in the land.

If animals are understood as calling out to God for food, it should not be surprising that they are also understood as capable of praising God. A series of texts in the Hebrew Bible, especially in the Psalms, contain passages that represent what Fretheim calls "nature's praise of God."[53] Such texts draw upon ancient Near Eastern hymnic traditions of representing various elements, including animals, praising one or more deities.[54] Although animals are not singled out in all of the biblical examples, they are referred to explicitly in a few passages. Psalm 148, for example, which is one of the longer examples of such texts in the Hebrew Bible, includes a refrain in which the "sea monsters" or "dragons" are to praise God (148:7). Three verses later, after references to praise from other element of nature, we find an adjuration to praise addressed to "the living creatures, and all animals, creeping things and birds of wing" (148:10). Comparable references to humans follow. Given the explicit reference to animals in this psalm, it is judicious to assume that animals are also included in more general calls to praise. When Psalm 69:34 calls on "skies and earth, seas and everything moving in them" to praise God, it seems certain that the moving elements include animals. A similar conclusion can be drawn about "the field and everything that is in it" in Psalm 96:12; "the sea and everything that fills it, the world and those who live in it" in Psalm 98:7; and "the sea and everything that fills it" in Isaiah 42:10. Although a reference to "everything that has breath" in Psalm 150:6 follows a series of references to musical instruments that are used to praise God, both the earlier reference to praise in the dome of the sky (150:1) and ancient Near

The Psalmist, the Primatologist, and the Place of Animals 163

Eastern iconographic associations between animals and music[55] support the conclusion that animals are praising God here, too, in this closing, climactic verse of the book of Psalms.

As Fretheim suggests in his discussion of this "language of nonhuman praise," these types of texts testify to some sort of belief "that God is able to sustain close relationship with" the nonhuman world.[56] Although many of these passages appear in biblical poetry rather than narrative, there is little reason to dismiss their relevance by considering them simply as exuberant expressions of poetic license. A more felicitous conclusion would be that such passages testify to some type of "interresponsiveness between God and nature in the Old Testament" (261). And the nature of the "nonverbal praise" (263) that various parts of the nonhuman world were believed capable of lifting up surely depended on perceptions of actual phenomena, including animals, such as the living creatures of the field, jackals, and ostriches assumed to be honoring God in Isaiah 43:20.

Not altogether unlike the primatologists, then, or some religious studies scholars, the psalmists sensed that things they saw happening among animals bore some relation to practices and emotions they saw among themselves. In the roar of lions, the flight of birds, and the surfacing and splashing of distant, mysterious sea creatures, the psalmists and other biblical writers heard or saw what they considered responses to a God who was believed to save—and also sometimes to judge—both human and animal. They heard and saw what Patton calls "animal veneration of God." This aspect of biblical religion does not appear everywhere, of course. The books of the Hebrew Bible, too, are a "heterogeneous multiplicity," as are both religions and animals; and the focus of biblical literature often does fall squarely on humans. But recognition of God's direct relationship to elements of nature, including animals, and of their response to God, is a dynamic in biblical literature that is too often missed. To characterize biblical religion by focusing solely upon relationships between humans and God, then, is to miss crucial features of the Hebrew Bible and to read it through the lens of human exceptionalism.

7

Reading the Hebrew Bible in an Age of Extinction

What does it mean to read the Bible in an age of extinction?

The question itself might seem improper. On the one hand, species extinctions are a natural part of evolutionary life. Thus one could ask whether the Bible has ever been read in a time when extinctions were not taking place. On the other hand, the Bible knows nothing about the evolution and extinction of species in a Darwinian sense. Pre-Darwinian readers who tried to correlate the fossil remains of extinct animals with their interpretations of the Bible inevitably ran into difficulties. When confronted with ancient bones and teeth that clearly came from creatures much larger than those known to him, the New England Puritan minister Cotton Mather (1663–1728) concluded "that they provided scientific confirmation for the accounts of antediluvian human giants found in the Bible" (cf. Gen. 6:4).[1] Similarly misguided attempts to reconcile evidence of extinct creatures with the Bible are scattered across history, going as far back as Augustine (354–430 CE).[2] Given this history of interpretations, it would not be surprising if biblical scholars responded to questions about animal extinction with little more than a reminder about the dangers of anachronism.

To ask about biblical interpretation and extinction in dialogue with animal studies, however, is not to deny the disjunction between assumptions held by the writers of biblical texts and assumptions held by post-Darwinian readers. It is rather to explore what it means to read the Bible at a time when we are increasingly aware, or should be aware, that we are contributing to what is now often called "the sixth mass extinction." The possibility of such an extinction event, or series of events, is more widely known today than it was even a few years ago, thanks in part to journalists who cover science and ecology.[3] I return below to further consideration of it. My interests here, however, are not primarily scientific but, rather, hermeneutical and ethical.

As with so many issues related to animals and the environment, the relationship of the Bible and biblical interpretation to anthropogenic species extinctions is ambiguous and contradictory. Influential ways of reading certain texts that I have mentioned already, such as the overemphasis on human dominion or rule over other creatures in Genesis 1:28, can foster a human exceptionalism that often leads to a lack of concern about our negative effects on endangered animals. Yet multiple passages from the Hebrew Bible can also be read as supporting, not simply kindness toward individual animals, but the flourishing of diverse types of animals living in a range of places. The environmental philosopher Holmes Rolston III even referred once to the story of Noah and the ark as "the first Endangered Species Project." Although this particular phrase may have been intended partly as humorous, Rolston took seriously the ways in which this "quaint" "parable" and other biblical texts could be read in support of species diversity.[4]

This tension between interpretations of the Bible that foster attention to species diversity and extinctions, and other interpretations that undermine such attention, shapes my concluding chapter. It will send me, as it sent Rolston, back to the story of Noah and several other texts below. First, however, I turn to contemporary discussions of animal extinctions. Many such discussions are technical and scientific, and I will touch upon them briefly. I am more interested, however, in the ways in which scholars shaped by or engaged with other disciplines help us think about reading in a time of extinction. In addition to Derrida's emphasis on the "heterogeneous multiplicity of the living," and Haraway's emphasis on multispecies entanglement, I want to highlight here Thom van Dooren's attention to story and place as crucial frames for the interpretation of, and responses to, animal extinctions.

Of Mass Extinctions and the Anthropocene

Scientists tell us that, over the history of life on earth, there have been at least five occasions when, according to fossil evidence, extinctions of species took place across the planet in a relatively short period, geologically speaking, and at a rate far exceeding that associated with normal evolutionary processes. Although less dramatic extinction events have also taken place, the most recent mass event is the disappearance of dinosaurs and many other species sixty-six million years ago, in what is usually called the Cretaceous-Paleogene (K-Pg) or Cretaceous-Tertiary (K-T) event. The end of the Cretaceous period is marked geologically by a thin layer of rock, called the K-Pg boundary, which separates assemblages of fossils and other sediments below the boundary from very different assemblages above it. This dramatic shift in forms of life is now often attributed, in part or in whole, to the impact of a large asteroid and the environmental consequences that followed.

Many scientists believe that we are now also entering or already living through another mass extinction event.[5] This time, however, the primary causes for extinctions follow from actions that humans have taken as both our numbers and the scale of our exploitation of the earth's resources have increased. Anthropogenic contributions to extinctions are diverse, and include habitat destruction, deforestation, modification and depletion of water systems, the introduction of so-called invasive species, overhunting and overfishing, various types of pollution, and, now, climate change. But the cumulative effect is disturbing: We have become the asteroid.

This thesis is sometimes conflated with another, more controversial, one: that we have now moved or are moving from an epoch known as the Holocene to another epoch sometimes referred to as the Anthropocene. On the extensive timescales of geological eons, eras, periods, and epochs, the Holocene emerged much more recently than the K-Pg boundary. It includes the emergence and growth of human civilizations, though not of our hominid species. The beginning of the Holocene, a little less than twelve thousand years ago, is defined primarily on the basis of geological criteria and related changes in climate, sea levels, and so forth. Its emergence, however, is also associated with extinctions. The transition from the preceding Pleistocene epoch corresponds with the decline and disappearance of numerous species, including such large mammals as mammoths and mastodons, woolly rhinoceroses, giant sloths and beavers, various species of large cats and ungulates, and many others. But if the end of the Pleistocene marks the beginning of the Holocene, what would mark the end of the Holocene? According to some scientists, the impact that humans have had already or are having now on the earth's climate, geochemical processes, water cycles, species distributions and extinctions, and so forth "are strong evidence that humankind, our own species, has become so large and active that it now rivals some of the great forces of Nature in its impact on the functioning of the Earth system." Thus they propose the term "Anthropocene" to suggest "that the Earth is now moving out of its current geological epoch" and that "humankind has become a global geological force in its own right."[6]

From the beginning, proposals for an Anthropocene have generated controversy. One set of disagreements involves "the birth of the Anthropocene."[7] When, and on what basis, should one say the Anthropocene epoch started? Paul Crutzen, the Nobel Prize winner credited with coining the term, suggested that it began in the late eighteenth century, on the basis of growing global concentrations of carbon dioxide and methane trapped in polar ice during that era.[8] Alternatively, one can focus on broad processes that go back to the origins of agriculture and its associated manipulation of the environment, or on narrower processes of geologic stratigraphy.[9] Such distinctions are not altogether irrelevant for biblical interpretation, since a decision to associate the beginning of the Anthropocene with the emergence of agriculture would include the world that produced the Bible within the Anthropocene, whereas alternative dates would not. It is striking, in fact, that the ecological theorist Timothy Morton appeals rhetorically to the account of Creation in Genesis 2–3, with its association between the origins of agriculture and God's curse on the ground (3:17–19), to buttress his suggestion that our current ecological crises are grounded in an "agrilogistics" that is continuous with the emergence of Mesopotamian agriculture.[10] But however one understands the origins of the Anthropocene, our contemporary reading of the Bible takes place within it.

If this first set of disagreements about the Anthropocene takes place in rather technical, scientific terms, a second set of controversies involves philosophical and political questions. Nearly all scholars participating in conversations about the Anthropocene acknowledge that we have entered an era when human impacts on the environment, including species extinctions, have reached unprecedented and devastating proportions. To the extent, however, that the term "Anthropocene" implies that the entire human race as such—"Anthropos"—contributes equally to these impacts, it obscures significant differences of geography, historical context, nation, class, race, gender, and so forth that have structured the modern industrial processes that exacerbate ecological destruction. Thus some scholars use the term "Capitalocene" to indicate that current ecological crises were produced less by humanity as such than by the specific processes set in motion by Western industrial capitalism and colonialism.[11]

Not everyone is convinced that this is sufficient reason to dismiss the notion of an Anthropocene. Dipesh Chakrabarty has suggested that, even though capitalism and colonialism played primary roles in getting us into our current ecological crisis, we are now in a species-wide situation of "shared catastrophe" that "cannot be reduced to a story of capitalism":

> While there is no denying that climate change has profoundly to do with the history of capital, a critique that is only a critique of capital is not sufficient for addressing questions relating to human history once the crisis of climate change has been acknowledged and the Anthropocene has begun to loom on the horizon of our present. The geologic now of the Anthropocene has become entangled with the now of human history.[12]

Unfortunately, our conventional ways of narrating history make it difficult for us to grapple with these realities, as Chakrabarty notes. Haraway, on the other hand, points out that a focus on the Anthropocene continues to privilege human exceptionalism, while ignoring the ways in which all of our activities and their consequences are "multispecies" events.[13]

In comparison with discussions about the Anthropocene, there is much less controversy over the reality of anthropogenic species extinctions. There are, to be sure, disagreements about periodization, since extinctions caused in whole or in part by humans may date as far back as the disappearance of Pleistocene megafauna.[14] The word "extinction," too, raises some difficulties: Should we apply the term to the moment when the last surviving individual of a species dies? Or can we only grasp the problem of extinction by noting how many species are in serious decline around the world, with some surviving only in numbers small enough that their continued existence is no longer likely without significant changes in human activity or even direct human intervention?[15] Notwithstanding such disagreements, nearly all researchers agree that animal species as well as plant species are threatened with extinction today on an unusually massive scale. And in nearly every case, such threats are being caused or exacerbated by humans.

Animal Studies, Species Extinctions, and the Importance of Story and Place

But how might animal studies help us read the Bible in the context of species extinctions? Surprisingly, species extinctions do not always receive much attention from scholars associated with animal studies. Framed as a crisis of biodiversity, species extinctions have traditionally been associated more closely with ecology and environmentalism. Although there is clearly some overlap between environmentalism and animal ethics, several tensions have historically separated them as well.[16] On one hand, environmentalists tend to focus on larger ecological systems and species rather than individual animals. On the other hand, thinkers associated with animal ethics sometimes adopt what Clare Palmer calls a "laissez-faire intuition," which she describes as "the idea that, while we have obligations to assist and care for domesticated animals, we have no such obligations toward animals in the wild."[17] Such an approach wishes no harm on wild animals, but it may take the view that the best thing we can do for them is, in the words of the animal rights theorist Tom Regan, "*let them be!*"[18] Regan acknowledges that many wild species face the threat of extinction, but that threat plays little role in his approach to animals. And although many thinkers associated with animal studies argue against the assumptions undergirding Regan's "rights" approach to animals, they sometimes seem equally content to leave the problem of extinctions alone.

A growing number of animal studies scholars, however, are giving more attention to what Deborah Bird Rose calls "the great unmaking of life" taking place today.[19] As a consequence, "extinction studies" has emerged as a shared area of writing and research across disciplines, including the humanities and social sciences.[20] And some of this literature, I want to suggest, offers useful hints for reframing biblical literature in an age of extinctions.

In his moving book *Flight Ways: Life and Loss at the Edge of Extinction*, Thom van Dooren predicts that "in the future—if humanity is here at all—extinction will be among the handful of themes that is understood to be central, perhaps even definitional, of our time."[21] Surprisingly, perhaps, van Dooren suggests that one important skill we need to (re)learn in this time of anthropogenic extinctions is to tell stories. The types of stories we tell, however, make a difference. Stories, after all, "are part of the world, and so they participate in its becoming. As a result, telling stories has consequences: one of which is that we will inevitably be drawn into new connections, and with them new accountabilities and obligations" (10). Storytelling is an ethical practice.

Over the course of five chapters, then, van Dooren tells stories about actual, living birds. But the *types* of stories he tells about these birds are significant. First, writing under the influence of Haraway, van Dooren writes stories that are "multispecies" in nature. The lives and deaths of the birds he writes about are entangled with, and impossible to understand apart from, other living creatures, including the creatures they eat and creatures that eat them. Among the creatures intertwined with the birds are humans: in every case, the birds whose stories van Dooren tells are threatened in some way by human activities. The nature of the threats, however, depends on the particular species of bird, the ways in which that species has evolved, and the specific places in which members of the species live. The threats faced by the albatrosses who unknowingly feed human garbage to their chicks is different from the threats faced by the penguins who search for old nesting grounds in places now inhabited by people, or the vultures who are poisoned by toxins introduced by humans into the dead bodies of animals (including human animals) that vultures scavenge. And the unraveling of life disclosed by van Dooren's stories does not affect only the birds. The disappearance of vultures, for example, increases the risks of disease among humans (especially the poor) and other animals who live with a growing number of corpses that the vultures formerly consumed.

As these examples suggest, van Dooren's stories are attentive not only to the particularities of species and companion species entanglements, but also to the particularities of *place*. Animals, including birds, live in specific places. This means, first of all, that they need space in which to live; and that space must meet the particular needs of the creatures living in it. This is one of the reasons why human-induced habitat loss is a much more significant component of the threats facing many species today than direct killing by humans, which played a larger role in the past. There simply is not enough livable space left for some animals to thrive in their species-specific ways. Some creatures, moreover, like the penguins in one of van Dooren's stories, or many species of sea turtle, are characterized by "site fidelity" (71): they "are philopatric, a term that literally means 'love of one's home' and in biology describes a process in which an animal returns to its place of birth or hatching to reproduce" (70). Thus van Dooren resists focusing exclusively on the notion of "habitat," which implies that any number of spaces sharing a particular type of habitat are interchangeable. Philopatric animals rather experience particular places more like a "home" (80). The animals create the stories of those places, and the animals' stories are created by the places in turn. Story, place, and species survival are inextricably intertwined.

Van Dooren therefore concludes with "a call for stories" (145). We need to learn "to tell different stories" (133), however, since the stories we have been telling do not always recognize that species are shared lives formed by generations of animals interacting and reproducing in particular places. We need to tell stories that take into account the suffering and loss that extinctions entail. We need to tell stories that cause us to ask about our "responsibility *here and now*" for addressing such suffering and loss (147; his emphasis). We need to tell stories that put aside human exceptionalism and refuse to grant too much significance to such distinctions as those between human and animal or, van Dooren notes, between science and the humanities. Van Dooren in fact advocates for new genres of storytelling in the age of anthropogenic extinctions, genres that he associates not only with animal studies but also the "environmental humanities" (147).

But what does this have to do with biblical interpretation? Here I return briefly to Haraway, who not only has influenced van Dooren but has been influenced by him in turn.[22] Like van Dooren, Haraway argues that, in order to find ways of fostering a more habitable, multispecies world, we need to learn to tell better stories involving multiple species in particular places. But if van Dooren's stories transgress the boundaries between science and the humanities and between humans and other animals (as Haraway's stories have done for years),[23] Haraway suggests that our stories need to be even more experimental: "we *must* change the story; the story *must* change" if our multispecies world is to survive and thrive.[24] We need, she tells us, more "speculative fabulation."[25] In the face of challenges associated with the Anthropocene, she turns for resources, not only to stories from science and the humanities, but also to stories from science fiction, visual art, novels, and, significantly for my purposes, myths. Haraway herself is most interested in myths that she calls "great chthonic tales." Although she makes passing references to ancient Near Eastern myths, she has little to say about biblical literature.[26] But it is this turn, or return, to elements of ancient myth, which Haraway recommends as part of her strategy for addressing our contemporary multispecies crises, that brings me back to biblical interpretation.

Retelling the Bible's Multispecies Stories

When Rolston refers to Noah's ark as "the first Endangered Species Project," he also blurs the line between science and the humanities. As Rolston sees it, the "motivation to save endangered species" is not simply "pragmatic, economic, political, and scientific" but also "moral, philosophical, and religious."[27] Although Rolston wishes to improve relations between science and religion, he is not claiming that the Bible is either a scientific document or a religious authority. By recalling the "parable" or "myth" of Noah and the ark, as well as several other biblical texts, Rolston tries rather to remind his readers that the survival of diverse life forms is an ancient value, indeed, an imperative. When God tells Noah to bring into the ark every type of animal, "every living thing, all flesh," God explicitly says this is to "keep them alive" (Gen. 6:19). The story's recognition of the value of all these types of animals, and not simply the ones that are useful to humans, has never been more important than today, Rolston suggests, when "the ancient myth" of mass extermination of animals "has, for the first time ever, become tragic fact." Now, more than ever, we need to remember that Noah "is commanded to save them all" (49). By retelling Noah's story in a time of endangered species, Rolston clearly hopes to remind us of what van Dooren later calls our "responsibility *here and now*": preserving species is our mandate, as it was Noah's.

This narrative emphasis on the survival of diverse forms of animal life is not simply biblical. We know that other ancient societies told similar versions of the Flood story, which included the preservation of all types of living things on a boat.[28] Rolston is not the only writer, moreover, to see in Noah's story a kind of parable for our need to address the plight of endangered species.[29] What I want to suggest here is that this way of retelling the Noah myth should become one part of a larger retelling of the Hebrew Bible's story of animal life. Such a retelling knits together texts from several different parts of the Bible, some of which I have discussed in earlier chapters. By reading these passages alongside one another in conscious response to extinction concerns, we may find to our surprise, not simply a Bible story, but a story about the Bible, that does not entirely support the versions of human exceptionalism that lead us to believe we can do whatever we wish without regard for our impact on other species. We discover, or rediscover, an ancient tradition that underscores the value of animal life in its "heterogeneous multiplicity," to recall Derrida's phrase; that acknowledges the homes of animals in places that are for them, rather than for us; and that casts a negative light on human responsibility for the disappearance of animals.

In such a context, Noah's story would be read, for example, alongside another text that Rolston also discusses: the first account of Creation in Genesis 1:1–2:4a. Among many points of contact between this account and the story of Noah, the most relevant for my purposes here is the shared emphasis on different "kinds" of plants and animals. In 1:12, the earth brings forth "plants yielding seed of every kind, and trees bearing fruit with the seed in it, of every kind." In 1:21 we find "the great sea monsters, and all the living creatures with which the waters swarm, of every kind, and all the winged birds of every kind." In 1:25 we find "living creatures of the earth of every kind, animals of every kind and all the things that creep on the earth of every kind." On two different days, when God looks upon this multiplicity of animals, "God saw that it was good"

(1:21, 25). These multiple "kinds" of animals are the "kinds" that Noah is commanded to keep alive. The Hebrew word for "kinds," *min*, is the same in both stories. The ancient writers who gave us these texts recognized the existence of diverse types of creatures, and they believed that God wanted those diverse types to be preserved.

But the writers also recognized that different types of creatures have to live in many different types of places. In Genesis 1 that recognition takes a very basic form: some creatures live in the waters, some live in the skies, and some move about on the land. This association of different types of animals with different types of spaces is taken further in both Psalm 104 and Job 38–41. There we find birds not only in the skies but in the branches (Ps. 104:12) and the trees (104:16–17). We find wild goats or ibexes in the mountains, and hyraxes among the rocks (104:18). We find wild animals in the forest at night (104:21), and Leviathan in the sea along with other living creatures (104:25–26). We find the wild ass in the plains and the mountains (Job 39:5–8) and the eagle high among the rocks (39:28). Even Behemoth has a place in the river and marsh, underneath the lotus plants (40:21–23). All of this is recognition of habitat, but it is more than that. As if anticipating van Dooren, the Psalmist notes that at least one species of bird, perhaps the stork, has its "home" or "house" in the fir trees, using the same word for "house," *bayit*, that is applied to human houses throughout the Hebrew Bible (Ps. 104:17). Lions, meanwhile, have a "dwelling place," where they lie down during the day (104:22). Many translations render this word "den," here and elsewhere; but a related word from the same root refers multiple times to the "dwelling place" not simply of humans but also of God, as well as of jackals.[30] Lions, jackals, and God all need specific dwelling places. In Job 38:40 as well, the lions are found in a "dwelling place"; while the wild ass has its "house" on the plains in 39:6. In the Bible's story of animals, then, creatures are not only diverse but are located in a wide range of places, often where people are not. And God has given them these places. Rab Judah remarks in a Midrash on Genesis, "It is not written, 'On the high mountains are the wild goats,' but 'The high mountains are for the wild goats.' Thus, for whose sake were the high mountains created? For the sake of the wild goats." As he goes on to note, God created the world even "for the sake of unclean things" (Bereshit Rabbah 12.9). Rab Judah's reading of Psalm 104 seems to conclude that God did not create the world only for us, with animals in the background. God created the various spaces of the world for diverse species of the world. We have our place, but it is one place among many.

Anticipating van Dooren again, the biblical texts that contribute to this story recognize that animals have stories, too. They look for food and drink (Ps. 104:11, 14, 21, 27; Job 38:39–41; 39:8, 29; 40:15, 20), avoid humans (Job 39:7), and laugh or play (Ps. 104:26; Job 39:18, 22; 40:20). They even cry out to God for food, as we see, for example, with roaring lions in Psalm 104:21 and young birds in Job 38:41. Like van Dooren's birds, they are often busy giving birth or tending their young (Job 38:41; 39:1–3, 14, 30). These young go on to live their own lives (39:4), contributing to the continuation of their kind that is essential for the survival of species. And this is as it should be, according to the Bible's story; for God has explicitly commanded them from the beginning to "be fruitful and multiply," "filling" both "the waters in the seas" and "the earth" (Gen. 1:22). The ongoing proliferation of animal life, in its "heterogeneous multiplicity," is thus mandated. It is therefore no wonder that, as we saw in chapter 6, the animals praise God (Ps. 148:7–10).

Now the story I have begun to retell, here and in the last couple of chapters, is *a* story about the Hebrew Bible and animal lives. It presents an alternative to more common ways of narrating the Bible's story, which focus on human "dominion" and "the image of God" (Gen. 1:26–27) to such an extent that our right to do whatever we wish with animals, and to do whatever we want for ourselves even at the risk of extinguishing animal kinds, is implicitly or explicitly justified. In telling the story this way, I do not want to be understood as denying that other stories about the Bible exist.

On the other hand, it is worth asking whether the story of the Bible I am retelling can account for features of the texts that some readers find troubling. For example, some ecological readers of the Bible express reservations about the story of Noah because it is not simply a story about the preservation of animal kinds, but also a story of death. God does, after all, kill many more people and animals than are saved on Noah's ark.[31] And it is true, as we have seen, that many biblical texts, including this one, represent God in frightening, perhaps even beastly, ways. But the story I am retelling here is not a theodicy, an attempt to justify some version of God in the face of suffering and evil. It is rather an account of the importance of preserving species, including the human species, even in situations where individual humans and animals die.

Moreover, it is not irrelevant to my "fabulation" (to recall Haraway's word) that mass death takes place in the story precisely because the earth has been "corrupted" and "filled with violence" (Gen. 6:11). Other biblical texts also associate the deaths of animals and plants with human violence. In Jeremiah 12:1, for example, the writer complains that those who act treacherously are thriving. But the impact of their misconduct does not fall only on other humans. In verse 4, the writer articulates something like a lament for the land and the life that should thrive on it. "How long," Jeremiah asks, "will the land mourn, and the vegetation throughout the field dry up? Because of the wickedness of those who live in it, the animals and the birds are swept away." Using a word for "wickedness" that is also applied to humans in the story of Noah (Gen. 6:5), and a word for the "land" that is identical to the "earth" "corrupted" in Genesis 6:11, the writer here understands the desolation of the earth and the disappearance of animals and birds to be consequences of human evil. He sees animals and birds being extinguished, and this is evidence that humans are acting immorally. Jeremiah 9:10, as well, articulates a lament for creation in the context of a devastation of Judah that has come about because of the transgressions of the people who live there. In addition to weeping for "mountains" and "pastures," the verse notes that "the voice of cattle is not heard, the birds of the skies and the animals have fled and are gone." A similar understanding appears in Hosea 4:3, where the prophet, after listing a series of human evils, exclaims, "Therefore the land [or 'earth'] mourns, and everything that lives on it withers. Also the living creatures of the field and the birds in the skies, and even the fish in the sea are disappearing!" Such texts understand human wickedness to be responsible, ultimately, for the vanishing of animals and birds.

This understanding of the disappearance of animals can be read back into the story of Noah as well. God may be the narrative agent of destruction in the Flood and in some of these other passages, but human actions are still the cause (Gen. 6:5–7, 11–13). The cumulative effect of human activity is a massive death of animals, including humans. And in this context, God commands Noah to take action to keep animal species alive.

But how far can we push the story I am telling? Could human responsibility for animal life be used to reinterpret even such notions as "the image of God"? It is a tempting possibility. Although many interpretations have been offered for the biblical understanding of "the image of God," it has managed to outfox scholars who have tried to capture it exegetically.[32] But if God creates all kinds of animals and demands their preservation, it is not hard to imagine that those who narratively embody the image of *that* God would orient their lives around this same priority. Far from being a justification for the rampant destruction of the earth and its species for our temporary benefit, this ancient belief that humans in some way represent God might have been interpreted as a call to radical ecological stewardship.

I do not choose that term, "stewardship," lightly. It is striking that the term "stewardship," which has long been debated among religious advocates for environmental responsibility, has recently resurfaced outside of religion among scholars wrestling with implications of living in the Anthropocene. "Earth stewardship in the Anthropocene" has been identified as a goal by scholars from a range of disciplines who are trying to figure out how, in a world structured by diverse cultures, traditions, histories, multispecies relations, and power relations among humans, we can respond to the catastrophic effects of human disruption of the environment.[33] If it is already the case that our activities are reshaping the earth and contributing to the disappearance of species, would it not be a positive step, we might ask, to own "our capacity to affect creation,"[34] and redirect our actions as stewards of a world created by a God in whose image we are likewise believed to be created?

In spite of these considerations, it is not at all clear that a plot emphasizing the creation of humans "in the image of God" will ultimately go far enough in "changing the story" to the extent that Haraway believes "the story *must* change." For although twenty-first century readers might understand this ancient notion of an "image of God" in many different ways, its implication of priority over other living creatures—and of God-given, ontological priority—seems likely to encourage the very human exceptionalism that has led to our extinction crises in the first place. Indeed, it is important to acknowledge that textual features celebrating the flourishing of animals and animal kinds are inextricably intertwined throughout these biblical myths with other features that, while perhaps useful in the ancient Near East, are easily exploited by the Bible's contemporary readers to justify inattention to species extinctions. The problem is not limited to "the image of God."

Consider, for example, the aftermath of the Flood. When the waters recede, "all the living creatures, and all the creeping things, and all the birds, everything that moves on the earth, went out by clans from the ark" (Gen. 8:19). The language here, like much biblical material we have seen, arguably destabilizes distinctions between humans and animals, since the word used for animal "clans" is used throughout the Hebrew Bible for human clans or families. And this destabilization continues in Genesis 9, where God makes a covenant not simply with humans but with "every living creature who is with you, with the birds, with the animals, and with all the living things of the earth who came with you out of the ark, every living thing of the earth" (9:10).

Between these two texts, however, another passage intrudes:

God blessed Noah and his sons and said to them, "Increase [or 'be fruitful'] and multiply, and fill the earth. Fear and dread of you will be on all the living creatures of the earth and on all the birds of the skies and on all that creeps on the ground and on all the fish of the sea. Into your hand they are given. Every moving thing that lives will be food for you. As I gave you green plants, it is all for you." (9:1–3)

The consequences of endless repetitions of such a passage, with its emphases on human population growth and eating animals, seem troubling indeed in an age of extinctions. No wonder the animals dread us.

There are, of course, few questions as volatile as the question of human overpopulation. Many progressives who in principle support environmental and animal concerns resist suggestions that human overpopulation is an ecological problem. Such suggestions are dismissed, partly for good reasons, as insensitive to, or even complicit with, histories of eugenics or other measures taken against reproduction among the poor, nonwhites, and the colonized. The problem, it is argued, is not population growth but the Euro-American exploitation of the earth's resources. Yet a growing number of environmentalists point out that, while uneven distribution of resources certainly needs to be addressed, the ecological consequences of having nine billion humans or more on the planet by the end of the twenty-first century are potentially devastating.[35] Even if the earth's carrying capacity makes it possible to support a larger human population, our continued growth and demands on earth's resources, including places where other animals live, are rapidly eliminating possibilities for many species to survive into the future. Partly in response, Haraway has recently proposed the provocative slogan "Make kin, not babies," as part of her project of telling new stories. One of her goals in coining such a slogan is "to unravel the ties of both genealogy and kin, and kin and species," allowing for multispecies—and not simply human species—flourishing overall.[36] Whether her slogan will find an audience is unclear, though it makes a good pairing with queer, feminist, and other reorganizations of kinship. But it reminds us that religious admonitions for humans to fill the earth are not helpful for telling new stories in an age of extinctions.

Unhelpful, too, is any religious encouragement to eat more animals. In the context of animal studies, questions about meat tend to focus on the cruelty that our modern system of animal agriculture visits on the billions of individual domesticated animals we eat, an important concern noted several times in earlier chapters. But diets that are heavy on meat are not simply cruel to the animals we raise on industrial farms. They also contribute directly to environmental destruction through such mechanisms as deforestation, habitat modification, chemical degradations of the environment, and climate change; and all of these same dynamics contribute to the extinctions of species.[37]

My point in raising these contemporary controversies is clearly not to resolve them here. Nor am I interested in launching an easy critique of biblical texts. The ancient writers who gave us those texts could not have imagined either our tremendous population growth or the horrors of contemporary factory farming. They were writing about the world they saw around them, not the one we inhabit. They likely never imagined it was possible for entire kinds of animals, whom they believed were created and considered good by God, to be wiped out, though they clearly recognized sinister implications in the disappearance of animals (Jer.12:1; Hos. 4:3). We, on the other hand, are increasingly aware of both the disappearance of species and the ways in which our actions are causing such disappearance. And that awareness should have an impact on our response to van Dooren's reminder of the "responsibility *here and now*" associated with the stories we tell. If "telling stories has consequences," as van Dooren argues, then it would be an evasion of responsibility to ignore the ways in which components of biblical stories lend themselves to plots that contribute to the disappearance of animal species.

Rather than emphasizing biblical texts that reaffirm human exceptionalism, we might focus instead on the interdependence of human and animal life presupposed by numerous other passages discussed throughout this book. Such passages include the scenes of devastation in the Flood story and in such books as Jeremiah and Hosea noted above, as well as multiple passages discussed in chapter 6. In these and other texts, the welfare of humans and the welfare of animals are inextricably intertwined. If our fates are linked to the fates of animals, as the Bible already recognizes, this is partly because, as Judith Butler notes, "the human animal is itself an animal. This is not an assertion concerning the type or species of animal the human is, but an avowal that animality is a precondition of the human, and there is no human who is not a human animal."[38] It might seem surprising to invoke Butler in this context, since the relevance of her influential writings for animal studies is contested.[39] But even if Butler is more focused on human than nonhuman life, she offers the phrase "precarious life" partly to provide what she calls "a non-anthropocentric framework for considering what makes life valuable."[40] One of her goals in using the term "precarious" is to suggest that violence can never be overcome if we pretend that vulnerability is an accidental feature of life. All of us are necessarily situated in a series of interdependent relationships to others, without which we can't survive. Those relationships make us who we are, but they also make us vulnerable to suffering.[41] Such relationships are not limited to our intimate relationships, though these are included. We exist in webs of relations that make up our neighborhoods, our cities, our religious traditions and other associations, our nations, and even—as the example of climate change shows—our entire earth. For we depend upon "a sustained and sustainable environment." This interdependence necessarily makes our lives precarious. And as Butler notes, "non-human life is also precarious life and . . . precariousness links human and non-human life in ethically significant ways."[42] For as Haraway's work reminds us, what Butler calls "precarious life" is inevitably a multispecies phenomenon. In a time of extinction, then, we do well to retell the Bible's story in ways that emphasize the interdependence of our precarious lives with those of other animals, rather than reaffirming human exceptionalism.

And in a time of extinction, it would be an evasion of responsibility to ignore the ancient demand to "keep alive" (Gen. 6:20) the diverse kinds of life that share the earth with us. Along with that demand, we need to remember biblical texts that, as we have seen, call attention with awe to striking features of various types of animal life, the specific places they use as homes, the ways in which they eat and are eaten, the ways in which they care for their young, and the sounds that they make. We may or may not any longer interpret such phenomena as evidence for a deity's provision of food, place, offspring, and salvation to this "heterogeneous multiplicity" of creatures, as some of the biblical writers did. But by learning to retell in new ways the stories of those who heard in the lion's roar, and the calls of young birds, a cry to God for food, we may find ourselves taking greater responsibility for ensuring that such cries do not disappear from the earth.

Notes

INTRODUCTION

1. Barbara J. King, *Being With Animals: Why We Are Obsessed with the Furry, Scaly, Feathered Creatures Who Populate Our World* (New York: Doubleday, 2010), 18; her emphasis. See also Pat Shipman, *The Animal Connection: A New Perspective on What Makes Us Human* (New York: Norton, 2011).

2. Barbara J. King, *Evolving God: A Provocative View on the Origins of Religion* (New York: Doubleday, 2007), 26.

3. On this distinction and its influence in biblical scholarship, see Theodore Hiebert, *The Yahwist's Landscape: Nature and Religion in Early Israel* (1996; Minneapolis: Fortress Press, 2008), 3–22.

4. Mary Douglas, *Purity and Danger: An Analysis of the Concepts of Pollution and Taboo* (1966; New York: Routledge, 2002), chapter 3, "The Abominations of Leviticus."

5. Walter Houston, *Purity and Monotheism: Clean and Unclean Animals in Biblical Law* (Sheffield, Eng.: Sheffield Academic Press, 1993); id., "What was the Meaning of Classifying Animals as Clean or Unclean?" in Andrew Linzey and Dorothy Yamamoto, eds., *Animals on the Agenda* (Urbana: University of Illinois Press, 1998).

6. See, e.g., Paula Wapnish and Brian Hesse, "Faunal Remains from Tel Dan: Perspectives on Animal Production at a Village, Urban, and Ritual Center," *Archaeozoologia* 4/2 (1991): 9–86; id., "Archaeozoology," in Suzanne Richard, ed., *Near Eastern Archaeology: A Reader* (Winona Lake, IN: Eisenbrauns, 2003); Brian Hesse, "Animal Husbandry and Human Diet in the Ancient Near East," in Jack Sasson, ed., *Civilizations of the Ancient Near East*, vol. 1 (New York: Simon & Schuster, 1995); "Animal Husbandry," in Eric Meyers, ed., *The Oxford Encyclopedia of Archaeology in the Near East* (Oxford: Oxford University Press, 1996); Melinda Zeder, "Sheep and Goats," in Myers, *Oxford Encyclopedia of Archaeology in the Near East*; Oded Borowski, *Every Living Thing: Daily Use of Animals in Ancient Israel* (Walnut Creek, CA: AltaMira Press, 1998); Philip J. King and Lawrence E. Stager, *Life in Biblical Israel* (Louisville: Westminster John Knox Press, 2001), 112–22; Brian Hesse and Paula Wapnish, "An Archaeozoological

Perspective on the Cultural Use of Mammals in the Levant," in Billie Jean Collins, ed., *A History of the Animal World in the Ancient Near East* (Leiden: Brill, 2002); Aharon Sasson, "The Pastoral Component of the Economy of Hill Country Sites in the Intermediate Bronze and Iron Ages: Archaeo-Ethnographic Studies," *Tel Aviv* 25 (1998): 3–51; id., "Reassessing the Bronze and Iron Age Economy: Sheep and Goat Husbandry in the Southern Levant as a Model Case Study," in Israel Finkelstein, Assaf Yasur-Landau, and Alexander Fantalkin, eds., *Bene Israel: Studies in the Archaeology of Israel and the Levant During the Bronze and Iron Ages in Honour of Israel Finkelstein* (Leiden: Brill, 2008); id., *Animal Husbandry in Ancient Israel: A Zooarchaeological Perspective on Livestock Exploitation, Herd Management and Economic Strategies* (Oakville, CT: Equinox, 2010). There also exist many technical reports on specific archaeological sites. For useful discussions of zooarchaeology from outside of biblical and ancient Near Eastern studies, see esp. Nerissa Russell, *Social Zooarchaeology: Humans and Animals in Prehistory* (Cambridge: Cambridge University Press, 2012); and Naomi Scott, *Beastly Questions: Animal Answers to Archaeological Issues* (London: Bloomsbury, 2014). Zooarchaeological evidence also needs to be interpreted, of course, and the conclusions scholars draw from it are diverse. For two quite different uses of zooarchaeological evidence by biblical scholars, compare Nathan MacDonald, *What Did the Ancient Israelites Eat?* (Grand Rapids, MI: Eerdmans, 2008) with Roland Boer, *The Sacred Economy of Ancient Israel* (Louisville: Westminster John Knox Press, 2015).

7. An impressive example is Brent Strawn, *What Is Stronger than a Lion? Leonine Image and Metaphor in the Hebrew Bible and the Ancient Near East* (Göttingen: Vandenhoeck & Ruprecht, 2005). See also Tova L. Forti, *Animal Imagery in the Book of Proverbs* (Leiden: Brill, 2008); Kenneth C. Way, *Donkeys in the Biblical World: Ceremony and Symbol* (Winona Lake, IN: Eisenbrauns, 2011); Benjamin A. Foreman, *Animal Metaphors and the People of Israel in the Book of Jeremiah* (Göttingen: Vandenhoeck & Ruprecht, 2011); Phillip Michael Sherman, "Animals," in Brent A. Strawn, ed., *The Oxford Encyclopedia of the Bible and Law* (Oxford: Oxford University Press, 2015); and for an early, underappreciated discussion of Israel's animal symbolism, Howard Eilberg-Schwartz, *The Savage in Judaism: An Anthropology of Israelite Religion and Ancient Judaism* (Bloomington: Indiana University Press, 1990), 115–40.

8. See, e.g., Gene M. Tucker, "Rain on a Land Where No One Lives: The Hebrew Bible on the Environment," *Journal of Biblical Literature* 116/1 (1997): 3–17; id., "The Peaceable Kingdom and a Covenant with the Wild Animals," in William P. Brown and S. Dean McBride, eds., *God Who Creates: Essays in Honor of W. Sibley Towner* (Grand Rapids, MI: Eerdmans, 2000); Richard Bauckham, *The Bible and Ecology* (Waco, TX: Baylor University Press, 2010); id., *Living With Other Creatures: Green Exegesis and Theology* (Waco, TX: Baylor University

Press, 2011); Patricia K. Tull, *Inhabiting Eden: Christians, the Bible, and the Ecological Crisis* (Louisville: Westminster John Knox Press, 2013), 91–108; and several of the essays in Norman C. Habel and Peter Trudinger, eds., *Exploring Ecological Hermeneutics* (Atlanta: Society of Biblical Literature, 2008).

9. Two volumes of essays that each include several articles by biblical scholars who explicitly engage contemporary animal studies are Stephen D. Moore, ed., *Divinanimality: Animal Theory, Creaturely Theology* (New York: Fordham University Press, 2014); and Jennifer Koosed, ed., *The Bible and Posthumanism* (Atlanta: Society of Biblical Literature, 2014). For an earlier, and often overlooked, contribution by a biblical scholar who takes into account scholarship about animals being done elsewhere in the humanities, see Heather A. McKay, "Through the Eyes of Horses: Representation of the Horse Family in the Hebrew Bible," in Alastair G. Hunter and Philip R. Davies, eds., *Sense and Sensitivity: Essays on Reading the Bible in Memory of Robert Carroll* (Sheffield, Eng.: Sheffield Academic Press, 2002).

10. The phrase "animal turn" is used explicitly, e.g., by Kari Weil, *Thinking Animals: Why Animal Studies Now?* (New York: Columbia University Press, 2012), 3–24. It has been picked up in biblical studies by Stephen D. Moore, "Introduction: From Animal Theory to Creaturely Theology," in Moore, ed. *Divinanimality*, 1–16. Michigan State University Press is publishing an entire series under the title The Animal Turn, edited by Linda Kaloff. In addition to Weil, other useful introductions to contemporary animal studies include Erica Fudge, *Animal* (London: Reaktion Books, 2002); Cary Wolfe, *Animal Rites: American Culture, the Discourse of Species, and Posthumanist Theory* (Chicago: Chicago University Press, 2003); id., "Human, All Too Human: 'Animal Studies' and the Humanities," *PMLA* 124/2 (2009): 564–75; Marianne DeKoven, "Guest Column: Why Animals Now?" *PMLA* 124/2 (2009): 361–69; Margo DeMello, *Animals and Society: An Introduction to Human–Animal Studies* (New York: Columbia University Press, 2012); Dawne McCance, *Critical Animal Studies: An Introduction* (Albany: State University of New York Press, 2013); Paul Waldau, *Animal Studies: An Introduction* (Oxford: Oxford University Press, 2013); Garry Marvin and Susan McHugh, eds., *Routledge Handbook of Human–Animal Studies* (New York: Routledge, 2014); and Matthew Calarco, *Thinking through Animals: Identity, Difference, Indistinction* (Stanford: Stanford University Press, 2015). Many other specialized studies and collections of essays also provide orientations to the field.

11. See, e.g., Paul Waldau and Kimberly Patton, eds., *A Communion of Subjects: Animals in Religion, Science, and Ethics* (New York: Columbia University Press, 2006); Celia Deane-Drummond and David Clough, eds., *Creaturely Theology: On God, Humans and Other Animals* (London: SCM Press, 2009); Celia Deane-Drummon, Rebecca Artinian-Kaiser, and David L. Clough, eds., *Animals as Religious Subjects: Transdisciplinary Perspectives* (London: Bloomsbury,

2013); Aaron S. Gross, *The Question of the Animal and Religion: Theoretical Stakes, Practical Implications* (New York: Columbia University Press, 2015); Donovan O. Schaefer, *Religious Affects: Animality, Evolution, and Power* (Durham, NC: Duke University Press, 2015). A much larger body of literature than this is devoted to the roles of, and attitudes toward, animals in various religious traditions, and to possibilities for rethinking those roles and attitudes.

12. Linda Kalof and Georgina M. Montgomery, eds., *Making Animal Meaning* (East Lansing: Michigan State University Press, 2011).

13. Claude Lévi-Strauss, *Totemism*, trans. Rodney Needham (Boston: Beacon Press, 1963), 89.

14. Helpful resources on animal ethics include Susan J. Armstrong and Richard G. Botzler, *The Animal Ethics Reader*, 2nd ed. (New York: Routledge, 2003); Clare Palmer, *Animal Ethics in Context* (New York: Columbia University Press, 2010); Lori Gruen, *Ethics and Animals: An Introduction* (Cambridge: Cambridge University Press, 2011); id., *Entangled Empathy: An Alternative Ethic for Our Relationships with Animals* (New York: Lantern Books, 2015); Tom L. Beauchamp and R. G. Frey, eds., *The Oxford Handbook of Animal Ethics* (Oxford: Oxford University Press, 2015); and Calarco, *Thinking through Animals*.

15. Among many sources, see, e.g., Gross, *Question of the Animal and Religion*; Ted Genoways, *The Chain: Farm, Factory, and the Fate of Our Food* (New York: Harper, 2014); Timothy Pachirat, *Every Twelve Seconds: Industrialized Slaughter and the Politics of Sight* (New Haven, CT: Yale University Press, 2011); Daniel Imhoff, ed., *The CAFO Reader: The Tragedy of Industrial Animal Factories* (Healdsburg, CA: Watershed Media; Berkeley: University of California Press [distributor], 2010); Jonathan Safran Foer, *Eating Animals* (New York: Little, Brown, 2009); Steve Striffler, *Chicken: The Dangerous Transformation of America's Fast Food* (New Haven, CT: Yale University Press, 2005); Matthew Scully, *Dominion: The Power of Man, the Suffering of Animals, and the Call to Mercy* (New York: St. Martin's Press, 2002), 247–86; Peter Singer, *Animal Liberation*, 3rd ed. (New York: HarperCollins, 2002), 95–183.

16. See, e.g., sources cited in chapter 7.

17. See, e.g., sources cited in chapter 6.

18. Ken Stone, *Practicing Safer Texts: Food, Sex and Bible in Queer Perspective* (London: T&T Clark, 2005), 23–45. See also Dale B. Martin, *Sex and the Single Savior: Gender and Sexuality in Biblical Interpretation* (Louisville: Westminster John Knox Press, 2006).

19. See, e.g., my "Gender Criticism: The Un-Manning of Abimelech," in Gale Yee, ed., *Judges and Method: New Approaches in Biblical Studies*, 2nd ed. (Minneapolis: Fortress Press, 2007); and "Queer Criticism," in Steven L. McKenzie and John Kaltner, eds., *New Meanings for Ancient Texts: Biblical Criticisms and Their Applications* (Louisville: Westminster John Knox Press, 2013).

20. Stephen D. Moore and Yvonne Sherwood, *The Invention of the Biblical Scholar: A Critical Manifesto* (Minneapolis: Fortress Press, 2011), 31.
21. DeMello, *Animals and Society*, 4–5.
22. Waldau, *Animal Studies*, 1, 10.
23. DeMello, *Animals and Society*, 19.
24. See, e.g., Athalya Brenner, *I Am . . . : Biblical Women Tell Their Own Stories* (Minneapolis: Fortress Press, 2004).
25. Weil, *Thinking Animals*, 6–7.
26. See, e.g. sources cited in chapter 6.
27. See esp., on this complex point, the work of Cary Wolfe, including *Animal Rites*; "Human, All Too Human"; *What Is Posthumanism?* (Minneapolis: University of Minnesota Press, 2010); and "Humane Advocacy and the Humanities: The Very Idea," in Marianne DeKoven and Michael Lundblad, *Species Matters: Humane Advocacy and Cultural Theory* (New York: Columbia University Press, 2012).
28. Calarco, *Thinking through Animals*. Page numbers cited parenthetically below in the text discussion refer to this source. For a review of Calarco's book that expands on the points made here, see Ken Stone, "How Do We Think Human/Animal Differences?" *Marginalia Review of Books*, March 14, 2016. http://marginalia.lareviewofbooks.org/how-do-we-think-humananimal-differences-by-ken-stone.
29. Singer, *Animal Liberation*; Tom Regan, *The Case for Animal Rights: Updated with a New Preface* (Berkeley: University of California Press, 2004); Paola Cavalieri, *The Animal Question: Why Nonhuman Animals Deserve Human Rights* (New York: Oxford University Press, 2001).
30. Paola Cavalieri and Peter Singer, eds., *The Great Ape Project: Equality beyond Humanity* (London: Fourth Estate, 1993).
31. Calarco, *Thinking through Animals*, 28.
32. Jacques Derrida, *The Animal That Therefore I Am*, ed. Marie-Louise Mallet, trans. David Wills (New York: Fordham University Press, 2008), esp. 3–18.
33. For an excellent example of a feminist philosophical study of animals written in dialogue with Derrida and emphasizing difference, see Kelly Oliver, *Animal Lessons: How They Teach Us to Be Human* (New York: Columbia University Press, 2009).
34. On the complex relations among animal-oriented critical theory, advocacy for animals, and advocacy for marginalized humans, see DeKoven and Lundblad, eds., *Species Matters*.
35. Calarco, *Thinking through Animals*, 45.
36. Giorgio Agamben, *The Open: Man and Animal*, trans. Kevin Attell (Stanford: Stanford University Press, 2004).
37. Calarco, *Thinking through Animals*, 53–54.
38. Ibid., 60. See Plumwood's essay "Being Prey," in James O'Reilly, Sean O'Reilly, and Richard Sterling, eds., *The Ultimate Journey: Inspiring Stories of*

Living and Dying (San Francisco: Travelers' Tales, 2000). Calarco also refers to Plumwood's essay in "We Are Made of Meat: Interview with Matthew Calarco" (2012), http://arzone.ning.com/profiles/blogs/we-are-made-of-meat-the-matthew-calarco-interview.

39. See also Plumwood's *Environmental Culture: The Ecological Crisis of Reason* (New York: Routledge, 2002).

40. Mel Y. Chen, *Animacies: Biopolitics, Racial Mattering, and Queer Affect* (Durham, NC: Duke University Press, 2012), 2.

41. Judith Halberstam, *Female Masculinity* (Durham, NC: Duke University Press, 1998), 13; my emphasis.

42. Ken Stone, "Wittgenstein's Lion and Balaam's Ass: Talking with Others in Numbers 22–25," in Koosed, ed., *Bible and Posthumanism*.

43. Aaron Gross, "Introduction and Overview: Animal Others and Animal Studies," in Aaron Gross and Anne Vallely, eds., *Animals and the Human Imagination: A Companion to Animal Studies* (New York: Columbia University Press, 2012), 5.

44. Holmes Rolston III, "Creation: God and Endangered Species," in Ke Chung Kim and Robert D. Weaver, eds., *Biodiversity and Landscapes* (Cambridge: Cambridge University Press, 1994), 48.

45. Gross, *Question of the Animal and Religion*, 13.

CHAPTER 1

1. Gila Kahila Bar-Gal, Charles Greenblatt, Scott R. Woodward, Magen Broshi, and Patricia Smith, "The Genetic Signature of the Dead Sea Scrolls," in David Goodblatt, Avital Pinnick, and Daniel R. Schwartz, eds., *Historical Perspectives: From the Hasmoneans to Bar Kokhba in Light of the Dead Sea Scrolls* (Leiden: Brill, 2001), 165–71.

2. See Gavin Moorhead, "Parchment Assessment of the Codex Sinaiticus," http://codexsinaiticus.org/en/project/conservation_parchment.aspx.

3. See Menahem Haran, "Bible Scrolls in Eastern and Western Jewish Communities from Qumran to the High Middle Ages," *Hebrew Union College Annual* 56 (1985): 21–62.

4. Menahem Haran, "Book-Scrolls at the Beginning of the Second Temple Period: The Transition from Papyrus to Skins," *Hebrew Union College Annual* 54 (1983): 112.

5. Agamben, *The Open*, 1–3.

6. Except where otherwise noted, translations from Hebrew are my own.

7. Gross, "Introduction and Overview," in id. and Vallely, eds., *Animals and the Human Imagination*, 1.

8. Susan Niditch, *"My Brother Esau Is a Hairy Man": Hair and Identity in Ancient Israel* (New York: Oxford University Press, 2008).

9. Gregory Mobley, "The Wild Man in the Bible and the Ancient Near East," *Journal of Biblical Literature* 116/2 (1997): 217–33.

10. On the challenge of translating Dinah's sexual shaming into English, see Lyn M. Bechtel, "What If Dinah Is Not Raped? (Genesis 34)," *Journal for the Study of the Old Testament* 62 (1994): 19–36.

11. See, e.g., Victor H. Matthews and Don C. Benjamin, *Social World of Ancient Israel 1250–1587 BCE* (Peabody, MA: Hendrickson, 1993), 52–66.

12. Portions of this reading of Jacob's story can be found in shorter form in Ken Stone, "Animating the Bible's Animals," in Danna Nolan Fewell, ed., *The Oxford Handbook of Biblical Narrative* (New York: Oxford University Press, 2016).

13. Donna Haraway, *When Species Meet* (Minneapolis: University of Minnesota Press, 2008), 73. See also Haraway, *The Companion Species Manifesto: Dogs, People, and Significant Otherness* (Chicago: Prickly Paradigm Press, 2003).

14. See, among many relevant sources, Juliet Clutton-Brock, *A Natural History of Domesticated Animals* (Austin: University of Texas Press, 1987); "How Domestic Animals Have Shaped the Development of Human Societies," in Linda Kalof, ed., *A Cultural History of Animals in Antiquity*, vol. 1 (New York: Berg, 2007); *Animals as Domesticates: A World View through History* (East Lansing: Michigan State University Press, 2012), 47–69; Paula Wapnish and Brian Hesse, "Faunal Remains from Tel Dan: Perspectives on Animal Production at a Village, Urban, and Ritual Center," *Archaeozoologia* 4/2 (1991): 9–86; "Archaeozoology," in Suzanne Richard, ed., *Near Eastern Archaeology: A Reader* (Winona Lake, IN: Eisenbrauns, 2003); Brian Hesse, "Animal Husbandry and Human Diet in the Ancient Near East," in Jack Sasson, ed., *Civilizations of the Ancient Near East*, vol. 1 (New York: Simon & Schuster, 1995); "Animal Husbandry," in Eric Meyers, ed., *The Oxford Encyclopedia of Archaeology in the Near East* (New York: Oxford University Press, 1996); Melinda Zeder, "Sheep and Goats," in Myers, *Oxford Encyclopedia of Archaeology in the Near East*; Oded Borowski, *Every Living Thing: Daily Use of Animals in Ancient Israel* (Walnut Creek, CA: AltaMira Press, 1998), 39–71; Philip J. King and Lawrence E. Stager, *Life in Biblical Israel* (Louisville: Westminster John Knox Press, 2001), 112–22; Brian Hesse and Paula Wapnish, "An Archaeozoological Perspective on the Cultural Use of Mammals in the Levant," in Collins, ed., *History of the Animal World in the Ancient Near East*; Aharon Sasson, "The Pastoral Component of the Economy of Hill Country Sites in the Intermediate Bronze and Iron Ages: Archaeo-Ethnographic Studies," *Tel Aviv* 25 (1998): 3–51; id., "Reassessing the Bronze and Iron Age Economy: Sheep and Goat Husbandry in the Southern Levant as a Model Case Study," in Israel Finkelstein, Assaf Yasur-Landau, and Alexander Fantalkin, eds., *Bene Israel: Studies in the Archaeology of Israel and the Levant during the Bronze and Iron Ages in Honour of Israel Finkelstein* (Leiden: Brill, 2008); id., *Animal Husbandry in*

Ancient Israel; MacDonald, *What Did the Ancient Israelites Eat?*; and Boer, *Sacred Economy of Ancient Israel*. On the broader cultural and historical significance of goats and sheep, see Joy Hinson, *Goat* (London: Reaktion Books, 2015), and Philip Armstrong, *Sheep* (London: Reaktion Books, 2016).

15. Sasson, "Reassessing the Bronze and Iron Age Economy," and *Animal Husbandry in Ancient Israel*.

16. Sasson, *Animal Husbandry in Ancient Israel*, 21.

17. This estimate is difficult to make for the ancient world, but the model that produces it comes from Aharon Sasson, "The Pastoral Component in the Economy of Hill Country Sites." Cf. Baruch Rosen, "Subsistence Economy in Iron Age I," in Israel Finkelstein and Nadav Na'aman, eds., *From Nomadism to Monarchy: Archaeological and Historical Aspects of Early Israel* (Jerusalem: Israel Exploration Society, 1994). For a summary of, and critical reflection on, both Sasson and Rosen, see MacDonald, *What Did the Ancient Israelites Eat*, 43–9.

18. See, e.g., Num. 27:17; 2 Sam. 5:2; 7:7–8; 1 Kgs 22:17; Pss. 23:1–4; 44:12, 23; 74:1; Isa. 56: 9–12; Jer. 3:15; 6:3; 10:21; 12:3, 10; 13:20; 23:1–8; 25:34–38; Ezek. 34; Zech. 11:4–17.

19. Calarco, *Thinking through Animals*, 6.

20. For convenient examples of Derrida's influence on the study of religion, see Yvonne Sherwood and Kevin Hart, eds., *Derrida and Religion: Other Testaments* (New York: Routledge, 2004); and Yvonne Sherwood, ed., *Derrida's Bible: Reading a Page of Scripture with a Little Help from Derrida* (New York: Palgrave Macmillan, 2004).

21. Derrida, *Animal That Therefore I Am*. Although Derrida refers to animals in many other writings, they receive particular attention in *The Beast and the Sovereign*, 2 vols., trans. Geoffrey Bennington (Chicago: University of Chicago Press, 2009–11); "'Eating Well,' or the Calculation of the Subject," in Elizabeth Weber, ed., *Points . . . : Interviews, 1974–1994*, trans. Peggy Kamuf et al. (Stanford: Stanford University Press, 1995); and "Violence against Animals," in Derrida and Elisabeth Roudinesco, *For What Tomorrow . . . : A Dialogue*, trans. Jeff Fort (Stanford: Stanford University Press, 2004). Among many discussions of Derrida's animal writings, see Calarco, *Thinking through Animals*; id., *Zoographies: The Question of the Animal from Heidegger to Derrida* (New York: Columbia University Press, 2008), 103–49; Cary Wolfe, *Animal Rites*; Michael Naas, "Derrida's Flair (For the Animals to Follow . . .)," *Philosophy Today* 40 (2010): 219–42; David Farrell Krell, *Derrida and Our Animal Others* (Bloomington: Indiana University Press, 2013); Judith Still, *Derrida and Other Animals: The Boundaries of the Human* (Edinburgh: University of Edinburgh Press, 2015); from the side of religious studies, Gross, *Question of the Animal and Religion*, 121–46; and from the side of biblical studies, Stephen D. Moore, "Introduction: From Animal Theory to Creaturely Theology," in Moore, ed., *Divinanimality*.

22. Derrida, "Violence against Animals," 66.

23. Derrida, *Animal That Therefore I Am*, 30.

24. Derrida, "'Eating Well,' or the Calculation of the Subject," 278.

25. Andrew Linzey and Dan Cohn-Sherbok, *After Noah: Animals and the Liberation of Theology* (Herndon, VA: Mowbray, 1997), 19.

26. Hiebert, *Yahwist's Landscape*, 34.

27. Robert Paul Seesengood, "What Would Jesus Eat? Ethical Vegetarianism in Nascent Christianity," in Koosed, ed., *Bible and Posthumanism*, 232.

28. E.g., Linzey and Cohn-Sherbok, *After Noah*, 17–34.

29. For my arguments along these lines in relation to gender, sexuality, and biblical interpretation, see *Practicing Safer Texts*, 23–45; "The Garden of Eden and the Heterosexual Contract," in Ellen T. Armour and Susan M. St. Ville, eds., *Bodily Citations: Religion and Judith Butler* (New York: Columbia University Press, 2006); and "Bibles That Matter: Biblical Theology and Queer Performativity," *Biblical Theology Bulletin* 38/1 (2008): 14–25.

30. See numerous examples throughout Strawn, *What Is Stronger than a Lion?*

31. Wolfe, *Animal Rites*, 8; his emphasis.

32. Derrida, "'Eating Well,' or the Calculation of the Subject,"280–1. Derrida uses the term "carnophallogocentrism" in several other places as well, including *Beast and the Sovereign*, 1: 15; *Acts of Religion*, ed. Gil Anidjar (New York: Routledge, 2002), 86 n. 32, 247; Daniel Birnbaum and Anders Olsson, "An Interview with Jacques Derrida on the Limits of Digestion," *e-flux* (2000) www.e-flux.com/journal/an-interview-with-jacques-derrida-on-the-limits-of-digestion.

33. Niditch, *My Brother Esau Is a Hairy Man*, 115.

34. Susan Haddox, "Favoured Sons and Subordinate Masculinities," in Ovidiu Creang, ed., *Men and Masculinity in the Hebrew Bible and Beyond* (Sheffield, Eng.: Sheffield Phoenix Press, 2010). On biblical distinctions between domesticated and wild animals see, e.g., Tucker, "Rain on a Land Where No One Lives," 10–11, and "The Peaceable Kingdom and a Covenant with the Wild Animals."

35. Carol Meyers, ed, *Women in Scripture: A Dictionary of Named and Unnamed Women in the Hebrew Bible, the Apocryphal/Deuterocanonical Books, and the New Testament* (Boston: Houghton Mifflin, 2000), 108, 143.

36. David Jobling, *The Sense of Biblical Narrative: Structural Analyses in the Hebrew Bible II* (Sheffield, Eng.: Sheffield Academic Press, 1986), 30–31; Pamela Milne, "The Patriarchal Stamp of Scripture: The Implications of Structuralist Analyses for Feminist Hermeneutics," in Athalya Brenner, ed. *A Feminist Companion to Genesis* (Sheffield, Eng.: Sheffield Academic Press, 1993), 161; Kelly Oliver, *Animal Lessons: How They Teach Us to Be Human* (New York: Columbia University Press, 2009), 143.

37. Danna Nolan Fewell and David M. Gunn, *Gender, Power, and Promise: The Subject of the Bible's First Story* (Nashville: Abingdon, 1993), 94

38. Carol J. Adams, *The Sexual Politics of Meat: A Feminist-Vegetarian Critical Theory* (New York: Continuum, 1991); id., *Neither Man nor Beast: Feminism and the Defense of Animals* (New York: Continuum, 1995).

39. Derrida, "'Eating Well,' or the Calculation of the Subject,"280.

40. Oliver, *Animal Lessons*, 145. On this association see also Still, *Derrida and Other Animals*; and, from a different philosophical perspective, Mary Midgley, *Animals and Why They Matter* (Athens: University of Georgia Press, 1983), 74–88.

41. Mark S. Roberts, *The Mark of the Beast: Animality and Human Oppression* (West Lafayette, IN: Purdue University Press, 2008), 61–91. Cf. David Nibert, *Animal Rights, Human Rights: Entanglements of Oppression and Liberation* (Lanham, MD: Rowman & Littlefield, 2002), 35–41; Still, *Derrida and Other Animals*, 249–303.

42. Mark G. Brett, *Genesis: Procreation and the Politics of Identity* (New York: Routledge, 2000); Christopher R. Heard, *Dynamics of Diselection: Ambiguity in Genesis 12–36 and Ethnic Boundaries in Post-Exilic Judah* (Atlanta: Society of Biblical Literature, 2001).

CHAPTER 2

1. www.statista.com/statistics/198100/dogs-in-the-united-states-since-2000. These estimates come from the American Pet Product Association.

2. www.statista.com/statistics/198102/cats-in-the-united-states-since-2000.

3. Among Haraway's books, dogs are central to both *When Species Meet* and *The Companion Species Manifesto*.

4. Useful sources on canine evolution, behavior, and cultural significance include James Serpell, ed., *The Domestic Dog: Its Evolution, Behaviour and Interactions with People* (Cambridge: Cambridge University Press, 1995); Marjorie Garber, *Dog Love* (New York: Simon & Schuster, 1996); Raymond and Lorna Coppinger, *Dogs: A New Understanding of Canine Origin, Behavior, and Evolution* (Chicago: University of Chicago Press, 2001); Douglas Brewer, Terence Clark, and Adrian Phillips, *Dogs in Antiquity: Anubis to Cerberus: The Origins of the Domestic Dog* (Warminster, Eng.: Aris & Phillips, 2001); Susan McHugh, *Dog* (London: Reaktion Books, 2004); Alice A. Kuzniar, *Melancholia's Dog: Reflections on Our Animal Kinship* (Chicago: University of Chicago Press, 2006); Adam Miklósi, *Dog Behaviour, Evolution, and Cognition* (New York: Oxford University Press, 2007); Alexandria Horowitz, *Inside of a Dog: What Dogs See, Smell, and Know* (New York: Scribner, 2009); Darcy F. Morey, *Dogs: Domestication and the Development of a Social Bond* (New York: Cambridge University Press, 2010); King, *Being with Animals*, 37–48; Brian Hare and Vanessa Woods, *The Genius of Dogs: How Dogs Are Smarter than You Think* (New York: Penguin Books, 2013); and Laura Hobgood-Oster, *A Dog's History*

of the World: Canines and the Domestication of Humans (Waco, TX: Baylor University Press, 2014).

5. Stephen Budiansky, *The Covenant of the Wild: Why Animals Chose Domestication* (New Haven, CT: Yale University Press, 1992).

6. Hobgood-Oster, *Dog's History of the World*.

7. Morey, *Dogs*, 25.

8. See Laura Hobgood-Oster, *Holy Dogs and Asses: Animals in the Christian Tradition* (Urbana: University of Illinois Press, 2008).

9. Simon J. M. Davis and François R. Valla, "Evidence for Domestication of the Dog 12,000 Years Ago in the Natufian of Israel," *Nature* 276 (1978): 610.

10. Eitan Tchernov and François R. Valla, "Two New Dogs, and Other Natufian Dogs, from the Southern Levant," *Journal of Archaeological Science* 24 (1997): 65–95.

11. Lawrence A. Stager, "Why Were Hundreds of Dogs Buried at Ashkelon?" *Biblical Archaeology Review* 17/3 (1991): 26–42; Paula Wapnish and Brian Hesse, "Pampered Pooches or Plain Pariahs? The Ashkelon Dog Burials," *Biblical Archaeologist* 56/2 (1993): 55–80.

12. Baruch Halpern, "The Canine Conundrum of Ashkelon: A Classical Connection?" in Lawrence E. Stager, Joseph A. Greene, and Michael D. Coogan, eds., *The Archaeology of Jordan and Beyond: Essays in Honor of James A. Sauer* (Winona Lake, IN: Eisenbrauns, 2000).

13. Morey, *Dogs*, 150–87.

14. See, e.g., Billie Jean Collins, "Animals in Hittite Literature," in Collins, ed., *History of the Animal World in the Ancient Near East*, 242; Benjamin R. Forster, "Animals in Mesopotamian Literature," in Collins, ed., *History of the Animal World*, 278, 280–81; Forster, "Animals in the Literatures of Syria-Palestine," in Collins, ed., *History of the Animal World*, 302.

15. See, e.g., A. Livingstone, "The Isin 'Dog House' Revisited," *Journal of Cuneiform Studies* 40 (1988): 54–60; Stager, "Why Were Hundreds of Dogs Buried at Ashkelon?"; Halpern, "The Canine Conundrum of Ashkelon"; Tallay Ornan, "The Goddess Gula and Her Dog," *Israel Museum Studies in Archaeology* 3 (2004): 13–30; Meir Edrey, "Dog Cult in Persian Period Judea," in Phillip Ackerman-Lieberman and Rakefet Zalashik, eds., *A Jew's Best Friend? The Image of the Dog throughout Jewish History* (Brighton, Eng.: Sussex Academic Press, 2013); Barbara Böck, *The Healing Goddess Gula: Towards an Understanding of Ancient Babylonian Medicine* (Leiden: Brill, 2014), 38–44.

16. E.g., Ornan, "The Goddess Gula and Her Dog," 18.

17. Böck, *Healing Goddess Gula*, 44.

18. Billie Jean Collins, "The Puppy in Hittite Ritual," *Journal of Cuneiform Studies* 42 (1990): 211–26. Cf. Jack Murad Sasson, "Isaiah LXVI 3–4a," *Vetus Testamentum* 26/2 (1976): 199–207.

19. Morey, *Dogs*, 183.

20. E.g., Hobgood-Oster, *Holy Dogs and Asses*; id., *Dog's History of the World*.

21. D. Winton Thomas, "*KELEBH* 'Dog': Its Origin and Some Usages of It in the Old Testament," *Vetus Testamentum* 10/4 (1960): 410–27.

22. Elaine Adler Goodfriend, "Could *keleb* in Deuteronomy 23:19 Actually Refer to a Canine?" in David P. Wright, David Noel Freedman and Avi Hurvitz, eds., *Pomegranates and Golden Bells: Studies in Biblical, Jewish, and Near Eastern Ritual, Law, and Literature in Honor of Jacob Milgrom* (Winona Lake, IN: Eisenbrauns, 1995), 389, 390, 392.

23. Joshua Schwartz, "Dogs in Jewish Society in the Second Temple Period and in the Time of the Mishnah and Talmud," *Journal of Jewish Studies* 55/2 (2004): 246, 248–49.

24. Edwin Firmage, "Zoology," in David Noel Freedman et al., eds., *The Anchor Bible Dictionary* (Garden City, NY: Doubleday, 1992), 6:1143; Borowski, *Every Living Thing*, 135.

25. Sophia Menache, "From Unclean Species to Man's Best Friend: Dogs in the Biblical, Mishnah, and Talmud Periods," in Ackerman-Lieberman and Zalashik, eds., *A Jew's Best Friend?* 40.

26. E.g., Menache, "Dogs: God's Worst Enemies?" *Society and Animals* 5/1 (1997): 23–44; id., "Dogs and Human Beings: A Story of Friendship," *Society and Animals* 6/1 (1998): 67–87.

27. Geoffrey David Miller, "Attitudes toward Dogs in Ancient Israel: A Reassessment," *Journal for the Study of the Old Testament* 32/4 (2008): 488.

28. Emmanuel Levinas, "The Name of a Dog, or Natural Rights," in id., *Difficult Freedom: Essays on Judaism*, trans. Sean Hand (Baltimore: Johns Hopkins University Press, 1990).

29. Some of the material that follows appears in a different context in my "The Dogs of Exodus and the Question of the Animal," in Moore, ed., *Divinanimality*.

30. In order to engage more easily the discussions of Levinas and others, my English translations in this chapter frequently follow the New Revised Standard Version (NRSV), especially where Levinas's essay is under discussion. Elsewhere in the chapter, I sometimes follow the NRSV and sometimes provide my own translation.

31. As translated in Jacob Z. Lauterbach, *Mekhilta de-Rabbi Ishmael: A Critical Edition, Based on the Manuscripts and Early Editions, with an English Translation, Introduction, and Notes*, vol. 2, 2nd ed. (Philadelphia: Jewish Publication Society, 2004), 466. See also *Exodus Rabbah* 31:9.

32. Derrida, *Animal That Therefore I Am*, 114.

33. See, e.g., John Llewelyn, "Am I Obsessed by Bobby? Humanism of the Other Animal," in Robert Bernasconi and Simon Critchley, eds., *Re-Reading Levinas* (Bloomington: Indiana University Press, 1991); id., *The Middle Voice of*

Ecological Conscience: A Chiasmic Reading of Responsibility in the Neighborhood of Levinas, Heidegger and Others (New York: St. Martin's Press, 1991), 49–67; David Clark, "On Being 'The Last Kantian in Nazi Germany,'" in Jennifer Ham and Matthew Senior, eds., *Animal Acts: Configuring the Human in Western History* (New York: Routledge, 1997); Wolfe, *Animal Rites*, 59–62; Peter Atterton, "Ethical Cynicism," in Matthew Calarco and Peter Atterton, eds., *Animal Philosophy: Ethics and Identity* (New York: Continuum, 2004); Kuzniar, *Melancholia's Dog*, 32–35; Calarco, *Zoographies*, 55–77; Aaron S. Gross, "The Question of the Creature: Animals, Theology, and Levinas' Dog," in Celia Deane-Drummond and David Clough, eds., *Creaturely Theology: On God, Humans and Other Animals* (London: SCM Press, 2009); Oliver, *Animal Lessons*, 41–42; Bob Plant, "Welcoming Dogs: Levinas and 'The Animal' Question," *Philosophy and Social Criticism* 37/1 (2011): 49–71; Deborah Bird Rose, *Wild Dog Dreaming: Love and Extinction* (Charlottesville: University of Virginia Press, 2011), 29–41; Karalyn Kendall, "The Face of a Dog: Levinasian Ethics and Human/Dog Co-evolution," in Noreen Giffney and Myra J. Hird, eds., *Queering the Non/Human* (New York: Routledge, 2016).

34. Clark, "On Being 'The Last Kantian in Nazi Germany,'" 166.
35. Levinas, "Name of a Dog," 151, 153.
36. Llewelyn, "Am I Obsessed With Bobby?" 235.
37. Clark, "On Being 'The Last Kantian in Nazi Germany,'" 169.
38. Levinas, "Interview," in Calarco and Atterton, eds., *Animal Philosophy*, 49.
39. The most significant exception I have seen is Deborah Bird Rose, who devotes several pages to the dogs of Exodus in *Wild Dog Dreaming*, 31–36. I want to thank Kate Rigby for calling Rose's work to my attention.
40. See, e.g., J. P. Hyatt, *Exodus* (Grand Rapids, MI: Eerdmans, 1980), 130, 245.
41. Derrida, *Animal That Therefore I Am*, 114.
42. James Serpell, "From Paragon to Pariah: Some Reflections on Human Attitudes to Dogs," in Serpell, ed., *Domestic Dog*, 252; Miller, "Attitudes toward Dogs in Ancient Israel," 495–96.
43. Thomas, "*KELEBH* 'Dog,'" 414–15; Goodfriend, "Could *keleb* in Deuteronomy 23:19 Actually Refer to a Canine?" 383.
44. Serpell, "From Paragon to Pariah."
45. Coppinger and Coppinger, *Dogs*.
46. Goodfriend, "Could *keleb* in Deuteronomy 23:19 Actually Refer to a Canine?" 389–90; Miller, "Attitudes toward Dogs in Ancient Israel," 500.
47. Houston, *Purity and Monotheism*, 190.
48. McHugh, *Dog*, 7–8.
49. As noted by Serpell, "From Paragon to Pariah."
50. Houston, *Purity and Monotheism*, 190. Cf. Menache, "From Unclean Species to Man's Best Friend," 42.

51. See esp. Stephanie Lynn Budin, *The Myth of Sacred Prostitution in Antiquity* (Cambridge: Cambridge University Press, 2009).

52. Goodfriend, "Could *keleb* in Deuteronomy 23:19 Actually Refer to a Canine?"

53. E.g., Stager, "Why Were Hundreds of Dogs Buried at Ashkelon?"; Edrey, "Dog Cult in Persian Period Judea."

54. Phyllis A. Bird, *Missing Persons and Mistaken Identities: Women and Gender in Ancient Israel* (Minneapolis: Fortress Press, 1997), 197–236.

55. Haran, "Bible Scrolls in Eastern and Western Jewish Communities," 36–37.

56. The laws in Leviticus 11 and Deuteronomy 14 are clearly important for an understanding of the Bible's animals. I devote relatively little attention to these laws here in part because the animals in them have already been studied more widely than most of the Bible's animals. But see, for discussion, Douglas, *Purity and Danger*; Michael Carroll, "One More Time: Leviticus Revised," in Bernhard Lang, ed., *Anthropological Approaches to the Old Testament* (Philadelphia: Fortress Press, 1985); Edwin Firmage, "The Biblical Dietary Laws and the Concept of Holiness," in J. A. Emerton, ed., *Studies in the Pentateuch* (Leiden: Brill, 1990); Jacob Milgrom, *Leviticus 1–16: A New Translation with Introduction and Commentary* (Garden City, NY: Doubleday, 1991), 643–742; Houston, *Purity and Monotheism*; id., "What was the Meaning of Classifying Animals as Clean or Unclean?"; John Sawyer, ed., *Reading Leviticus: A Conversation with Mary Douglas* (Sheffield, Eng.: Sheffield Academic Press, 1996); Jean Soler, "The Semiotics of Food in the Bible," in Carole Counihan and Penny Van Esterik, eds., *Food and Culture: A Reader* (New York: Routledge, 1997). For earlier comments of my own about these passages, see Stone, *Practicing Safer Texts*, 46–67.

57. See, e.g., Menahem Haran, "Seething a Kid in Its Mother's Milk," *Journal of Jewish Studies* 30/1 (1979): 23–35. Haran notes that this interpretive tradition is quite old, going back as far as Philo and Clement of Alexandria and continuing through such influential figures as Ibn Ezra, Ramban, and Calvin. For a more recent survey of interpretations of this challenging text, see Stefan Schorch, "'A Young Goat in Its Mother's Milk'? Understanding an Ancient Prohibition," *Biblical Interpretation* 60 (2010): 116–30.

58. Susan Ackerman, *Under Every Green Tree: Popular Religion in Sixth-Century Judah* (Atlanta: Scholars Press, 1992), 101–63; id., "Child Sacrifice: Returning God's Gift," *Bible Review* 9/3 (1993): 20–29, 56; Susan Niditch, *War in the Hebrew Bible: A Study in the Ethics of Violence* (Oxford: Oxford University Press, 1993); Jon D. Levenson, *The Death and Resurrection of the Beloved Son: The Transformation of Child Sacrifice in Judaism and Christianity* (New Haven, CT: Yale University Press, 1995); Francesca Stavrakopoulou, *King Manasseh and Child Sacrifice: Biblical Distortions of Historical Realities* (Berlin: Walter de Gruyter, 2004); Jason Tatlock, "The Place of Human Sacrifice in the Israelite Cult," in

Christian Eberhart, ed., *Ritual and Metaphor: Sacrifice in the Bible* (Atlanta: Society of Biblical Literature, 2011).

59. Derrida, *Animal That Therefore I Am*, 115.

60. Derrida, "'Eating Well,' or the Calculation of the Subject," 279; his emphasis.

61. For an attempt to sort through possible reasons for the donkey's unusual status in this regard, see Way, *Donkeys in the Biblical World*, 178–83.

62. See, e.g., F. Charles Fensham, "The Dogs in Ex. XI 7," *Vetus Testamentum* 16/4 (1966): 504–7.

63. Schwartz, "Dogs in Jewish Society in the Second Temple Period," 261–2.

64. McHugh, *Dog*, 42; cf. Menache, "Dogs: God's Worst Enemies?" 27.

65. Calarco, *Thinking through Animals*, 6.

66. Ibid., 11. Helpful discussions of the ethical implications of Darwin's theories for our relations with animals include James Rachels, *Created from Animals: The Moral Implications of Darwinism* (Oxford: Oxford University Press, 1990); and Lisa H. Sideris, *Environmental Ethics, Ecological Theology, and Natural Selection* (New York: Columbia University Press, 2003). For two interesting but quite different theological attempts to take seriously those implications, see Elizabeth A. Johnson, *Ask the Beasts: Darwin and the God of Love* (London: Bloomsbury, 2014), for a Roman Catholic feminist perspective, and Ronald E. Osborn, *Death before the Fall: Biblical Literalism and the Problem of Animal Suffering* (Downers Grove, IL: IVP Academic, 2014), for a neo-evangelical perspective.

67. On the prevalence of this view in England, see Keith Thomas, *Man and the Natural World: Changing Attitudes in England 1500–1800* (Oxford: Oxford University Press, 1983).

68. Derrida, "Violence against Animals," 66.

69. McKay, "Through the Eyes of Horses," 127–28.

70. For one influential critique, see Robert Allen Warrior, "Canaanites, Cowboys, and Indians: Deliverance, Conquest, and Liberation Theology Today," in David Jobling, Tina Pippin, and Ronald Schleifer, eds., *The Postmodern Bible Reader* (Oxford: Blackwell, 2001).

CHAPTER 3

1. Derrida, *Animal That Therefore I Am*, 42.

2. For examples, see John Byron, *Cain and Abel in Text and Tradition: Jewish and Christian Interpretations of the First Sibling Rivalry* (Leiden: Brill, 2011).

3. Hermann Gunkel, *Genesis* (Macon, GA: Mercer University Press, 1997), 43.

4. Gerhard von Rad, *Genesis* (Philadelphia: Westminster Press, 1972), 104.

5. For the Talmud, see b. Sanhedrin 59b. For more contemporary examples of such a reading, see Richard H. Schwartz, *Judaism and Vegetarianism* (1982; rev.

ed., New York: Lantern Books, 2001), 2–3; Andrew Linzey, "The Bible and Killing for Food," in Armstrong and Botzler, eds., *Animal Ethics Reader*, 286–90; and, from biblical scholarship, J. W. Rogerson, "What Was the Meaning of Animal Sacrifice?" in Andrew Linzey and Dorothy Yamamoto, eds., *Animals on the Agenda* (Urbana: University of Illinois Press, 1998), 11–13, 16–17; cf. James Barr, "Man and Nature: The Ecological Controversy and the Old Testament," *Bulletin of the John Rylands Library* 55/1 (1972), 21.

6. W. Sibley Towner, *Genesis* (Louisville: Westminster John Knox Press, 2001), 59.

7. Yvonne Sherwood, "Cutting Up Life: Sacrifice as a Device for Clarifying—and Tormenting—Fundamental Distinctions between Human, Animal, and Divine," in Jennifer Koosed, ed., *Bible and Posthumanism* (Atlanta: Society of Biblical Literature, 2014), 247.

8. Derrida, *Animal That Therefore I Am*, 16; his emphasis. Page numbers cited immediately below in the text refer to this source.

9. See Carl Kerényi, *The Heroes of the Greeks* (London: Thames & Hudson, 1959), 79–81.

10. Derrida, "'Eating Well,' or the Calculation of the Subject,"279; his emphasis.

11. See, e.g., Tom Regan, *The Case for Animal Rights: Updated with a New Preface* (Berkeley: University of California Press, 2004); Cavalieri, *The Animal Question*; Paul Waldau, *Animal Rights: What Everyone Needs to Know* (Oxford: Oxford University Press, 2011).

12. McCance, *Critical Animal Studies*, x, 148.

13. Derrida, "Force of Law: The 'Mystical Foundation of Authority,'" in *Acts of Religion*, ed. Gil Anidjar (London: Routledge, 2002), 246. Page numbers cited immediately below in the text refer to this source.

14. Ibid. Feminist texts that make this point in dialogue with Derrida include Still, *Derrida and Other Animals*; Oliver, *Animal Lessons*; but see also earlier texts by Midgley, *Animals and Why They Matter*; Adams, *Sexual Politics of Meat*; id., *Neither Man nor Beast*.

15. Derrida, "'Eating Well,' or the Calculation of the Subject,"280–81.

16. Derrida, *Beast and the Sovereign*, 1: 15. For other references to "carnophallogocentrism" in Derrida's work, see sources cited in chapter 1.

17. For an example of such appreciative critique, see Élisabeth de Fontenay, *Without Offending Humans: A Critique of Animal Rights*, trans. Will Bishop (Minneapolis: University of Minnesota Press, 2012), 14–17.

18. Derrida, *Animal That Therefore I Am*, 55, 101.

19. Gross, *Question of the Animal and Religion*, 132. Page numbers cited immediately below in the text refer to this source, chapter 5 of which, "Disavowal,

War, Sacrifice" (121–46), provides a powerful reading of Derrida, animals, and religion.

20. Derrida, "Force of Law," 247; his emphasis.

21. E.g., Jonathan Klawans, "Sacrifice in Ancient Israel: Pure Bodies, Domesticated Animals, and the Divine Shepherd," in Waldau and Patton, eds., *Communion of Subjects*, 65–66. Cf. Kimberly Patton, "Animal Sacrifice: Metaphysics of the Sublimated Victim," in Waldau and Patton, *Communion of Subjects*, 391–92.

22. Sherwood, "Cutting Up Life," 251. Cf. Seesengood, "What Would Jesus Eat?" 232.

23. See, e.g., Collins, ed., *History of the Animal World in the Ancient Near East*; JoAnn Scurlock, "The Techniques of the Sacrifice of Animals in Ancient Israel and Ancient Mesopotamia: New Insights through Comparison, Part 1," *Andrews University Seminary Studies* 44/1 (2006): 13–49; id., "The Techniques of the Sacrifice of Animals in Ancient Israel and Ancient Mesopotamia: New Insights through Comparison, Part 2," *Andrews University Seminary Studies* 44/2 (2006): 241–64; Ingvild Sælid Gilhus, *Animals, Gods and Humans: Changing Attitudes to Animals in Greek, Roman and Early Christian Ideas* (London: Routledge, 2006); Maria-Zoe Petropoulou, *Animal Sacrifice in Ancient Greek Religion, Judaism, and Christianity, 100 BC to AD 200* (Oxford: Oxford University Press, 2008); Jennifer Wright Knust and Zsuzsanna Várhelyi, eds., *Ancient Mediterranean Sacrifice* (Oxford: Oxford University Press, 2011); Anne Porter and Glenn M. Schwartz, eds., *Sacred Killing: The Archaeology of Sacrifice in the Ancient Near East* (Winona Lake, IN: Eisenbrauns, 2012).

24. Ronald S. Hendel, "Prophets, Priests, and the Efficacy of Ritual," in Wright et al., eds., *Pomegranates and Golden Bells*.

25. The most frequently cited examples are René Girard, *Violence and the Sacred*, trans. Patrick Gregory (Baltimore: Johns Hopkins University Press, 1977), and Walter Burkert, *Homo Necans: The Anthropology of Ancient Greek Sacrificial Ritual and Myth*, trans. Peter Bing (Berkeley: University of California Press, 1983). But see also Nancy Jay, *Throughout Your Generations Forever: Sacrifice, Religion, Paternity* (Chicago: University of Chicago Press, 1992).

26. Gary Anderson, "Sacrifice and Sacrificial Offerings (OT)," in David Noel Freedman et al., eds., *The Anchor Bible Dictionary* (New York: Doubleday, 1992), 5: 872.

27. For discussions of terminology and categories, see Baruch A. Levine, *In the Presence of the Lord: A Study of Cult and Some Cultic Terms in Ancient Israel* (Leiden: Brill, 1974); Jacob Milgrom, *Leviticus 1–16: A New Translation with Introduction and Commentary* (Garden City, NY: Doubleday, 1991); and, more succinctly, Patrick D. Miller, *The Religion of Ancient Israel* (Louisville: Westminster John Knox, 2000), 106–30.

28. See, e.g., the classic study of George Buchanan Gray, *Sacrifice in the Old Testament: Its Theory and Practice* (Oxford: Clarendon Press, 1925), 2–3.

29. Moshe Halbertal, *On Sacrifice* (Princeton, NJ: Princeton University Press, 2012).

30. Anderson, "Sacrifice and Sacrificial Offerings (OT)," 874–75.

31. For further discussion see, in addition to Anderson (ibid.), the sources listed in notes 27 and 28 above.

32. Anderson, "Sacrifice and Sacrificial Offerings (OT)," 873. On the reference from Aquinas, see Victor Turner, "Sacrifice as Quintessential Process: Prophylaxis or Abandonment?" *History of Religions* 16/3 (1977): 189–215.

33. See, e.g., Michael Carroll, "One More Time: Leviticus Revisited," in Bernhard Lang, ed., *Anthropological Approaches to the Old Testament* (Philadelphia: Fortress Press, 1985), 117–26; Edwin Firmage, "The Biblical Dietary Laws and the Concept of Holiness," in J. A. Emerton, ed., *Studies in the Pentateuch* (Leiden: Brill, 1990); Milgrom, *Leviticus 1–16*, 643–742; Houston, *Purity and Monotheism*; id., "What was the Meaning of Classifying Animals as Clean or Unclean," in Linzey and Yamamoto, eds., *Animals on the Agenda*; John F. A. Sawyer, ed., *Reading Leviticus: A Conversation with Mary Douglas* (Sheffield, Eng.: Sheffield Academic Press, 1996). For an attempt of my own to engage Douglas's work, see *Practicing Safer Texts*, 46–67.

34. On difficulties identifying animals on the list, see Borowski, *Every Living Thing*, 186–89.

35. Derrida, *Animal That Therefore I Am*, 40.

36. William K. Gilders, *Blood Ritual in the Hebrew Bible* (Baltimore: Johns Hopkins University Press, 2004).

37. See Nicole J. Ruane, *Sacrifice and Gender in Biblical Law* (Cambridge: Cambridge University Press, 2013).

38. Saul Olyan, *Rites and Rank: Hierarchy in Biblical Representations of Cult* (Princeton, NJ: Princeton University Press, 2000), 4. See also Gilders, *Blood Ritual in the Hebrew Bible*.

39. See sources cited in chapter 2, n. 58, above.

40. Levenson, *Death and Resurrection of the Beloved Son*, 14.

41. Niditch, *War in the Hebrew Bible*, 28–55.

42. JoAnn Scurlock, "Animal Sacrifice in Ancient Mesopotamian Religion," in Collins, ed., *History of the Animal World in the Ancient Near East*, 389.

43. Stephanie Dalley, *Myths from Mesopotamia: Creation, the Flood, Gilgamesh and Others* (Oxford: Oxford University Press, 1989), 33, 114.

44. Gilhus, *Animals, Gods and Humans*, 115.

45. Milgrom, *Leviticus 1–16*, 440. Cf. Miller, *Religion of Ancient Israel*, 126–28; Walter Eichrodt, *Theology of the Old Testament*, trans. J. A. Baker (Philadelphia: Westminster Press, 1961), 1:142–3; Menahem Haran, *Temples and Temple Service*

in Ancient Israel: An Inquiry into Biblical Cult Phenomena and the Historical Setting of the Priestly School (Winona Lake, IN: Eisenbrauns, 1985), 17.

46. Henri Hubert and Marcel Mauss, *Sacrifice: Its Nature and Function*, trans. W. D. Halls (Chicago: University of Chicago Press, 1964 [1898]).

47. Jonathan Z. Smith, "The Domestication of Sacrifice," in Robert G. Hammerton-Kelly, ed., *Violent Origins: Ritual Killing and Cultural Formation* (Stanford: Stanford University Press, 1987), 199.

48. Jonathan Klawans, "Sacrifice in Ancient Israel," 67. Cf. Klawans, *Purity, Sacrifice, and the Temple: Symbolism and Supersessionism in the Study of Ancient Judaism* (Oxford: Oxford University Press, 2006), 59.

49. See Jack W. Vancil, "Sheep, Shepherd," in Freedman et al., eds., *Anchor Bible Dictionary*, 5: 1188–89.

50. Eilberg-Schwartz, *Savage in Judaism*, 115–40.

51. See, e.g., Num. 27:17; 2 Sam. 5:2; 7:7–8; 1 Kgs 22:17; Pss. 23:1–4; 44:12, 23; 74:1; Isa. 56: 9–12; Jer. 3:15; 6:3; 10:21; 12:3, 10; 13:20; 23:1–8; 25:34–38; Ezek. 34; Zech. 11:4–17.

52. Klawans, *Purity, Sacrifice, and the Temple*, 61.

53. Ibid., 73–4.

54. E.g., King and Stager, *Life in Biblical Israel*, 34.

55. For my own attempt at such an analysis, see "Animal Difference, Sexual Difference, and the Daughter of Jephthah," *Biblical Interpretation* 24 (2016): 1–16.

56. See esp. Mieke Bal, *Death and Dissymmetry: The Politics of Coherence in the Book of Judges* (Chicago: University of Chicago Press, 1988).

57. Adams, *Sexual Politics of Meat*, 59.

58. Yi-Fu Tuan, *Dominance and Affection: The Making of Pets* (New Haven, CT: Yale University Press, 1984), 167.

59. Derrida, *Animal That Therefore I Am*, 25; his emphasis.

60. Klawans, "Sacrifice in Ancient Israel," 65.

61. Derrida, *Animal That Therefore I Am*, 101.

CHAPTER 4

1. Moses Maimonides, *The Guide of the Perplexed*, trans. Shlomo Pines (Chicago: University of Chicago Press, 1963), 3.17 (2: 472–73).

2. Elijah Judah Schochet, *Animal Life in Jewish Tradition: Attitudes and Relationships* (New York: KTAV, 1984), 207.

3. Maimonides,. *Guide of the Perplexed*, 3.17 (2: 473–4).

4. See, e.g., Noah J. Cohen, *Tsa'ar Ba'ale Hayim: The Prevention of Cruelty to Animals: Its Bases, Development and Legislation in Hebrew Literature*, 2nd ed. (Jerusalem: Feldheim, 1976), 47–48; J. David Bleich, "Judaism and Animal Experimentation," in Martin D. Yaffe, ed., *Judaism and Environmental Ethics: A*

Reader (Lanham, MD: Lexington Books, 2001), 336; Schwartz, *Judaism and Vegetarianism*, rev. ed., 19; Dan Cohn-Sherbok, "Hope for the Animal Kingdom: A Jewish Vision," in Waldau and Patton, eds., *Communion of Subjects*, 83.

5. See the numerous references in Cohen, *Tsa'ar Ba'ale Hayim*.

6. E.g., Andrew Linzey and Dan Cohn-Sherbok, *After Noah*, 24; Stephen H. Webb, *On God and Dogs: A Christian Theology of Compassion for Animals* (Oxford: Oxford University Press, 1998), 23.

7. See, e.g., Baruch A. Levine, *Numbers 21–36: A New Translation with Introduction and Commentary* (New York: Doubleday, 2000), 137–275.

8. See, e.g., George H. van Kooten and Jacques van Ruiten, eds., *The Prestige of the Pagan Prophet Balaam in Judaism, Early Christianity, and Islam* (Leiden: Brill, 2008); Judith R. Baskin, *Pharaoh's Counsellors: Job, Jethro, and Balaam in Rabbinic and Patristic Tradition* (Chico, CA: Scholars Press, 1983).

9. Michael S. Moore, *The Balaam Traditions: Their Character and Development* (Atlanta: Scholars Press, 1990), 101.

10. Élisabeth de Fontenay, "A Golden Bough to Translate the Beasts," in *Animality. Inaesthetics 2*, ed. Wilfried Dickhoff and Marcus Steinweg, http://inaesthetics.org/index.php/main/issue/2/3.

11. Levine, *Numbers 21–36*, 139.

12. Cyrus H. Gordon and Gary A. Rendsburg, *The Bible and the Ancient Near East*, 4th ed. (New York: Norton, 1997), 106.

13. Jill Bough, *Donkey* (London: Reaktion Books, 2011), 7.

14. Clutton-Brock, *Natural History of Domesticated Animals*, 91; Albano Beja-Pereira et al., "African Origins of the Domestic Donkey," *Science* 304 (June 2004): 1781.

15. Way, *Donkeys in the Biblical World*. See also Way's "Animals in the Prophetic World: Literary Reflections on Numbers 22 and 1 Kings 13," *Journal for the Study of the Old Testament* 34/1 (2009): 47–62.

16. Strawn, *What Is Stronger Than a Lion?*

17. See also Forti, *Animal Imagery in the Book of Proverbs*; Foreman, *Animal Metaphors and the People of Israel in the Book of Jeremiah*; and Deborah O'Daniel Cantrell, *The Horsemen of Israel: Horses and Chariotry in Monarchic Israel (Ninth–Eighth Centuries B.C.E.)* (Winona Lake, IN: Eisenbrauns, 2011).

18. See Jo Ann Hackett, *The Balaam Text from Deir 'Allā* (Chico, CA: Scholars Press, 1980); Moore, *Balaam Traditions*, 66–96; Levine, *Numbers 21–36*, 241–75.

19. Way, *Donkeys in the Biblical World*, 60–67. Page numbers cited below in the text discussion refer to this source.

20. Ibid., 65–66.

21. George Savran, "Beastly Speech: Intertextuality, Balaam's Ass and the Garden of Eden," *Journal for the Study of the Old Testament* 64 (1994): 33–55. See also Cameron B. R. Howard, "Animal Speech as Revelation in

Genesis 3 and Numbers 22," in Habel and Trudinger, eds., *Exploring Ecological Hermeneutics*.

22. David Marcus, *From Balaam to Jonah: Anti-prophetic Satire in the Hebrew Bible* (Atlanta: Scholars Press, 1995).

23. Way, *Donkeys in the Biblical World*, 192–3.

24. Strawn, *What Is Stronger than a Lion?* 45.

25. Jennifer L. Koosed and Robert Paul Seesengood, "Daniel's Animal Apocalypse," in Moore, ed., *Divinanimality*, 182.

26. Way, *Donkeys in the Biblical World*, 192. Cf. Mordechai Cogan, *1 Kings: A New Translation with Introduction and Commentary* (New York: Doubleday, 2001), 371.

27. Cogan, *1 Kings*, 374.

28. Ken Stone, "Wittgenstein's Lion and Balaam's Ass: Talking with Others in Numbers 22–25," in Koosed, ed., *Bible and Posthumanism*.

29. Steven L. McKenzie, *How to Read the Bible: History, Prophecy, Literature—Why Modern Readers Need to Know the Difference and What it Means for Faith Today* (New York: Oxford University Press, 2005), 7.

30. Athalya Brenner, "Jonah's Poem out of and within its Context," in Philip R. Davies and David J. Clines, eds., *Among the Prophets: Language, Image and Structure in the Prophetic Writings* (Sheffield, Eng.: Sheffield Academic Press, 1993), 192.

31. Marcus, *From Balaam to Jonah*, 3–4.

32. Cf. Koosed and Seesengood, "Daniel's Animal Apocalypse," in Moore, ed., *Divinanimality*.

33. Robert Gordis, *The Book of God and Man: A Study of Job* (Chicago: University of Chicago Press, 1978).

34. McKay, "Through the Eyes of Horses," 133.

35. As Jared Beverly notes, this reference is one of many animal images that appear in the erotic poems of Song of Songs. Gazelles and deer are especially common. Beverly is completing a dissertation on this imagery at Chicago Theological Seminary in dialogue with both animal studies and queer theory, but some of his work has been shared in "Loving Animals: A Queer Zoological Reading of Song of Songs" (paper presented at the Annual Meeting of the Society of Biblical Literature, San Diego, November 22–25, 2014).

36. Haraway actively mingles texts from the biological and animal sciences, the humanities and social sciences, various art forms, and even online discussion groups throughout *When Species Meet* and other texts. For Despret and Hearne, see Vinciane Despret, "Sheep Do Have Opinions," in Bruno Latour and Peter Weibel, eds., *Making Things Public: Atmospheres of Democracy* (Cambridge, MA: MIT Press, 2005); "The Becomings of Subjectivity in Animal Worlds," *Subjectivity* 23 (2008): 123–39; and *What Would Animals Say If We Asked the Right*

Questions? trans. Brett Buchanan (Minneapolis: University of Minnesota Press, 2016). Vicki Hearne, *Adam's Task: Calling Animals by Name* (New York: Skyhorse, 2016 [1986]); *Animal Happiness: A Moving Exploration of Animals and Their Emotions* (New York: HarperCollins, 1994); "A Taxonomy of Knowing: Animals Captive, Free-Ranging, and at Liberty," *Social Research* 62 (1995): 441–56; and *Bandit: Dossier of a Dangerous Dog* (New York: HarperCollins, 1991).

37. Gary A. Phillips and Danna Nolan Fewell, "Ethics, Bible, Reading As If," in Danna Nolan Fewell and Gary A. Phillips, eds., *Bible and Ethics of Reading*, Semeia 77 (Atlanta: Society of Biblical Literature, 1997), 3–4.

38. Melinda A. Zeder, "The Domestication of Animals," *Journal of Anthropological Research* 68/2 (2012): 177.

39. Tull, *Inhabiting Eden*, 102–3.

40. Menahem Haran, "Seething a Kid in Its Mother's Milk," *Journal of Jewish Studies* 30/1 (1979), 35. For a more recent survey of interpretations of this challenging text, see Stefan Schorch, "'A Young Goat in Its Mother's Milk'? Understanding an Ancient Prohibition," *Biblical Interpretation* 60 (2010): 116–30

41. Haran, "Seething a Kid in Its Mother's Milk," 29.

42. Cohn-Sherbok, "Hope for the Animal Kingdom," 82; Tull, *Inhabiting Eden*, 94; Webb, *On God and Dogs*, 21–22; Scully, *Dominion*, 93.

43. Cf. Sherman, "Animals," in Strawn, ed., *Oxford Encyclopedia of the Bible and Law*.

44. Gross, *Question of the Animal and Religion*, 154.

45. Maimonides, *Guide of the Perplexed*, 3.48 (2:599).

46. Calarco, *Thinking through Animals*, 6.

47. Among many accounts of animals and Aristotle, see Gary Steiner, *Anthropocentrism and Its Discontents: The Moral Status of Animals in the History of Western Philosophy* (Pittsburgh: University of Pittsburgh Press, 2010), 53–92. Cf. Alasdair Cochrane, *An Introduction to Animals and Political Theory* (London: Palgrave, 2010).

48. Kathy Rudy, *Loving Animals: Toward a New Animal Advocacy* (Minneapolis: University of Minnesota Press, 2011).

49. See, e.g., Schaefer, "Do Animals Have Religion?"; id., *Religious Affects*; Lori Gruen, *Entangled Empathy: An Alternative Ethic for Our Relationships with Animals* (New York: Lantern Books, 2015).

50. Jeremy Bentham, *An Introduction to the Principles of Morals and Legislation* (1823), rev. ed. (Oxford: Clarendon Press, 1879), 311.

CHAPTER 5

1. Pierre J. P. Van Hecke, "Pastoral Metaphors in the Hebrew Bible and in Its Ancient Near Eastern Context," in Robert Gordon and Johannes de Moore, *The Old Testament in Its World* (Leiden: Brill, 2005), 201.

2. Timothy Morton, *Dark Ecology: For a Logic of Future Coexistence* (New York: Columbia University Press, 2016), 49. Morton's phrase builds on Terry O'Connor, *Animals as Neighbors: The Past and Present of Commensal Species* (East Lansing: Michigan State University Press, 2013), though O'Connor is primarily focused on animals who fall somewhere between the wild and the domesticated.

3. See, e.g., Borowski, *Every Living Thing*, 186, 205–6.

4. See, e.g., Tucker, "Rain on a Land Where No One Lives," 10.

5. Recent discussions on this large and complex topic include Roderick Frazier Nash, *Wilderness in the American Mind* (1967), 5th ed. (New Haven, CT: Yale University Press, 2014); Jedidiah Purdy, *After Nature: A Politics for the Anthropocene* (Cambridge, MA: Harvard University Press, 2015); Emma Marris, *Rambunctious Garden: Saving Nature in a Post-Wild World* (New York: Bloomsbury, 2015); Paul Wapner, *Living through the End of Nature: The Future of American Environmentalism* (Cambridge, MA: MIT Press, 2010); Jamie Lorimer, *Wildlife in the Anthropocene: Conservation after Nature* (Minneapolis: University of Minnesota Press, 2015).

6. Kerry Harris and Yannis Hamilakis, "Beyond the Wild, the Feral, and the Domestic: Lessons from Prehistoric Crete," in Garry Marvin and Susan McHugh, eds., *Routledge Handbook of Human–Animal Studies* (New York: Routledge, 2014), 98.

7. Derrida, *Animal That Therefore I Am*, 31.

8. Nash, *Wilderness in the American Mind*, xx.

9. See Richard W. Bulliet, *Hunters, Herders, and Hamburgers: The Past and Future of Human–Animal Relationships* (New York: Columbia University Press, 2005; Tim Ingold, *The Perception of the Environment: Essays on Livelihood, Dwelling and Skill* (New York: Routledge, 2000); and the helpful discussion of Ingold's work in Gross, *Question of the Animal and Religion*, 95–120.

10. Nash, *Wilderness in the American Mind*, xx.

11. For an attempt to use this framework in the context of queer biblical interpretation, see my "The Ostrich Leaves Her Eggs to the Earth: Queer Animals of God in the Book of Job," in Tat-siong Benny Liew, ed., *Reading Ideologies: Essays on the Bible & Interpretation in Honor of Mary Ann Tolbert* (Leiden: Brill, 2011). For a focus on the book of Isaiah with more attention to sociohistorical contexts, see my "Jackals and Ostriches Honoring God: The Zoological Gaze in the Isaiah Scroll," in Jon L. Berquist and Alice Hunt, eds., *Focusing Biblical Studies: The*

Crucial Nature of the Persian and Hellenistic Periods: Essays in Honor of Douglas A. Knight (London: T&T Clark, 2012).

12. Adrian Franklin, *Animals and Modern Cultures: A Sociology of Human–Animal Relations in Modernity* (London: Sage, 1999), 62. Page numbers cited parenthetically in the text discussion that follows refer to this source.

13. See, e.g., Hal Whitehead and Luke Rendell, *The Cultural Lives of Whales and Dolphins* (Chicago: University of Chicago Press, 2015); Carl Safina, *Beyond Words: What Animals Think and Feel* (New York: Holt, 2015), esp. 295–409; Maddalena Bearzi and Craig B. Stanford, *Beautiful Minds: The Parallel Lives of Great Apes and Dolphins* (Cambridge, MA: Harvard University Press, 2008).

14. See also Harriet Ritvo, *The Animal Estate: The English and Other Creatures in the Victorian Age* (Cambridge, MA: Harvard University Press, 1987), esp. 205–88.

15. Tucker, "Rain on a Land Where No One Lives," 10.

16. Strawn, *What Is Stronger than a Lion*, 26. Strawn provides a full list of passages that refer to lions on 357–74. As he notes, there are additional passages that may allude to lions without mentioning them explicitly.

17. Enemies as lions: Pss. 7:2 (Hebrew 7:3); 10:9; 17:12; 22:13, 21 (Hebrew 22:14, 22); 34:10 (Hebrew 34:11); 35:17; 57:4 (Hebrew 57:5); 58:6 (Hebrew 58:7). God as protector from wild animals: Ps. 22:20–21 (Hebrew 22:21–22).

18. See also Hugh Pyper, "The Lion King: Yahweh as Sovereign Beast in Israel's Imaginary," in Koosed, ed., *Bible and Posthumanism*.

19. Ibid., 64.

20. Ibid., 68; Derrida, *Beast and the Sovereign*, 1: 49.

21. Norman Habel, *An Inconvenient Text: Is a Green Reading of the Bible Possible?* (Adelaide, Australia: ATF Press, 2009), 33.

22. Joseph Blenkinsopp, "Cityscape to Landscape: The 'Back to Nature' Theme in Isaiah 1–35," in Robert D. Haak and Lester L. Grabbe, eds., *Every City Shall Be Forsaken: Urbanism and Prophecy in Ancient Israel and the Near East* (Sheffield, Eng.: Sheffield Academic Press, 2001).

23. Tucker, "The Peaceable Kingdom and a Covenant with the Wild Animals," 223.

24. See Robert Barry Leal, "Negativity towards Wilderness in the Biblical Record," *Ecotheology* 10/3 (2005): 364–81. Cf. Bauckham, *Bible and Ecology*, 103–40.

25. For "wild cats" I follow the translation of a difficult term by Blenkinsopp, "Cityscape to Landscape," 40; id., *Isaiah 1–39: A New Translation with Introduction and Commentary* (New York: Doubleday, 2000), 276, 280.

26. Though the nature of these creatures, sometimes referred to in translations as "satyrs" (KJV) or "goat demons" (NRSV), is obscure, something other than simple goats seems to be in view. See Blenkinsopp, *Isaiah 1–39*, 280, 453–54.

27. Blenkinsopp, "Cityscape to Landscape," 41–42; id., *Isaiah 1–39*, 448–49, 453–54.

28. Leal, "Negativity towards Wilderness in the Biblical Record," 369, and sources cited there.

29. Blenkinsopp, *Isaiah 1–39*, 454.

30. On this important biblical theme, see Jon D. Levenson, *Creation and the Persistence of Evil: The Jewish Drama of Divine Omnipotence* (Princeton, NJ: Princeton University Press, 1988).

31. Tucker, "The Peaceable Kingdom and a Covenant with Wild Animals," 222.

32. See Bernd U. Schipper, "Egyptian Background to the Psalms," in William P. Brown, ed., *The Oxford Handbook of the Psalms* (Oxford: Oxford University Press, 2014). For a translation of the Egyptian hymn, see Miriam Lichtheim, *Ancient Egyptian Literature: Volume II: The New Kingdom*, 2nd rev. ed. (Berkeley: University of California Press, 2006), 96–100.

33. See, e.g., discussions of the psalm in relation to Creation themes in Levenson, *Creation and the Persistence of Evil*; Ronald A. Simkins, *Creator and Creation: Nature in the Worldview of Ancient Israel* (Peabody, MA: Hendrickson, 1994); Terence E. Fretheim, *God and World in the Old Testament: A Relational Theology of Creation* (Nashville: Abingdon, 2005); Ellen F. Davis, *Scripture, Culture, and Agriculture: An Agrarian Reading of the Bible* (Cambridge: Cambridge University Press, 2009); and William P. Brown, *The Seven Pillars of Creation: The Bible, Science, and the Ecology of Wonder* (Oxford: Oxford University Press, 2010).

34. Levenson, *Creation and the Persistence of Evil*, 57.

35. See MacDonald, *What Did the Ancient Israelites Eat?* 19–31.

36. For this understanding of the verb more often translated "create," see James Barr, *Biblical Faith and Natural Theology* (Oxford: Oxford University Press, 1993), 84.

37. See Levenson, *Creation and the Persistence of Evil*, 55–57.

38. Barr, *Biblical Faith and Natural Theology*, 84; his emphasis.

39. Elizabeth Johnson, *Ask the Beasts*, 273–75.

40. I explore this radicality further in "Job" in Deryn Guest et al., eds., *The Queer Bible Commentary* (London: SCM Press, 2006), which also discusses some of the points made here.

41. The book's inclusion of multiple points of view is articulated well in Carol A. Newsom, *The Book of Job: A Contest of Moral Imaginations* (Oxford: Oxford University Press, 2003).

42. On the book's use of Creation and nature imagery, see Carol A. Newsom, "The Book of Job," in Leander Keck et al., eds. *The New Interpreter's Bible*, vol. 4 (Nashville: Abingdon Press, 1996); id., *Book of Job*; Kathryn Schifferdecker, *Out of the Whirlwind: Creation Theology in the Book of Job* (Cambridge, MA:

Harvard University Press, 2008); Brown, *Seven Pillars of Creation*, 115–40; Brian R. Doak, *Consider Leviathan: Narratives of Nature and the Self in Job* (Minneapolis: Fortress Press, 2014); and Norman C. Habel, *Finding Wisdom in Nature: An Eco-Wisdom Reading of the Book of Job* (Sheffield, Eng.: Sheffield Phoenix, 2014).

43. See Levenson, *Creation and the Persistence of Evil*; Bernard F. Batto, *Slaying the Dragon: Mythmaking in the Biblical Tradition* (Louisville: Westminster John Knox Press, 1992); John Day, *God's Conflict with the Dragon and the Sea* (Cambridge: Cambridge University Press, 1985); Simkins, *Creator and Creation*. For a creative theological reading of the Bible's representation of relationships between deity and chaos, see Catherine Keller, *Face of the Deep: A Theology of Becoming* (New York: Routledge, 2003.

44. Newson, "Book of Job," 602.

45. Edward L. Greenstein, "In Job's Face / Facing Job," in Fiona Black, Roland Boer, and Erin Runions, eds., *The Labour of Reading: Desire, Alienation, and Biblical Interpretation* (Atlanta: Society of Biblical Literature, 1999), 307–8.

46. Newsom, "Book of Job," 609.

47. Borowski, *Every Living Thing*, 190.

48. This passage uses different Hebrew terminology for the ostrich than most of the other passages that refer to it, but scholars generally agree that an ostrich is envisaged.

49. Norman C. Habel, *The Book of Job* (Philadelphia: Westminster Press, 1985), 347.

50. Newsom, "Book of Job," 615; cf. Day, *God's Conflict with the Dragon and the Sea*, 62–87.

51. Brown, *Seven Pillars of Creation*, 130.

52. Marvin H. Pope, *Job* (Garden City, NY: Doubleday, 1973), 323–24; Habel, *Book of Job*, 565–56.

53. Timothy K. Beal, *Religion and Its Monsters* (New York: Routledge, 2002), 50.

54. Levenson, *Creation and the Persistence of Evil*, 17.

55. Cf. Day, *God's Conflict with the Dragon and the Sea*, 83, 87.

56. Beal, *Religion and Its Monsters*, 51–2

57. Derrida, *Animal That Therefore I Am*, 31.

58. Tova Forti, "Of Ships and Seas, and Fish and Beasts: Viewing the Concept of Universal Providence in the Book of Jonah through the Prism of Psalms," *Journal for the Study of the Old Testament* 35/3 (2011): 370.

59. E.g., Anne Benvenuti, *Spirit Unleashed: Reimagining Human–Animal Relations* (Eugene, OR: Cascade Books, 2014), 12–13.

60. See, e.g., Lisa Sideris, *Environmental Ethics, Ecological Theology, and Natural Selection* (New York: Columbia University Press, 2002). Cf. James Rachels, *Created from Animals: The Moral Implications of Darwinism* (New York: Oxford University Press, 1990).

61. Derrida, *Beast and the Sovereign*, 1: 13.

CHAPTER 6

1. See, e.g., Hiebert, *Yahwist's Landscape*; Simkins, *Creator and Creation*; Fretheim, *God and World in the Old Testament*; Davis, *Scripture, Culture, and Agriculture*. For an earlier criticism of these now discredited ways of thinking about the Bible and nature, see James Barr, "Man and Nature: The Ecological Controversy and the Old Testament," *Bulletin of the John Rylands University Library* 55/1 (1972): 9–32; as well as Barr, *Biblical Faith and Natural Theology*.

2. Kimberley Patton, "'He Who Sits in the Heavens Laughs': Recovering Animal Theology in the Abrahamic Traditions," *Harvard Theological Review* 93/4 (2000): 422–23; her emphasis.

3. Levenson, *Creation and the Persistence of Evil*, 17.

4. Patton, "'He Who Sits in the Heavens Laughs,'" 402–3; her emphasis. Page numbers cited parenthetically in the discussion that follows refer to this.

5. Jane Goodall, *Reason for Hope: A Spiritual Journey* (New York: Soko Publications, 1999), 174.

6. Donovan O. Schaefer, "Do Animals Have Religion? Interdisciplinary Perspectives on Religion and Embodiment," *Anthrozoös* 25 (2012), supplement: 173–89. Page numbers cited parenthetically in the discussion that follows refer to this.

7. Schaefer, *Religious Affects*, 206–7.

8. Ibid., 212.

9. Gross, *Question of the Animal and Religion*, 115. Page numbers cited parenthetically in the discussion that follows refer to this.

10. E.g., Tim Ingold, *The Perception of the Environment: Essays on Livelihood, Dwelling and Skill* (London: Routledge, 2000).

11. Deane-Drummond et al., eds., *Animals as Religious Subjects*.

12. Schaefer, "Do Animals Have Religion," 174.

13. Cf. Agamben, *The Open*, 33–38, *passim*.

14. Calarco, *Thinking through Animals*, 6.

15. There is a very large literature here. For accessible summary discussions, see Frans de Waal, *Are We Smart Enough to Know How Smart Animals Are?* (New York: Norton, 2016); Safina, *Beyond Words*; Virginia Morrell, *Animal Wise: The Thoughts and Emotions of Our Fellow Creatures* (New York: Crown, 2013); Jonathan Balcombe, *Second Nature: The Inner Lives of Animals* (New York: Palgrave Macmillan, 2010). In addition to primates, elephants have played an important role in these discussions. See, e.g., Cynthia Moss, *Elephant Memories: With a New Afterword* (Chicago: University of Chicago Press, 2000 [1988]); Joyce Poole, *Coming of Age with Elephants* (New York: Hyperion, 1996); Katy Payne, *Silent Thunder: In the Presence of Elephants* (New York: Penguin Books, 1998); G. A.

Bradshaw, *Elephants on the Edge: What Animals Teach Us about Humanity* (New Haven, CT: Yale University Press, 2009); Caitlin O'Connell, *Elephant Don: The Politics of a Pachyderm Posse* (Chicago: University of Chicago Press, 2015); Safina, *Beyond Words*, 5–135; Caitrin Nicol, "Do Elephants Have Souls?" *The New Atlantis: A Journal of Technology & Society* (2013), www.thenewatlantis.com/publications/do-elephants-have-souls. For a perspective from the side of religious studies, see Jacob J. Erickson, "Elephant Orphans and Ecological Spiritualities: An Earth Day Reflection," *Religion Dispatches* (April 22, 2015), http://religiondispatches.org/elephant-orphans-and-ecological-spiritualities. On animals that are frequently eaten by humans, see now Barbara J. King, *Personalities on the Plate: The Lives and Minds of Animals We Eat* (Chicago: University of Chicago Press, 2017).

16. Frans de Waal, *The Bonobo and the Atheist: In Search of Humanism among the Primates* (New York: Norton, 2013), 16.

17. Jane Goodall, *In the Shadow of Man (1971)*, rev. ed. (Boston: Houghton Mifflin, 1988), 35–37.

18. See de Waal, *Are We Smart Enough*, 63–94, and Safina, *Beyond Words*, 191–99.

19. Goodall, *Through a Window: 30 Years with the Chimpanzees of Gombe* (London: Weidenfeld & Nicolson, 1990), 15.

20. See, e.g., William McGrew, *The Cultured Chimpanzee: Reflections on Cultural Primatology* (Cambridge: Cambridge University Press, 2004). For a path-breaking paper on this topic see A. Whiten et al., "Cultures in Chimpanzees," *Nature* 399 (17 June 1999): 682–85.

21. Goodall, *Through a Window*, 83–94. The implications of such discoveries for our own self-understanding are thoughtfully explored in Ronnie Zoe Hawkins, "Seeing Ourselves as Primates," *Ethics & the Environment* 7/2 (2002): 60–103.

22. See, e.g., Eugene Linden, *Silent Partners: The Legacy of the Ape Language Experiments* (New York: Ballantine, 1986); Sue Savage-Rumbaugh and Roger Lewin, *Kanzi: The Ape at the Brink of the Human Mind* (New York: John Wiley & Sons, 1994); Roger Fouts, *Next of Kin: My Conversations with Chimpanzees* (New York: Avon, 1997); Jerry H. Gill, *If a Chimpanzee Could Talk: And Other Reflections on Language Acquisition* (Tucson: University of Arizona Press, 1997), 9–28; Hearne, *Adam's Task*, 18–41; Fudge, *Animal*, 117–28; Barbara J. King, *The Dynamic Dance: Nonvocal Communication in African Great Apes* (Cambridge, MA: Harvard University Press, 2004); Elizabeth Hess, *Nim Chimpsky: The Chimp Who Would Be Human* (New York: Bantam Dell, 2008); W. A. Hillix and Duane Rumbaugh, *Animal Bodies, Human Minds: Ape, Dolphin, and Parrot Language Skills* (New York: Kluwer Academic/Plenum, 2010); Andrew R. Halloran, *The Song of the Ape: Understanding the Language of Chimpanzees* (New York: St. Martin's Press, 2012); de Waal, *Are We Smart Enough*, 95–117.

23. See esp. King, *Dynamic Dance*, and Halloran, *Song of the Ape*.
24. Hearne, *Adam's Task*, 39.
25. Frans. de Waal, *Chimpanzee Politics: Power and Sex among Apes* (1982), 25th anniversary ed. (Baltimore: Johns Hopkins University Press, 2007), 4.
26. Frans. de Waal, *Primates and Philosophers: How Morality Evolved* (Princeton, NJ: Princeton University Press, 2006), 8. Among his other work see, for similar themes, *Good Natured: The Origins of Right and Wrong in Humans and Other Animals* (Cambridge, MA: Harvard University Press, 1996); *The Age of Empathy: Nature's Lessons for a Kinder Society* (New York: Three Rivers Press, 2009); and *Bonobo and the Atheist*.
27. De Waal, *Good Natured*, 17.
28. De Waal, *Bonobo and the Atheist*, 235.
29. Ibid., 213.
30. King, *Evolving God*, 41.
31. Barbara King, "Seeing Spirituality in Chimpanzees," *Atlantic*, March 29, 2016, www.theatlantic.com/science/archive/2016/03/chimpanzee-spirituality/475731, makes this clear.
32. King, *Dynamic Dance*, 221–22; her emphasis.
33. King, *Evolving God*, 51; her emphasis. Page numbers cited parenthetically in the discussion that follows refer to this.
34. King, *Being with Animals*, 29.
35. Barbara J. King, *How Animals Grieve* (Chicago: University of Chicago Press, 2013).
36. Goodall, *Through a Window*, 178–79.
37. Ibid., 202.
38. Goodall, *Reason for Hope*, 189.
39. Jane. Goodall, "Primate Spirituality," in Bron Taylor, ed., *The Encyclopedia of Religion and Nature* (New York: Continuum, 2005), 1304.
40. Goodall, *Reason for Hope*, 189.
41. Goodall, "Primate Spirituality," 1303–4. See also Goodall's interview with Patton and Paul Waldau, "The Dance of Awe," in Patton and Waldau, *Communion of Subjects*.
42. De Waal, *Bonobo and the Atheist*, 199.
43. King, *Being with Animals*, 159.
44. Stewart Guthrie, "Animal Animism: Evolutionary Roots of Religious Cognition," in Ilkka Pyysiäinen and Veikko Anttonen, eds., *Current Approaches to the Cognitive Science of Religion* (New York: Continuum, 2002).
45. Schaefer, *Religious Affects*, 200–201, *passim*. See also James B. Harrod, "The Case for Chimpanzee Religion," *Journal for the Study of Religion, Nature and Culture* 8/1 (2014): 8–45.
46. Barbara Smuts, "Encounters with Animal Minds," *Journal of Consciousness Studies* 8/5–7 (2001): 301.

47. Mark Bekoff, *Minding Animals: Awareness, Emotions, and Heart* (New York: Oxford University Press, 2002); id., "Wild Justice, Cooperation, and Fair Play: Minding Manners, Being Nice, and Feeling Good," in Robert W. Sussman and Audrey R. Chapman, eds., *The Origins and Nature of Sociality* (New York: Aline de Gruyter, 2004); id., *The Emotional Lives of Animals* (Novato, CA: New World Library, 2007); Bekoff and Jessica Pierce, *Wild Justice: The Moral Lives of Animals* (Chicago: University of Chicago Press, 2009). See also Dale Peterson, *The Moral Lives of Animals* (London: Bloomsbury, 2011).

48. Fretheim, *God and World in the Old Testament*, 123.

49. Ibid., 204.

50. McKenzie, *How to Read the Bible*, 7, 10; his emphasis.

51. Adele Berlin, "A Rejoinder to John A. Miles, Jr., with Some Observations on the Nature of Prophecy," *Jewish Quarterly Review* 66/4 (1976): 227–35.

52. Brenner, "Jonah's Poem," 192.

53. Fretheim, *God and World in the Old Testament*, 249–68.

54. Ibid., 259–60. Cf. Delbert R. Hillers, "A Study of Psalm 148," *Catholic Biblical Quarterly* 40 (1978): 323–34.

55. See Brent A. Strawn and Joel M. LeMon, " 'Everything That Has Breath': Animal Praise in Psalm 150:6 in the Light of Ancient Near Eastern Iconography," in Susanne Bickel, ed., *Bilder als Quellen / Images as Sources: Studies on Ancient Near Eastern Artefacts and the Bible Inspired by Othmar Keel* (Göttingen: Vandenhoeck & Ruprecht, 2007).

56. Fretheim, *God and World in the Old Testament*, 249, 255.

CHAPTER 7

1. Mark V. Barrow Jr., *Nature's Ghosts: Confronting Extinction from the Age of Jefferson to the Age of Ecology* (Chicago: University of Chicago Press, 2009), 27.

2. On Augustine, see Claudine Cohen, *The Fate of the Mammoth: Fossils, Myth, and History*, trans. William Rodarmor (Chicago: University of Chicago Press, 2002), 23–26. Cf. Paul Semonin, *American Monster: How the Nation's First Prehistoric Creatures Became a Symbol of National Identity* (New York: New York University Press, 2000).

3. See, e.g., Sarah Kaplan, "Earth Is on Brink of a Sixth Mass Extinction, Scientists Say, and It's Humans' Fault," *Washington Post*, June 22, 2015, www.washingtonpost.com/news/morning-mix/wp/2015/06/22/the-earth-is-on-the-brink-of-a-sixth-mass-extinction-scientists-say-and-its-humans-fault. For a valuable book-length account by a science journalist, see Elizabeth Kolbert, *The Sixth Extinction: An Unnatural History* (New York: Holt, 2014).

4. Holmes Rolston III, "Creation: God and Endangered Species," in Ke Chung Kim and Robert D. Weaver, eds., *Biodiversity and Landscapes* (Cambridge: Cambridge University Press, 1994), 48.

5. See, e.g., Gerardo Ceballos et al., "Accelerated Modern Human-Induced Species Losses: Entering the Sixth Mass Extinction," *Science Advances* 1/5 (2015), http://advances.sciencemag.org/content/1/5/e1400253.full; Kolbert, *Sixth Extinction*; Anthony D. Barnosky, *Dodging Extinction: Power, Food, Money, and the Future of Life on Earth* (Berkeley: University of California Press, 2014); Eric Chivian and Aaron Bernstein, *Sustaining Life: How Human Health Depends on Biodiversity* (Oxford: Oxford University Press, 2008); Stephen M. Meyer, *The End of the Wild* (Cambridge, MA: MIT Press, 2006); Chris D. Thomas et al., "Extinction Risk from Climate Change," *Nature* 427 (January 2004): 145–48; Edward O. Wilson, *The Future of Life* (New York: Random House, 2002). And see too www.iucn.org and www.biologicaldiversity.org.

6. Will Steffen et al., "The Anthropocene: Conceptual and Historical Perspectives," *Philosophical Transactions of the Royal Society* 369 (2011), 843. See also Will Steffen, Paul J. Crutzen, and John R. McNeill, "The Anthropocene: Are Humans Now Overwhelming the Great Forces of Nature?" *Ambio* 36/8 (2007): 614–21.

7. Jeremy Davies, *The Birth of the Anthropocene* (Berkeley: University of California Press, 2016).

8. Paul J. Crutzen, "Geology of Mankind," *Nature* 415 (January 2002), 23.

9. For a focus on agriculture, see Bruce D. Smith and Melinda A. Zeder, "The Onset of the Anthropocene," *Anthropocene* 4 (2013): 8–13. For a focus on stratigraphy, see Jan Zalasiewicz et al., "Are We Now Living in the Anthropocene?" *GSA Today* 18/2 (2008): 4–8. For additional analysis, see Davies, *Birth of the Anthropocene*.

10. Morton, *Dark Ecology*, 38–40.

11. Jason W. Moore, ed., *Anthropocene or Capitalocene? Nature, History, and the Crisis of Capitalism* (Oakland, CA: PM Press, 2016). Cf. Ashley Dawson, *Extinction: A Radical History* (New York: O/R Books, 2016).

12. Dipesh Chakrabarty, "The Climate of History: Four Theses," *Critical Inquiry* 35/2 (2009): 218, 221, 212.

13. Donna Haraway, "Anthropocene, Capitalocene, Plantationocene, Chthulucene: Making Kin," *Environmental Humanities* 6 (2015): 159–65; id., "Staying with the Trouble: Anthropocene, Capitalocene, Chthulucene," in Moore, ed., *Anthropocene or Capitalocene?*; Haraway et al., "Anthropologists Are Talking—About the Anthropocene," *Ethnos* 81/3 (2016): 535–64. As I was completing this manuscript, Haraway republished these arguments in her book *Staying with the Trouble: Making Kin in the Chthulucene* (Durham, NC: Duke University Press, 2016), which I have only partly been able to take into account here.

14. For discussion see Paul L. Koch and Anthony D. Barnosky, "Late Quaternary Extinctions: State of the Debate," *Annual Review of Ecology, Evolution, and Systematics* 37 (2006): 215–50.

15. See Barnosky, *Dodging Extinction*, for helpful discussion of such issues. The most influential list of species threatened with extinction to varying degrees remains the IUCN Red List of Threatened Species: www.iucn.org/resources/conservation-tools/iucn-red-list-threatened-species.

16. See the excellent discussion by Anna L. Peterson, *Being Animal: Beasts and Boundaries in Nature Ethics* (New York: Columbia University Press, 2013). For a helpful earlier discussion, see Sideris, *Environmental Ethics, Ecological Theology, and Natural Selection*. For a stark way of framing these issues, see Eugene C. Hargrove, ed., *The Animal Rights/Environmental Ethics Debate: The Environmental Perspective* (Albany: State University of New York Press, 1992).

17. Palmer, *Animal Ethics in Context*, 63.

18. Regan, *Case for Animal Rights*, 361; his emphasis.

19. Deborah Bird Rose, "Multispecies Knots of Ethical Time," *Environmental Philosophy* 9/1 (2012): 128.

20. See, e.g., http://extinctionstudies.org; Deborah Bird Rose, *Wild Dog Dreaming*; and now Ursula K. Heine, *Imagining Extinction: The Cultural Meanings of Endangered Species* (Chicago: University of Chicago Press, 2016).

21. Thom van Dooren, *Flight Ways: Life and Loss at the Edge of Extinction* (New York: Columbia University Press, 2014), 5. Page numbers cited parenthetically in the discussion that follows refer to this source.

22. See, e.g., Haraway, "Staying with the Trouble," 41–42.

23. In addition to *When Species Meet* and *Companion Species Manifesto*, see, e.g., Haraway's earlier *Primate Visions: Gender, Race, and Nature in the World of Modern Science* (New York: Routledge, 1989) and *Simians, Cyborgs, and Women: The Reinvention of Nature* (New York: Routledge, 1991).

24. Haraway, "Staying with the Trouble," 45; her emphasis.

25. Ibid., 35–36; id., "Anthropocene, Capitalocene, Plantationocene, Chthulucene," 160.

26. Ibid., 61, n. 61.

27. Rolston, "Creation," 48.

28. See, e.g., Dalley, *Myths from Mesopotamia*, 29–31, 110–12.

29. See, e.g., Charles C. Mann and Mark L. Plummer, *Noah's Choice: The Future of Endangered Species* (New York: Knopf, 1995); Scully, *Dominion*, 368–75.

30. See, e.g., for God, Deut. 26:15; Jer. 25:30; Zech. 2:13 (Hebrew 2:17); Ps. 26:8; 68:5 (Hebrew 68:6); 2 Chron. 30:27; 36:15; and for jackals, Jer. 9:11 (Hebrew 9:10); 10:22; 49:33; 51:37.

31. Cf. Habel, *Inconvenient Text*, 11–16.

32. For a convenient discussion by a biblical scholar with ecological commitments, see Norman Habel, *The Birth, the Curse and the Greening of the Earth: An Ecological Reading of Genesis 1–11* (Sheffield, Eng.: Sheffield Phoenix Press, 2011), 35–38.

33. Laura Ogden et al., "Global Assemblages, Resilience, and Earth Stewardship in the Anthropocene," *Frontiers in Ecology and the Environment* 11/7 (2013): 341–47.

34. Diane Jacobson, "Biblical Bases for Ecojustice Ethics," in Dieter T. Hessel, ed., *Theology for Earth Community: A Field Guide* (Maryknoll, N.Y.: Orbis Books, 1996), 48.

35. See, e.g., Philip Cafaro and Eileen Crist, *Life on the Brink: Environmentalists Confront Overpopulation* (Athens: University of Georgia Press, 2012).

36. Haraway, "Anthropocene, Capitalocene, Plantationocene, Chthulucene," 161.

37. Cf. Tony Weis, *The Ecological Footprint: The Global Burden of Industrial Livestock* (New York: Zed Books, 2013); Barnosky, *Dodging Extinction*.

38. Judith Butler, *Frames of War: When Is Life Grievable?* (New York: Verso, 2009), 19.

39. Cf. Chloë Taylor, "The Precarious Lives of Animals: Butler, Coetzee, and Animal Ethics," *Philosophy Today* 52/1 (2008): 60–72; Oliver, *Animal Lessons*, 42–44; James Stanescu, "Species Trouble: Judith Butler, Mourning, and the Precarious Lives of Animals," *Hypatia* 27/3 (2012): 567–82; Richard Iveson, "Domestic Scenes and Species Trouble: On Judith Butler and Other Animals," *Journal for Critical Animal Studies* 10/4 (2012): 20–40.

40. Pierpaolo Antonello and Roberto Farneti, "Antigone's Claim: A Conversation with Judith Butler," *Theory and Event* 12/1 (2009), https://muse-jhu-edu.cts.idm.oclc.org/article/263144.

41. See further Butler, *Precarious Life: The Powers of Mourning and Violence* (New York: Verso, 2004); id., *Giving an Account of Oneself* (New York: Fordham University Press, 2005).

42. In Antonello and Farneti, "Antigone's Claim."

Index

Aaron, 105
Abraham, 31, 73, 87, 89, 95, 143, 145
adam, 38, 156, 158, 160, 161
Adam and Eve, 34, 39, 41–42, 49;
  naming of animals and Eve, 38, 68;
  talking snake, 38, 100–101
Adams, Carol, 88
Agamben, Giorgio: on anthropogenesis/
  anthropological machine, 12, 13, 147;
  The Open, 23
American Sign Language, 149
Amos: 1:2, 122; 5:19, 102; 5:22, 74
Anderson, Gary, 74, 76
animal ethics: vs. animal hermeneutics,
  17, 106, 115; and Balaam's donkey,
  16–17, 92–93, 109–15; and
  environmentalism, 169; and Levinas,
  51–52, 53
animal extinctions: as anthropogenic,
  18–19, 166–67, 168–69, 170, 171,
  173, 176–77, 178–80; Cretaceous-
  Paleogene (K-Pg) event, 166; sixth
  mass extinction, 6, 164–65, 166
animal hermeneutics: vs. animal ethics,
  17, 106, 115; in biblical interpretation,
  28–44; Gross on, 24, 28, 93; and
  human self-understanding, 24,
  28–29. *See also* companion species;
  human-animal binary
animal religion, 142–47, 149, 151, 152,
  153, 154–63
animal rights, 11, 12, 64, 71
animals: and affect, 6, 112–14, 145–46,
  148, 150, 152–53, 154, 163; boundary
  with humans, 10–14, 15, 16, 25, 28,
  33–40, 58–59, 62–63, 64–65, 68,
  69–70, 73–74, 80–81, 87, 112, 146,
  147, 148–50, 157, 171, 178; clean vs.
  unclean animals, 3, 58, 60–61, 62,
  77, 118, 196n56; cognitive abilities,
  6, 144, 145, 146, 148; communicative
  abilities, 3, 10, 151–52, 154, 155;
  compassion regarding, 110–15, 146;
  domesticated vs. wild, 17, 41, 56, 63,
  68, 76, 77, 84, 109, 117–18, 119, 121,
  130, 134, 169; eating of, 4, 6, 11, 30–
  31, 39, 40, 41, 42, 49, 52, 66–67, 71,
  72, 77, 82, 85, 89–90, 112, 178, 179;
  and human self-understanding, 24,
  28–29; and places, 171, 174–75; and
  the poor, 58, 63, 65; relationship with
  God, 2, 17, 82, 87, 91, 103, 104–5,
  106, 111, 116, 117, 118, 121, 122, 123,
  124–25, 127, 128–29, 130–31, 133–38,
  139, 140–45, 155–63, 172, 173–76, 178,
  181, 206n17; as religious/theological
  subjects, 18, 142–43; subordination
  to humans, 2, 4–5, 6, 36–37, 38, 130,
  131, 138, 139, 165, 175, 176–77, 178;
  tool-making by, 148; treatment by
  humans, 4–5, 6, 11, 13, 15–16, 17, 18,
  34, 35–36, 37, 39, 40, 42, 58, 59–61,
  63, 64–65, 66–90, 91–92, 97, 99–
  100, 106, 108, 109–15, 111, 146, 160;
  women associated with, 41–43, 63–
  64, 68, 87–88, 107
animal sacrifice, 60–61, 63, 66–90;
  and companion species, 76–77,

83–84; Derrida on, 16, 60, 66, 67, 68–74, 83, 86, 146; differentiation of humans regarding, 79–80; and domestication, 76–78, 83, 84–86, 87; eligibility of animals, 59, 76–79, 81, 86, 111; and gender, 80; and God, 37, 66–67, 73, 75, 79, 80, 81–82, 85, 87, 160; vs. grain offerings, 75, 79; vs. human sacrifice, 15–16, 59, 60, 65, 80–81, 87–89; Israelite daily offerings, 78, 83; Klawans on, 16, 67, 83–90; as *minchah*, 75; multivalence of biblical sacrifice, 74–76; as sin offerings, 79; as smelled by God, 81–82, 87; specificity in, 78–79; as *zebach*, 76

animal species: diversity of, 165, 169; and God, 91, 144; preservation of, 165, 172–74, 175–77, 181; species difference vs. differences among humans, 15, 25, 28, 40–44, 63. See also animal extinctions; companion species

animal studies: vs. animal behavior disciplines, 8; and animal extinctions, 169–70; Calarco on, 10–13; and cats, 45–46; definitions of, 8–9; difference approach in, 10, 11–12; and dogs, 45–46; identity approach in, 10–11; indistinction approach in, 10, 12–13; methodological diversity in, 8–9, 14; relationship to biblical interpretation, 3–4, 5, 6–8, 14–15, 17–18, 19, 24, 28, 29, 34, 36, 44, 53, 63–65, 67, 92–93, 108–9, 118–19, 121, 142–45, 155, 164–65, 169–70, 172–81; zoological gaze in, 17, 118–25, 129, 130, 139, 155

animal symbolism, 1, 2, 3–4, 5, 14
antelope, 77
Anthropocene, 166, 167–68, 172, 177
anthropocentrism, 5, 7, 9, 10, 13, 36, 52–53, 64
Aquinas, Thomas: on offering vs. sacrifice, 76; on subjugation of animals, 113

Aristotle, 43, 112–13
ark of the covenant, 103
Asclepius, 47
Ashkelon, 57
Atrahasis, 82
Augustine, St., 164

Babylon, 126, 127, 158; Babylonian exile, 128, 129
Balaam's donkey, 93–100, 113; and animal ethics, 16–17, 92–93, 109–15; and avoidance of *tsaar baalei chayyim*, 92, 114–15; as faithful, 99–100; God's relationship with Balaam, 93, 94, 95, 99, 100, 103, 104; vs. other biblical animals, 95–106, 114; vs. other biblical donkeys, 95–96, 97, 98–99, 114; vs. other subjugated equines, 97, 106–9; vs. talking snake of Genesis, 100–101; vs. Xanthus, 96, 100
Balak, 93, 94, 95
Barr, James, 132
Bathsheba, 42
Beal, Timothy, 136, 138
bears, 102, 103, 104, 117, 121, 123, 125
behemoth, behemah, 118, 136, 156, 158, 160, 161
Behemoth, 135–36, 139, 174
Bekoff, Mark, 154
Bellerophon and Pegasus, 69, 70, 82
Bentham, Jeremy: on suffering, 114
Bereshit Rabbath 12.9, 174
Beverly, Jared, 203n35
Bilhah, 41, 43
Bird, Phyllis, 57
birds, 111, 131, 138, 145, 161, 170, 175; sacrifice of, 76–77, 78, 79. See also ostriches
Blenkinsopp, Joseph, 125–27
Böck, Barbara, 47
Bonn-Oberkassel dog, 46
bonobos, 148, 150
Bough, Jill, 97
Brenner, Athalya, 160

Brown, William, 136
Budiansky, Stephen, 46
Butler, Judith: on life as precarious, 180

Cain and Abel, 34, 37, 66–67, 75, 79; Derrida on, 16, 34, 66, 67, 68–70
Calarco, Matthew: on animal studies, 10–13; on human-animal binary, 15, 25, 34, 62, 112, 148
Calvin, John, 150, 196n57
camels, 26, 27, 28, 77, 107
Canaanites: slaughter of, 64
capitalism/Capitalocene, 168
cats: as companion species, 45–46; role in animal studies, 45
cattle, 3, 22, 27, 28, 30, 32, 117; sacrifice of, 76–77, 78–79
Cavalieri, Paola, 11
cave paintings of animals, 1
Chakrabarty, Dipesh: on capitalism, 168
chayot, 118
Chen, Mel Y., 14
cherem, 81
Chimera, 16, 68–69, 73–74, 82
chimpanzees, 144, 148, 149–50, 152–53, 154
Christianity: significance of animals for, 4, 22–23, 33, 143–44
1 Chronicles 29:11, 161
2 Chronicles 9:21, 155
Clark, David, 52, 53–54
Clement of Alexandria, 111, 196n57
Coetzee, J. M.: *Disgrace*, 46
Cogan, Mordechai, 104
companion species: dogs, 15, 29, 45–46, 77, 117; donkeys, 96, 117; goats, 15, 30–33, 45, 117, 190n17; Haraway on, 14–15, 25, 28–30, 45; and sacrifice, 76–77, 83–84; sheep, 15, 30–33, 45, 117, 190n17
compassion regarding animals, 110–15, 146
Coppinger, Raymond and Lorna: on village dogs, 55, 56
Cretaceous-Paleogene (K-Pg) event/ Cretaceous-Tertiary (K-T) event, 166

Crutzen, Paul: on the Anthropocene, 167

Daniel: 6:22, 103; 6:24, 103–4; 7, 106; Daniel and the lions, 2, 103–4, 105
Darwin, Charles, 10, 62–63, 139, 150, 164
David, 31–32, 42, 54, 95, 117
Dawkins, Richard, 150, 151
Dead Sea Scrolls, 21
deer, 77, 134
Deleuze, Gilles, 12
DeMello, Margo, 8, 9
Derrida, Jacques: on Adam naming the animals, 68; on animal sacrifice, 16, 60, 66, 67, 68–74, 83, 86, 146; on animals as homogeneous set, 69, 78; *The Animal That Therefore I Am*, 16, 34, 36, 45, 66, 68–74; on animal vs. human differences, 11–12, 13, 34–36, 63, 69–71, 119; *The Beast and the Sovereign*, 72, 123, 139; on Bellerophon and Pegasus, 69, 70; on Bentham, 114; on Cain and Abel, 16, 34, 66, 67, 68–70; on carnivorous virility, 42; on carnophallogocentrism, 40–41, 42, 72; on the Chimera, 16, 68–69, 70; "Eating Well", 60, 71; "Force of Law", 71, 73; on heterogeneous multiplicity of the living, 35, 38, 70, 119, 138, 146, 165, 173; on human-animal binary, 15, 25, 35, 69–70; vs. Klawans, 86, 88–89, 90; on Levinas, 51, 52, 53, 59–60, 72, 96; on neologism *animot*, 70, 73; on non-criminal putting to death, 71, 81, 89; on philosophy and animals, 69, 73; on the Western subject, 71–72
Descartes, René, 72
Despret, Vinciane, 108
Deuteronomy: 4:24, 81, 82; 5:14, 110; 7:14, 33; 7:22, 124; 9:3, 81; 14:0, 196n56; 14:3, 77; 14:3–21, 58; 14:4–5, 77; 14:6, 77; 14:21, 77, 111; 22:1–

Index

3, 110; 22:4, 110; 22:6–7, 111; 22:10, 111; 23:5, 93; 23:18, 56–57; 25:4, 110; 28:53–57, 127; 32:22, 81; 32:24, 124; 33:17, 134

De Waal, Frans: *Chimpanzee Politics*, 149–50; on chimpanzees, 153; on human-animal boundary, 148; on morality and animals, 18, 150–51; on religion, 151, 152, 154

dietary laws, 3, 27, 58, 77, 146, 196n56

Dinah, 27

dogs: burials of, 46–47; as companion species, 15, 29, 45–46, 77, 117; domestication of, 30, 35, 46, 54–55, 56; dung and biblical scrolls, 57–58; in Exodus, 15, 49–62, 50, 63, 64, 65, 109, 195n39; and Gula-Ninisina, 47; and healing, 47; and human dignity, 50–51; and human hierarchy, 54–55; and insults, 54; and prostitutes, 56–57; role in animal studies, 45; as scavengers, 55–56; sense of smell, 46; and temple payments, 56–57

domestication: and animal sacrifice, 76–78, 83, 84–86, 87; of dogs, 30, 35, 46, 54–55, 56; domesticated vs. wild animals, 17, 41, 56, 63, 68, 76, 77, 84, 109, 117–18, 119, 121, 130, 134, 169

donkeys, 26, 27, 28, 32, 63, 77, 111; burials of, 98; as companion species, 96, 117; in Covenant Code, 58, 109; and lions, 102, 103, 104; in metaphors, 44, 107; redemption in Exodus, 60–61. *See also* Balaam's donkey

Douglas, Mary, 56, 83; on food laws and unclean animals, 3; *Purity and Danger*, 3, 77

eagles, 135, 139
Edom, 24, 32, 43, 126–27
Egyptian plagues, 105, 156, 157
Eilberg-Schwartz, Howard, 84
Elisha/Elijah, 101–3, 104, 105, 123; ravens of, 102, 105, 134

Enkidu, 25
environmentalism, 169, 178–79
Esau: and Edom, 24, 43; hairiness of, 23, 25, 26, 41; masculinity of, 41; relationship with Jacob, 24, 26–27, 32, 39–40, 43
evolution of life, 139, 150
Exodus: 3:1, 31; 3:11–16, 156; 4:20, 95; 7:8–12, 105; 8:17–18, 156; 9:4, 156; 9:5, 156; 9:9–10, 156; 9:21, 156; 9:22, 156; 11:4–7, 34, 51, 53, 57–58, 61–62; 11:5, 61, 62; 11:6, 50, 61; 11:7, 50, 61, 62, 155–56; 12:12, 34; 12:29–32, 34; 12:32, 156; 12:38, 156; 13:1–2, 88; 13:12–13, 99; 13:13, 60–61; 13:15, 61, 155–56; 14, 158; 14:23–15:1, 156; 14:30, 142; 15, 157, 158; 15:10, 158; 16:13, 105; 17:2–6, 156; 19:13, 156; 20:17, 42, 43; 20:30, 56; 21:1–23:33, 58–59; 22:29–30, 59, 61, 80, 88; 22:30, 111; 22:31, 49, 50, 51, 53, 54, 55, 56, 57–58, 60, 61, 77; 23:4–5, 109; 23:11, 110; 23:12, 110; 23:19, 111; 23:29, 124; 24:17, 81; 25, 110; 29:1–35, 78; 29:18, 82; 29:25, 82; 29:36, 78; 29:38–42, 81; 29:38–46, 78; 29:41, 78, 82; 29:43, 78; 29:45, 78; 34:19–20, 59, 60–61, 61, 80, 88, 99; 34:26, 111; Covenant Code, 58, 109; silent dogs of, 15, 49–62, 50, 63, 64, 65, 109, 195n39

Ezekiel: 1:11, 158; 5:10, 127; 14:13, 158; 14:17, 158; 14:19, 158; 14:21, 158; 20:25–26, 59, 80; 23:19–21, 44; 23:20, 98, 107; 25:13, 158; 29:8, 158; 29:11, 158; 34, 85; 34:11–12, 84; 34:13–14, 84; 34:16, 84; 36:11, 158; 41:22, 81; 44:7, 81; 44:16, 81

farmers, 3, 121
feminism, 12, 15, 63, 71–72, 106, 132
Fewell, Danna Nolan, 42
fish, 77
Flood, the, 111, 121, 124, 134, 157–58, 180; Noah's ark, 2, 18–19, 82, 158, 165, 172–73, 175–76, 178

Fontenay, Élisabeth de, 96, 100
Forti, Tova, 138
Francis, St., 145
Franklin, Adrian: on Bible's zoological gaze, 17; on culture, 119–20; on whale and dolphin watching, 120; on the zoological gaze, 17, 119–21
Fretheim, Terence, 157, 162, 163
Freud, Sigmund, 150

gazelles, 77
gender and ethnic differences vs. species difference, 15, 25, 28, 40–44, 62
Genesis, 1:0, 63; 1:1–2:4a, 36, 173; 1:2, 126, 158; 1:12, 173; 1:21, 38, 173–74; 1:22, 35, 175; 1:24, 37; 1:24–26, 118; 1:25, 37, 173–74; 1:26–27, 175; 1:26–28, 4, 130, 138, 139; 1:27, 36–37; 1:28, 35, 36–37, 38, 131–32, 165; 1:30, 37; 1:31, 37; 2–3, 167; 2:4b–3:24, 37; 2:7, 38; 2:16, 66; 2:18, 38; 2:19, 38, 68; 2:20, 118; 2:23, 38, 42, 68; 3:4, 38; 3:4–5, 101; 3:5, 38; 3:6, 136; 3:7, 101; 3:12, 136; 3:14, 118; 3:14–15, 101; 3:17–19, 167; 3:20, 38, 42, 68; 3:21, 39; 3:22, 37, 38; 3:22–23, 101; 4:3–5, 75; 4:4–5, 66, 68; 6:4, 164; 6:5, 176; 6:5–7, 176; 6:11, 176; 6:11–13, 176; 6:12–13, 158; 6:17, 38; 6:19, 172; 6:20, 181; 7:11, 158; 7:14, 118; 7:15, 38; 7:21, 118; 8:1, 158; 8:19, 178; 8:21, 67, 82; 9:1–3, 178; 9:2, 121, 131; 9:3, 66; 9:9–17, 111, 124, 158; 9:10, 118, 178; 9:11, 158; 9:15–17, 158; 12:16, 31; 13:2, 31; 13:5–8, 31; 16:12, 43, 107, 134, 161; 20:14, 31; 21:25–30, 31; 22:2, 80; 22:3, 95; 25:11, 25; 25:25, 25; 25:27, 25; 27:3–4, 39; 27:9, 23, 25, 31; 27:9–10, 39; 27:11, 25; 27:16, 23, 25; 29:6, 41; 30:32, 26; 30:37–42, 26; 30:37–43, 31; 30:43, 26, 43; 31:10–13, 31; 31:41, 41; 31:41–43, 32; 32:14–15, 27, 32; 32:28, 23, 24, 27; 32:32, 27; 33:13, 27, 32; 33:17, 27; 34:0, 107; 34:5, 27; 34:16, 27; 34:23, 27; 34:28, 27; 35:10, 23, 24; 38, 57; 38:17, 31; 49:14–15, 107

Gideon, 122, 142
Gilgamesh, 25, 57, 82
Gilhus, Ingvild, 82
goats: as companion species, 15, 30–33, 45, 117, 190n17; goatskins and biblical scrolls, 14, 21, 44; herding of, 30–32, 33, 41, 84, 85; mountain goats, 131, 134, 161; prohibition against boiling young goat in its mother's milk, 58, 111, 196n57; and Rebekah, 23, 25–26, 39–40; sacrifice of, 76–77, 78–79, 85
God, 32–33, 50, 104; and animal sacrifice, 37, 66–67, 73, 75, 79, 80, 81–82, 85, 87, 160; and avoidance of *tsaar baalei chayyim*, 92, 111, 114–15; commandment to increase and multiply, 2, 35, 36, 38, 132, 175; commandment to sacrifice Isaac, 80; as creator, 2, 18–19, 36–39, 41, 68, 101, 111, 118, 121, 126, 130, 132, 136, 140, 156, 157, 158, 167, 173–74; vs. dogs of Exodus, 56–57, 62; and human sacrifice, 80–81; humans as image of, 4, 36, 175, 177–78; as lion, 116–17, 121, 122–23; as predator, 116–17, 121, 122–23; providence of, 91; relationship with animals, 2, 17, 82, 87, 91, 103, 104–5, 106, 111, 116, 117, 118, 121, 122, 123, 124–25, 127, 128–29, 130–31, 133–38, 139, 140–45, 155–63, 172, 173–76, 178, 181, 206n17; relationship with Balaam, 93, 94, 95, 99, 100, 103, 104; relationship with Behemoth and Leviathan, 135–38, 139; relationship with humans, 16, 33, 91, 93, 94, 95, 99, 100, 103, 104–5, 116–17, 121, 122, 128, 129, 130, 131, 132–36, 139, 140–41, 143, 155–56, 157–60, 161, 163, 175–77, 206n17; relationship with Jonah, 104–5; as shepherd, 33, 84, 85–86, 87, 116, 123; Ten Commandments, 110; "Thou shalt not kill" command, 59–60; as unpredictable, 103

Goliath, 54, 117
Goodall, Jane, 18, 144, 145, 148, 152–54
Goodfriend, Elaine, 57
Gordon, Cyrus, 96, 100
great apes, 11, 35, 46, 148–49, 150. *See also* chimpanzees
Greenstein, Edward, 133–34
Gross, Aaron: on animal hermeneutics, 24, 28, 93; on animals and human communities, 23–24, 28, 44; on compassion for animals, 146; on Derrida and sacrifice, 72–73; *The Question of the Animal and Religion*, 19; on religious actors, 146–47; on treatment of animals by humans, 111
Gula-Ninisina, 47
Gunkel, Hermann, 66
Gunn, David, 42
Guthrie, Stewart, 154

Habel, Norman, 135
Halberstam, Judith, 14
Halbertal, Moshe: *On Sacrifice*, 75
Hamilakis, Yannis, 118
Hamor, 27, 107
Haran, Menahem, 22, 111, 196n57
Haraway, Donna, 12, 31, 108, 176; on animal-human contact zone, 29; on companion species, 14–15, 25, 28–30, 45; on dogs, 46; on human-animal distinction, 34; on human exceptionalism, 168; on multispecies events, 165, 171–72, 179; on myths, 172; on naturecultures, 29, 30, 84; on species extinction, 19; *Staying with the Trouble*, 213n13; on telling new stories, 172, 177, 179; *When Species Meet*, 203n36
Harris, Kerry, 118
Harris, Sam, 151
Hearne, Vicki, 108, 149
Heidegger, Martin, 60
Hobgood-Oster, Laura, 46
Holocaust, 50–52
Holocene, 166–67, 167

Homer's *Iliad*, 96
Homer's *Odyssey*: Argos in, 46
horses, 44, 77, 98, 106, 107, 135; Achilles' horse Xanthus, 96, 100; Bellerophon and Pegasus, 69, 70, 82
Hosea: 2:12, 124; 2:18, 124; 4:3, 19, 176, 179; 5:14, 122; 6:6, 74; 8:9, 134, 161; 11:10, 122; 13:0, 117; 13:5, 116; 13:6a, 116; 13:6c, 116; 13:7–8, 121; 13:8, 102
Houston, Walter, 56
Hubert, Henri, 83
human-animal binary, 28, 33–40, 73; Calarco on, 15, 25, 34, 62, 112, 148; Derrida on, 15, 25, 35, 69–70
human exceptionalism, 36, 163, 165, 168, 171, 173, 177, 178, 180, 181
human overpopulation, 178–79
human sacrifice: vs. animal sacrifice, 15–16, 59, 60, 65, 80–81, 87–89; child sacrifice, 16, 42–43, 59, 80–81, 87–88, 89; daughter of Jephthah, 42–43, 80–81, 87–88, 89; God's commandment to sacrifice Isaac, 80
human self-understanding and animals, 24, 28–29
hyenas, 134
Hymn to Aten, 130, 131
hyraxes, 131, 161, 174

ibexes, 21, 77, 130, 161, 174
Ibn Ezra, 196n57
Ingold, Tim, 146
Instruction of Any, 103
Isaac, 23, 25, 26, 31, 39–40, 80, 95
Isaiah: 1:3, 100; 1:11, 74; 5:29–30, 122; 11:1–5, 124; 11:6–8, 106, 124–25; 13:19, 126; 13:21–22a, 126, 206n26; 30:17, 81; 31:4, 122; 32:14, 161; 34:9–10, 126; 34:11, 126; 34:12, 126; 34:13, 126; 34:16b, 127; 34:17, 127; 37:35, 142; 38:13, 122; 42:10, 162; 43, 155; 43:16, 128; 43:17, 128; 43:18, 128; 43:19, 128; 43:19b–21, 128–29, 130; 43:20, 163; 43:21, 128, 129; 46:1, 118; 49:14, 129; 56:10, 48; 56:10–11, 54; 65:25, 125; 66:3, 74

Ishmael, 43, 107
Islam, 143–44
Israel: dogs in, 46–49; goats and sheep in, 15, 31, 32, 33; kingship in, 122; origins of, 24–28
Issachar, 107
IUCN Red List of Threatened Species, 214n15

jackals, 126, 127–29, 130, 134, 163, 174
Jacob, 25–28, 36, 41; Isaac's blessing of, 14, 23, 31–33, 39–40; as Israel, 14, 24, 26, 31–33, 43; relationship with Esau, 24, 26–27, 32, 39–40, 43
Jephthah's daughter, 42–43, 80–81, 87–88, 89
Jeremiah: 2:15, 122; 2:23–24, 107; 2:24, 98, 161; 5:6, 122; 5:8, 98, 107; 6:20, 74; 7:20, 158; 7:21–2, 74; 9:10, 176; 9:11, 127; 10:22, 127; 12:1, 176, 179; 12:4, 18–19; 12:8, 123; 12:9, 123; 13:23, 123; 14:6, 98, 161; 15:3, 55, 124; 19:19, 127; 21:6, 158; 25:30, 122, 123; 25:38, 122; 27:5–6, 158; 28:14, 158; 31:27, 158; 32:10, 158; 32:12, 158; 36:29, 158; 49:19, 122; 49:29, 127; 49:32, 127; 49:33, 127; 50:3, 158; 50:11, 107; 50:17, 122; 50:39, 127; 50:44, 122; 51:17, 122; 51:34–35, 122; 51:37, 127; 51:62, 158
Jerusalem, 127–28
Jezebel, 55
Job, 132–33; 10:16, 122; 16:9, 122; 24:5, 134, 161; 30:1, 48, 55; 30:29, 127, 134; 38:0–39, 130; 38:0–41, 17, 111, 119, 139, 140; 38:2, 133; 38:3, 133; 38:8, 133; 38:9, 133; 38:16, 133; 38:17, 133; 38:30, 175; 38:39, 133–34; 38:39–41, 175; 38:40, 174; 38:41, 161, 175; 39:1–3, 175; 39:5–6, 134; 39:5–8, 161, 174; 39:6, 174; 39:7, 134, 175; 39:8, 175; 39:9–12, 134; 39:13–18, 128, 134; 39:14, 175; 39:14–16, 134; 39:17, 135; 39:18, 175; 39:19–25, 135; 39:22, 175; 39:26–30, 135, 138; 39:27, 135; 39:28, 174; 39:29, 175; 39:30, 135; 40:7, 135–36; 40:15, 136, 175; 40:17, 136; 40:19, 137; 40:20, 175; 40:21–23, 174; 41:1–2, 136–37; 41:5, 136–37; 41:7–8, 136–37; 41:9, 137; 41:9–11, 137–38; 41:11, 137; 41:25, 137; 41:34, 138
Joel: 1:4–20, 105–6; 1:18, 162; 1:20, 162; 2:22, 162; 3:16, 122
Johnson, Elizabeth, 132
Jonah: 1:17, 159; 3:7–8, 159; 4:7, 159; 4:11, 159, 160; as satire, 101, 104–5, 159–60
Jonathan, 122
Joseph (son of Jacob), 27
Joshua: 2, 57; 10:21, 62; 13:22, 93
Judaism: avoidance of *tsaar baalei chayyim*/suffering of living creatures in, 92, 111, 114–15; dietary laws, 3, 27, 58, 77, 146, 196n56; and parchment scrolls, 22; significance of animals for, 4, 22–23, 33, 143–44
Judges: 1:14, 95; 6:21, 81; 7:7, 142; 8:22–23, 122; 11, 43; 11:29–30, 81; 11:35, 89; 11:35–36, 81; 11:39, 81; 13:19, 31; 14:4–5, 123; 14:8, 105; 15:4–5, 105; 15:6, 88; 19, 43, 95; 19:29, 88

Kant, Immanuel, 72
King, Barbara, 18; on animals in the Bible, 2; *Being with Animals*, 1–2, 152; on cave paintings of animals, 1; on chimpanzees, 153, 154; on great apes, 151–52; *How Animals Grieve*, 152
1 Kings: 4:29, 19; 4:33, 19; 10:22, 155; 13, 101, 102, 103, 104, 105; 13:9, 102; 13:24, 100, 102; 13:25, 102; 13:28, 102; 16:4, 55; 17:4, 102, 134; 17:6, 102, 134; 18:38, 81; 21:19, 55; 21:23, 102; 21:23–24, 55; 22:20–23, 104; 22:38, 55, 57, 102; man of God in, 101, 102, 103, 104, 105
2 Kings: 1:10–14, 81; 2:11, 102; 2:23–25, 101–2, 105; 2:24, 123; 4:22, 95; 4:24, 95; 8:12, 54; 8:13, 54; 9:10, 55, 102; 9:35–6, 102; 9:35–37, 55; 17, 104; 17:23–26, 103; 17:25, 124; 19:34, 142

Klawans, Jonathan: on animal sacrifice, 16, 67, 83–90; vs. Derrida, 86, 88–89, 90; on principle of *imitatio Dei*, 85–86, 87; on Psalm 23, 16
Koosed, Jennifer, 103

Laban, 26, 31, 32
Lamentations: 2:3, 81; 2:20, 127; 3:10, 102, 122, 123; 4:3, 127, 134; 4:10, 127
language, 9, 10, 149, 152
Leah, 26, 31, 32, 41, 43
leopards, 121, 123, 125
Levenson, Jon, 81, 130, 136–37, 143
Leviathan, 131, 135–36, 139, 143, 161, 174
Levinas, Emmanuel: and animal ethics, 51–52, 53; Derrida on, 51, 52, 53, 59–60, 72, 96; on dogs and human dignity, 50–52; on Exodus and human freedom, 64; "The Name of a Dog, or Natural Rights", 15, 49–54, 57, 59–60, 61, 63, 64, 96; on prohibition on murder, 59–60
Levine, Baruch, 96
Lévi-Strauss, Claude, 5
Leviticus: 1:3–9, 79; 1:9, 81–82; 1:10–13, 79; 1:14–17, 79; 3:6–11, 79; 3:11, 81; 3:12–16, 79; 3:16, 81; 4:1–21, 78; 4:22–26, 78; 5:6, 79; 5:7–10, 79; 5:11–13, 79; 8:1–36, 78; 9:24, 81; 10:2, 81; 11, 118, 196n56; 11:1–47, 58; 11:2, 77; 11:3, 77; 11:4–8, 77; 11:39–40, 77; 16, 79; 17:10–16, 55; 17:15–16, 77; 21:6, 81; 21:8, 81; 21:17, 80, 81; 21:21, 80, 81; 21:22, 80, 81; 22:8, 77; 22:10–16, 80; 22:25, 80, 81; 22:27, 111; 22:28, 85, 111, 112, 113–14; 25:7, 110; 26:6, 124; 26:29, 127; 26:31, 82; 27:27, 61
Lilith, 126–27
lions, 125, 174, 206n17; and Daniel, 2, 103–4, 105; and donkeys, 102, 103, 104; God as lion, 116–17, 121, 122–23; God as providing food for, 121–22, 131, 133, 135, 139, 161, 162, 175; lion symbolism, 40, 97, 116–17, 121–24

Llewelyn, John, 52
locusts, 105–6
London, Jack: *Call of the Wild*, 46

Maimonides, Moses: on animals vs. humans, 91–92, 112–14; on divine providence, 91; on emotions among animals, 112–14; on forbidden foods, 112; *Guide of the Perplexed*, 91, 112; on treatment of animals, 91–92, 97, 108, 109, 112–14
Malachi: 1:7, 81; 1:12, 81
Marcus, David: on anti-prophetic satire, 101, 104, 105, 109
masculinity, 40, 41, 43, 72
Mather, Cotton, 164
Mauss, Marcel, 83
McCance, Dawne, 71
McHugh, Susan, 62
McKay, Heather: on Balaam's donkey, 108–9, 114; on subjugated equines, 106–9; "Through the Eyes of Horses", 63, 106–9
McKenzie, Steven, 104, 159
Mekhilta of Rabbi Ishmael, 50
Micah: 1:8, 127; 6:6–8, 74
Midrash, 174
Milgrom, Jacob, 82
Miller, Geoffrey, 48–49
Moore, Michael, 94
Moore, Stephen, 7–8, 185n10
morality, 150, 154, 155
Morey, Darcy, 47
Morton, Timothy, 167; on neighbor species, 117
Moses, 31–32, 33, 61, 62, 95, 128, 156
mules, 106

Nabal, 32
Nancy, Jean-Luc, 60
Nash, Roderick: on wilderness, 119
Nathan, 42, 86
Nebuchadnezzar, 158
nephesh, 37, 38, 55, 110
Niditch, Susan, 25, 41, 81

Nineveh, 127, 159, 160
Noah: animal sacrifices of, 67; and animals' fear of humans, 66, 121
Noah's ark, 2, 18–19, 82, 157–58, 175–76, 178; and endangered species, 18, 165, 172–73
Numbers: 3:13, 88; 8:17, 88; 11:31–33, 105; 16:35, 81; 18:15, 60–61, 88; 19, 78; 21:6, 105; 22:12, 94; 22:18, 93; 22:20, 94; 22:21, 94; 22:22, 94; 22:23, 94; 22:25, 94; 22:27, 94; 22:28, 92, 94; 22:29, 94; 22:30, 95, 100, 114; 22:31, 95; 22:32, 92; 22:32–33, 95; 22:35, 99; 28:2, 81; 28:24, 81; 31:8, 93; 31:16, 93. *See also* Balaam's donkey

Oliver, Kelly, 43
Olyan, Saul, 80
orangutans, 148
original sin, 150
ostriches, 126, 127–29, 130, 134–35, 138, 139, 163, 208n48
oxen, 106, 109, 110, 111, 122

Pachirat, Timothy, 89
Palmer, Claire, 169
parchment, 21–23, 44; and canonization of biblical texts, 22; vs. papyrus, 22
Passover, 34, 76, 79, 155–56; silent dogs of Exodus, 15, 49–62, 50, 63, 64, 65, 109, 195n39
Patton, Kimberly: on divine-animal relations, 142–45, 146, 147, 153, 163; "He Who Sits in the Heavens Laughs", 142–45; on Jonah, 159
Pegasus, 69, 70, 82
Philo, 111, 196n57
philopatric animals, 171
Pierce, Jessica, 154
Pleistocene, 166–67, 168
Plumwood, Val, 12, 13
Proverbs: 12:10, 110; 17:12, 102; 26:11, 54; 27:23, 110; 28:15, 102; 30:18, 138, 139
Psalm 2:4, 142
Psalm 7:2, 206n17

Psalm 8:5–8, 130
Psalm 10:9, 206n17
Psalm 17: 17:8, 141; 17:12, 206n17
Psalm 18:8, 81
Psalm 22: 22:13, 206n17; 22:16, 54; 22:20, 54; 22:20–21, 206n17; 22:21, 206n17
Psalm 23, 16, 33, 84, 89
Psalm 24:1, 160–61
Psalm 32:19, 99
Psalm 34:10, 206n17
Psalm 35:17, 206n17
Psalm 36: 36:5, 140; 36:5–6, 160; 36:5–6a, 157; 36:5–9, 140–42, 154–55; 36:6, 18, 141, 157, 158, 161
Psalm 40:6, 74
Psalm 44:19, 127
Psalm 50:10, 118, 160
Psalm 57: 57:1, 141; 57:4, 206n17
Psalm 58:6, 206n17
Psalm 59: 59:6, 54, 55; 59:14, 55
Psalm 68:22–23, 55
Psalm 69:34, 162
Psalm 74:14, 137
Psalm 96:12, 162
Psalm 98:7, 162
Psalm 103:30, 161
Psalm 104, 17, 111, 119, 138, 139, 140, 162, 174–75; 104:3–9, 133; 104:5–26, 174; 104:10–12, 130; 104:11, 161, 175; 104:12, 161, 174; 104:14–15, 131, 161; 104:16–17, 130, 174; 104:17, 161, 174; 104:18, 161, 174; 104:20, 131; 104:21, 91, 133, 161, 175; 104:22, 174; 104:22–23, 131; 104:25, 131, 161; 104:26, 131, 137, 143, 161, 175; 104:27, 175; 104:27–28, 161; 104:27–30, 131–32, 161; 104:29–30, 38
Psalm 119:166, 162
Psalm 145:15–16, 161–62
Psalm 146:9, 111
Psalm 147:9, 91, 162
Psalm 148: 148:7, 162; 148:7–10, 175; 148:10, 118, 162
Psalm 150: 150:1, 162–63; 150:6, 162–63

Pyper, Hugh, 122–23

Rab Judah, 174–75
Rachel, 26, 31, 32, 41, 43
Rad, Gerhard von, 66
Ramban, 196n57
ravens, 102, 105, 134, 135, 139
Rebekah, 23, 25–26, 31, 39–40
Regan, Tom, 11, 169
Revelation: animals in, 2
Rolston, Holmes, III: on Noah's ark and endangered species, 18, 165, 172–73
Rose, Deborah Bird, 169; *Wild Dog Dreaming*, 195n39
Rudy, Kathy, 93; on animal affect, 113; *Loving Animals*, 113
Ruth 4:11, 32

Sabbath, 110
Sabbath year, 110
Samson, 105, 123; wife of, 88
1 Samuel: 6, 103; 8:6–22, 122; 9–10, 95; 11, 88; 11:5–7, 43; 16:11, 31; 16:19, 31; 16:20, 95; 17:15, 31; 17:20, 31; 17:28, 31; 17:33–37, 117; 17:34, 102; 17:34–37, 31; 17:43, 54; 23:14, 54; 24:1–2, 131; 25:2, 32
2 Samuel: 1:23, 122; 3:8, 54; 9:8, 54; 12, 86; 12:3, 42, 89; 16:9, 54; 17:8, 102; 22:9, 81
Sasson, Aharon, 30
satire, 101, 104–5, 109, 159
Saul, 43, 88, 95, 117, 122
Savran, George, 101
Schaefer, Donovan, 153, 154; "Do Animals Have Religion?", 145; on Jonah, 159; *Religious Affects*, 145–46
Schochet, Elijah Judah, 91–92
Scurlock, JoAnn, 81
Second Temple period, 22
Seesengood, Robert, 39, 103
sheep, 26–27, 60–61, 110, 111; as companion species, 15, 25, 29, 30–33, 45, 117, 190n17; herding of, 30–32, 33, 41, 84, 85; sacrifice of, 76–77, 78, 79, 85
shepherd imagery, 84–86, 88; God as shepherd, 33, 84, 85–86, 87, 116, 123
Sherwood, Yvonne, 7–8, 67, 74
Simkins, Ronald, 158
Singer, Peter, 11
slaves, 25, 26, 28, 41, 42, 43, 64, 65, 89
Smith, Jonathan Z., 83
Smuts, Barbara, 154
snakes, 38–39, 100–101, 105
Sodom and Gomorrah, 126
Solomon, 155; wisdom of, 19
Song of Songs 1:9, 98, 107, 203n35
Strawn, Brent, 97, 103; on biblical lions, 121–22

Talmud, 22, 66, 143; Avodah Zarah 3b, 143
Thomas, D. Winton, 48, 49
tool-making, 148
Towner, W. Sibley, 67
tsaar baalei chayyim: avoidance of, 92, 111, 114–15
Tuan, Yi-Fu, 88–89
Tucker, Gene, 121, 125, 130, 131, 132
Tull, Patricia, 110

van Dooren, Thom: *Flight Ways*, 170; on place, 171, 174; on species extinction, 19; on species preservation, 173; on storytelling, 165, 170–72, 175, 179–80

Waldau, Paul, 8–9
Way, Kenneth, 104; on Balaam's donkey, 99–100, 114; on biblical donkeys, 98–99, 109; on donkey burials, 98; *Donkeys in the Biblical World*, 97–100
Weil, Karl, 9
wild animals: vs. domesticated animals, 17, 41, 56, 63, 68, 76, 77, 84, 109, 117–18, 119, 121, 130, 134, 169; wild asses, 98, 134, 139, 161, 174; wild

goats, 174; wild oxen, 134, 139. *See also* lions
wilderness and desolation, 125–29, 130
Wolfe, Cary, 40
wolves, 123, 125
women: associated with animals, 41–43, 63–64, 68, 87–88, 107; and biblical law, 42; creation of, 41–42
Woolf, Virginia: *Flush*, 46

Xanthus, 96, 100

Zechariah: 1:8, 106; 6:1–7, 106; 9:9, 95, 106
Zephaniah 2:13–15, 127
Zilpah, 41, 43
zooarchaeology/archaeozoology, 3, 30, 32

The authorized representative in the EU for product safety and compliance is:
Mare Nostrum Group
B.V Doelen 72
4831 GR Breda
The Netherlands